PRENTICE-HALL
CONTEMPORARY COMPARATIVE POLITICS SERIES
JOSEPH LaPALOMBARA, Editor

published

forthcoming

D1367435

MICHAEL ROSKIN

Lycoming College

Prentice-Hall, Inc.
Englewood Cliffs, N.J. 07632

OTHER GOVERNMENTS OF EUROPE

SWEDEN, SPAIN, ITALY, YUGOSLAVIA, AND EAST GERMANY

Library of Congress Cataloging in Publication Data

ROSKIN, MICHAEL (date)
    Other governments of Europe.

    (Prentice-Hall series in contemporary comparative politics)
    Bibliography: p.
    Includes index.
        1. Sweden—Politics and government.   2. Spain—Politics and government.
3. Italy—Politics and government.   4. Yugoslavia—Politics and government.
5. Germany, East—Politics and government.   I. Title.
JN5.R67   320.3   76-39983
ISBN 0-13-642959-9

to my wife, Therese

OTHER GOVERNMENTS OF EUROPE:
SWEDEN, SPAIN, ITALY, YUGOSLAVIA, AND EAST GERMANY
Michael Roskin

© 1977 by Prentice-Hall, Inc., Englewood Cliffs, New Jersey

Printed in the United States of America

10   9   8   7   6   5   4   3

PRENTICE-HALL INTERNATIONAL, INC., London
PRENTICE-HALL OF AUSTRALIA PTY. LIMITED, Sydney
PRENTICE-HALL OF CANADA, LTD., Toronto
PRENTICE-HALL OF INDIA PRIVATE LIMITED, New Delhi
PRENTICE-HALL OF JAPAN, INC., Tokyo
PRENTICE-HALL OF SOUTHEAST ASIA PTE. LTD., Singapore
WHITEHALL BOOKS LIMITED, Wellington, New Zealand

CONTENTS

FOREWORD

The series in Contemporary Comparative Politics is unabashedly committed to several goals. We assume that the undergraduate student is by and large not interested in becoming a political scientist but is planning to follow other pursuits. This being so, we aim to expose these students to aspects of politics that will be salient to them throughout their lives. In order to make this point stick though, we believe it is necessary to avoid using the so-called "grand theories" of political science as organizing frameworks. Such "theories" are subtle forms of misinformation; they mislead students—and sometimes others—into believing that we know more about political systems and processes than is actually the case.

It is also our assumption that only the rare undergraduate wishes to master the workings of any single political system. Even where such interest may be present, the study of single countries rarely leads to anything resembling systematic comparative analysis. Therefore, we have sought to focus on a wide range of interesting and important aspects of politics that individual volumes in this series treat comparatively.

We also believe that those aspects of politics included in this series should be treated from both an institutional and a behavioral perspective. Political science will remain a hobbled discipline as long as those who write or consume it elect one of these orientations or the other. Political science will become or remain an arid discipline if we neglect to treat the normative side of politics. The authors of this series are neither bare-facts empiricists nor "cloud-ninety" political moralists. They are prepared to use whatever forms of comparative analysis are available to permit us better to understand the relationships between political institutions, behavior, values, and man's condition. The range of understanding we seek to achieve is reflected in the core of the series (Joseph LaPalombara, *Politics within Nations*) and in the titles of individual series volumes.

Because no series can encompass all areas of politics, we have had to make choices. Some of these choices introduce the reader to aspects of politics not often treated on a comparative basis. Our published volumes on political violence, political corruption, legal culture, and the military and politics, fall into this category. Other choices expose the reader to more traditional aspects of government and politics treated in a fresh comparative perspective. Series volumes on national legislatures, bureaucracies, and elections fall into this category.

A visitor from a distant planet, or an unwary student, could come away from our textbooks on comparative politics believing that the world consists only of the United States, Britain, France, West Germany, the Soviet Union, and China. On the other hand, where many nations from different continents are all treated in one volume, the analysis itself is doomed to superficiality and simplistic, misleading generalizations.

The beauty of this short book by Michael Roskin is that it concentrates on five countries that are similar in many respects but also sufficiently different to permit useful contrasts and comparisons. All five countries are European; they are rarely treated by textbooks in comparative politics. They are found at different levels of economic and political development, and the author helps to open our eyes to some of the reasons for these differences and variations. As Roskin moves from one country to another we come to appreciate the particular texture and rich variation in modes of political participation and problem solving.

A particularly appealing aspect of this book is Roskin's method of comparison. He asks essentially the same questions about each country, and he then provides illuminating answers. His list of questions is clearly not exhaustive, but each question is interesting and important. The book itself convincingly shows us why it is essential to include the smaller or less powerful nations in our comparative analyses. This achievement conforms exactly to the spirit of this series.

JOSEPH LAPALOMBARA

New Haven

PREFACE

This short book is not by an expert, nor is it intended for experts. Indeed, if I had been a specialist on any one of the five countries, chances are I would have not undertaken to write about the other four. The book grew not out of research expertise but rather out of classroom lectures in a first course in Comparative Politics that I attempted to enliven by including material from countries besides Britain, France, West Germany, and the Soviet Union. To tell the truth, I was getting a little tired of the same old Big Four every year. I started collecting material and soon had enough to begin a book aimed at the level of the sophomores who take my European Politics.

I can honestly claim in-depth familiarity with only one of the five countries, Yugoslavia, where I studied for a year. The other lands I have visited for varying lengths of time; consequently, I had to pick a lot of other persons' brains. The most delightful country for doing this is Spain, where Spanish generosity helps visiting academics with ideas, publications, and meals. Of course, you never want to interrupt a Spanish intellectual once he starts talking. On Spain, outstanding assistance came from Juan Linz of Yale; Amando de Miguel, Salustiano del Campo, and Julián Marías of Madrid; and Juan F. Marsal and Santiago Terribas of Barcelona. Some officers of the U.S. Information Service achieve rare rapport with their host country's intellectual life and serve as true bicultural intermediaries. I was fortunate to find two such men in Spain: Lee Johnson of the U.S. Embassy in Madrid and Allen Rogers of the American cultural center in Barcelona.

In Italy I benefited greatly from talks with Milan sociologist Guido Martinotti and Larry Gray, an American graduate student in Rome whose grasp of Italian politics is phenomenal.

In Yugoslavia I gained valuable insights from Vera Erlich and Rudi Supek of Zagreb, and Firdus Djinić and Branko Pribićević of Belgrade. Another bicultural USIS man, Edmund Bator, facilitated contacts in Belgrade.

My introduction to Sweden came from a graduate-student colleague of my Belgrade days, Lars Nord, who specializes on Yugoslav foreign policy at the University of Uppsala. In Stockholm, the efficient Swedish Institute arranged useful talks with Sture Lindmark of the *Svenska Dagbladet* and Krister Wahlbaeck of Stockholm University. Ruth Link, editor of *Sweden Now*, and Robert Skole, provided an American viewpoint on Sweden. The Swedish Information Service in New York must be ranked as one of the best of such efforts.

In East Berlin I was well received by Waldemar Damp (later an official of the GDR Embassy in Washington) and Gerwin Schweiger. Important documentation on East Germany was provided by the West German Information Center in New York.

Lycoming College, in the person of Dean James R. Jose, came through with a travel grant that enabled me to visit Europe in 1974.

My greatest thanks go to Joseph LaPalombara of Yale, editor of this series, who gently dissuaded me from some of my more intemperate statements and prompted me to rethink what politics is all about. Writing a book under his guidance was an important educational experience for me. Any errors in this book are my own, probably the result of not heeding his advice.

MICHAEL ROSKIN

Williamsport, Pa.

TO
EXPAND
HORIZONS
1

The five countries considered in this book—Sweden, Spain, Italy, Yugoslavia, and East Germany—are usually neglected in the undergraduate study of politics. This is unfortunate, for the addition of these five systems to students' "data banks" or "intellectual tool kits" will make them a good deal more sophisticated in the study of comparative politics in general and European politics in particular. They will have a broader range of instances and examples at their disposal and will thus be able to compare more validly. Their horizons will expand to encompass a greater variety of political experiences, including some fascinating ones to which undergraduates (and even graduate students) are not much exposed.

Typically students begin comparative politics with a first course on the "Big Four"—Britain, France, West Germany, and the Soviet Union.[1] This is not a bad choice, but these systems leave a lot out. Among them are no thoroughgoing social democracies, no right-wing dictatorships, no chronically chaotic systems, and no variants of communism. To stop with the Big Four is to remain narrow. More recently, students may have shifted to or added texts that approach comparative politics not on a country-by-country basis, but topic by topic, each in cross-national perspective.[2] Both approaches tend to overlook a rich vein of data on the margins of Europe.

What can we learn from a study of Sweden, Spain, Italy, Yugoslavia, and East Germany?

Britain is often presented as a highly developed political system, stable,

[1] For example, Roy C. Macridis and Robert E. Ward, eds., *Modern Political Systems: Europe*, 3rd ed. (Englewood Cliffs, N.J.: Prentice-Hall, 1972); and Samuel H. Beer and Adam B. Ulam, eds., *Patterns of Government: The Major Political Systems of Europe*, 3rd ed. (New York: Random House, 1973). There are several other good texts.

[2] For example, Joseph LaPalombara, *Politics Within Nations* (Englewood Cliffs, N.J.: Prentice-Hall, 1974); and Peter H. Merkl, *Modern Comparative Politics* (New York: Holt, Rinehart and Winston), 1970.

durable, a "welfare state." Once we study Sweden, however, we may conclude that it, not Britain, is a better example of the modern welfare state. Indeed, Britain in the 1970s is wracked by so many serious problems—civil war in Northern Ireland, urban terrorism, major inflation, unruly labor unions, and a general decline of civility—that we may wish to use it as an example of political decay rather than as one of Europe's most highly developed systems. A look at Sweden helps us put Britain in perspective. We may even conclude that Sweden, not Britain, should serve as the prototypical Northern European welfare state.

France used to be studied in terms of the turmoil of the Third and Fourth Republics, a view (not undeserved) that tended to emphasize the shaky, unstable nature of the French system. This may no longer be quite as accurate as it once was. De Gaulle's Fifth Republic rewrote the rules of the political game in France; a powerful president no longer needs a tumultuous National Assembly in order to govern. The French economy has soared to nearly West German levels. The French system is no longer a good example of the unstable politics of proportional representation systems with weak executives, but a good example is at hand: Italy, which in many ways resembles the "classic" France of the Third and Fourth Republics. This classic pattern is well worth studying, not only because it represents a historical type, but also because a number of polities, in Europe and elsewhere, are still caught up in such a system. Italy is a much better representative of a Latin European, or Mediterranean, system than is present-day France.

If the study of Italy is a little like taking a time machine back a few decades into France, the study of Spain is somewhat like taking a time machine back a century or more. The author does not say this to ridicule Spain—in fact, he is extremely fond of Spain—but rather because in Spain we can see some of the deep-seated social, political, and economic problems that formerly plagued France and still unsettle Italy. Studying Spain we can learn something about the volatility of Latin European politics—its passion, inflexibility, and extremism—which earlier split France and Italy into two antagonistic camps, and to a certain extent still does. Taking Latin Europe as a pattern, we can then see how France has modernized almost out of this pattern; how Spain has been trapped in it; and how Italy is making an unsteady transition within it.

Until recently, the initial study of Communist systems has focused exclusively on the Soviet Union. China is now sometimes added. But the Soviet Union may not be the best example of a Communist (or, as they like to call themselves, "Socialist") system, nor is the Soviet emphasis on extreme centralization necessarily the only approach Communist systems may take. East Germany is actually a more highly developed Communist system than the Soviet Union. East Germans enjoy the highest standard of living of the Soviet bloc; their industry and agriculture are more efficient than are those of the Soviets. This author is of the opinion that the Soviet Union's problems grow from an effort to impose an advanced, complex system onto a relatively backward, undisciplined population.

Coercion and inefficiency must accompany such an attempt. In an already industrialized, hard-working, and disciplined population like that of East Germany, such a system works more efficiently and with less coercion. Prussians make better Communists than do Russians. A better example of how communism should work, then, might be found in East Germany than in the Soviet Union.

The centralization and tight control of Soviet-type systems may not be the only way to "build socialism," as the Communists like to describe their current phase. Yugoslavia, kicked out of the Soviet camp in 1948, has evolved its own brand of communism, which stresses decentralization and "worker self-management" within a market economy. Supply and demand, not central directives, determine much of Yugoslav development. Although beset by numerous problems, including serious friction between its regions, Yugoslavia's maverick path stands as a rebuke to Soviet conceptions of "socialism."

THREE GROUPS OF THREE

In sum, then, knowledge of these five countries rounds out our picture of Europe, supplementing the already well-known systems of Britain, France, West Germany, and the Soviet Union. Further, taking these nine countries together, they fall rather neatly into the following three groups of three to enhance our ability to compare:

The Northern European pattern: Sweden, Britain, West Germany.

The Latin European pattern: Italy, France, Spain.

The East European pattern: East Germany, Soviet Union, Yugoslavia.

Any such construction is bound to be somewhat artificial, but we can learn a lot from such groupings. Within each group a country might be more or less advanced; but in each group politics tends to revolve around a key question, albeit with numerous variations.

Northern European politics, and here we could include Denmark and Norway as well, tends to revolve around the question, "How much welfare?", that is, typically a Social Democratic party proposes extensive welfare measures and these are opposed by conservative parties. Elections endorse first one view, then the other, and gradually the system grows into a welfare state.

Latin European systems have not fully solved some of their basic problems of legitimacy. Large sectors of the population frankly despise the ruling conservative regime and obey only reluctantly. Here the key question is not welfare but, "Should this system exist?" Internal strife and even civil war erupt intermittently between conservative defenders of a traditional order and leftist opponents. One-man rule often results from this conflict. Portugal and Greece also fit into this pattern.

The East European systems sweep the questions of welfare and legitimacy under the carpet and instead impose a new key political question, "How much centralization?" The participants in this debate tend to be the ruling elite rather than the broad masses, but often the participants speak for the ethnic, industrial, or intellectual sectors of the society from which they sprang. The Communist systems of Eastern Europe have not settled the issue of whether to have complete centralization, the perfection of Stalinism, or to decentralize somewhat and bring in Western concepts of profitability, efficiency, and consumer demand. Yugoslavia has gone the farthest in the latter direction, but many other East European systems quietly entertain such ideas, too.

We will discuss these three patterns in more detail in the last chapter. They are introduced here to start the student thinking in comparative terms.

SOME STATISTICAL COMPARISONS

To begin this comparative process, let us consider some recent (1973) statistics for our nine European countries plus the United States (see Table 1–1).

Table 1–1   Size and Population

	Area in Square Miles	Population in Millions	Inhabitants per Square Mile
Soviet Union	8,599,300	249	30
United States	3,615,125	205	58
West Germany	95,959	60	625
Britain	94,211	56	599
Italy	116,313	55	472
France	210,039	52	247
Spain	194,885	35	179
Yugoslavia	98,766	21	215
East Germany	41,648	17	418
Sweden	173,666	8	48

Some differences stand out immediately. In the first place, Sweden, with the third largest area in Western Europe (after France and Spain), is far more thinly populated than most European countries not counting the Soviet Union, the bulk of which lies in Asia. Sweden has fewer inhabitants per square mile than the United States, although not as few as Finland or Norway. But the rest of Europe, we quickly observe, is crowded. West Germany and Britain have about ten times the population density of the United States. The most crowded country in Europe is little Holland, which jams an amazing average of 1,040 persons on to a square mile.

But we also may notice that area, population, and density mean little in terms of economic vitality, standard of living, or system of goverment. We cannot say, for example, that Sweden is rich and democratic because her people have enough room to spread out into. In the first place, nine Swedes out of ten live in the southern third of Sweden, where the climate is mildest. Secondly, a country can be rich and democratic and also crowded. West Germany, for example, has thirteen times the population density of Sweden. On the other hand, the Soviet Union, although no longer poor, has room to spare in Siberia. Thus population density figures do not tell us much. Large areas of Sweden, the Soviet Union, the United States, Spain, and Yugoslavia cannot sustain much population either because they are too cold or too arid, or lack resources. Thus even nations with plenty of territory invariably have their populations concentrated in certain areas.

Perhaps more revealing comparisons come from the economic side. The 1972 gross national products (GNP) for ten nations, as a whole and per capita are shown in Table 1–2.

Table 1–2   Economy

	1972 GNP in Millions of Dollars	Per Capita GNP, 1972
United States	1,158,000	$5,546
Sweden	41,686	5,129
West Germany	259,848	4,211
France	199,679	3,862
Britain	154,224	2,759
East Germany	46,400	2,730
Italy	118,170	2,176
Soviet Union	478,000	1,930
Spain	45,840	1,329
Yugoslavia	21,588	1,043

Sometimes more recent figures show the United States actually behind Sweden in per capita GNP, but by the time cost of living is calculated, Sweden comes out with about seven-eighths of U.S. real per capita income.

Although the differences in per capita income in Europe are large, from $1,000 per Yugoslav to $5,000 per Swede, we should remember that on a world scale all these ten countries are rather well off. Economists sometimes use the figure of $1,000 per capita GNP to separate "have" from "have-not" countries, and much of the world's population produces per capita GNPs of less than $200. Yugoslavia may be one of the poorest countries of Europe, but in the world she occupies a middle position.

Within Europe, the richer countries (Sweden, West Germany, and France) are all north of the poorer countries (Italy, Spain, and Yugoslavia). The philosopher Montesquieu theorized that colder climates produce more vigorous people than do warm climates.[3] We need not accept this theory to appreciate the fact that North-South differences do play a major role, especially internally, within the three Mediterranean countries considered here. In the respective Souths of Spain, Italy, and Yugoslavia, higher temperatures, lower rainfall, and scanty resources may indeed help foster the poverty that seems to be endemic there. In fact, if the northern thirds of Spain, Italy, and Yugoslavia were studied as separate entities, they would resemble much of Northern Europe economically.

Our chart also reveals that Great Britain is no longer so great in comparison with Sweden, West Germany, and France. How could the once-mighty British economy decline? It actually did not decline; it merely failed to grow as fast as the economies of its Continental neighbors. Indeed, from 1963 to 1973, Britain's annual economic percentage growth rate was the lowest in all of Europe. Percentage annual average growth rates from 1963 to 1973 in constant dollars were[4]

Yugoslavia	6.6
Spain	6.3
France	5.7
Soviet Union	5.5
Italy	4.8
West Germany	4.7
United States	3.9
East Germany	3.6
Sweden	3.4
Britain	2.7

Japan's economy, by the way, grew at a rate of 10.5 percent annually during this same period.

In terms of growth, our two poorest countries, Spain and Yugoslavia, are now the top two. This is partly explained by the relatively small increment it takes to register a big percentage gain when the starting figure is low. But our chart also shows the new-found economic vitality of two countries that had languished for centuries as backwaters of Europe. Some already highly developed economies, on the other hand, such as the United States' and Sweden's, scored only modest percentage gains; this is normal for such countries because it takes a much greater increase to register a large percentage rise.

Still, Britain's poor showing demonstrates some of the interrelationships between politics and economics. Outside of the European Economic Community (better known as the Common Market) until 1973, beset by numerous

---

[3] Baron de Montesquieu, *The Spirit of the Laws*, trans. by Thomas Nugent (New York: Hafner, 1949), pp. 221–25.

[4] United States Arms Control and Disarmament Agency, *World Military Expenditures and Arms Trade, 1963–1973* (Washington: Government Printing Office, 1975).

strikes and labor indiscipline, Britain's economy languished while others soared. At the same time, the civil war in Northern Ireland and rising domestic violence eroded British traditions of civility and respect for law. Conservative and Labor governments came into office promising sweeping changes but delivering little. Economic decay fostered political decay, which in turn led to more economic decay. A so-called developed country does not automatically and forever stay developed. Similar problems threatened Italian democracy as Italy's economy turned sour in the mid-1970s.

Some economists are skeptical about GNP figures, especially for cross-national comparisons. GNP, for example, does not indicate standard of living or level of industrialization. Kuwait and Libya had huge GNPs due to their oil wealth, but they were still underdeveloped by most other measures. Inflation and changing currency parities can make measuring one country's per capita GNP against another's deceptive. GNP does not include much of women's work. The GNP of Communist countries, which do not even publish Western-style GNP figures, has to be estimated, and there is often considerable variation among estimators on this. To get around some of the problems associated with GNP measures, economist Theodore Caplow suggests using "one of the best simple indicators of development, the number of telephones per capita."[5] Using 1971 figures on telephones per 100 inhabitants we find[6]

United States	60.4
Sweden	55.7
Britain	28.9
West Germany	24.9
Italy	18.8
France	18.5
Spain	15.1
East Germany	12.7
Soviet Union	4.9
Yugoslavia	4.0

The Communist countries, the bottom three, may argue that they do not wish to invest in such bourgeois luxuries as telephones but easily could if they wanted to. A country's planners may deliberately try to hold down private ownership of telephones and invest its funds in industry. It may further be argued that some countries are now in a catch-up phase of their telephone networks and that these figures are changing. Nonetheless, compared to per capita GNP, the United States, Sweden, and Yugoslavia are in about their proper rank order. But West Germany changes places with Britain, and France with

---

[5] Theodore Caplow, "Are the Poor Countries Getting Poorer?" *Foreign Policy*, 3 (Summer 1971), 92–93.

[6] Statistical Office of the United Nations, *Statistical Yearbook 1972* (New York: United Nations Publishing Service, 1973), pp. 506–508.

Italy, compared to their respective per capita GNPs. The Soviet Union and East Germany are way out of place, probably evidence that they do indeed regard private telephones as luxury items.

Are telephones a trivial measure? Before we dismiss this approach we should ask ourselves what are the social, political, and economic effects of having almost everyone able to pick up a phone and call almost anyone else in the country. Those who stress the communications approach to politics argue that such networks are the foundations of national community.[7]

If we wish to focus on a more life-or-death matter than telephones, let us look at precisely that. Infant mortality is often taken as a good measure of a country's health-delivery system. The infant mortality rate reflects not so much the latest and most expensive medical technology as it does the number and availability of physicians and clinics throughout the entire country. In addition to being available before, during, and after birth, medical help must also be affordable. Another contributing factor is the attitude of the population, that is, whether or not they actually use the medical care available. Figures from 1970 and 1971 show infant mortality per 1,000 live births as[8]

Sweden	11.1
France	14.4
Britain	17.9
East Germany	18.0
United States	19.2
Soviet Union	22.6
West Germany	23.3
Spain	27.9
Italy	28.3
Yugoslavia	55.2

Here we see that the welfare states of Western Europe—even France has comprehensive national health insurance—deliver medical care more completely than does the United States, which still contains pockets of people who cannot afford and/or mistrust medical services. West Germany's rate is puzzling, for Germany's public health services go back to the 1890s. One explanation may be the large numbers of foreign workers in West Germany; many of these workers bring their families and have children there with less medical attention than German citizens receive. Spain's and Italy's rather high infant mortality rates are not surprising; medical services are unevenly developed in those two countries. What is a little surprising is that the Spanish rate is actually a little lower than the Italian rate, a measure of the decay of Italian hospitals. Yugoslavia's high rate is in part a measure of the extreme backwardness of her

[7] See Karl W. Deutsch, *Nationalism and Social Communication: An Inquiry into the Foundations of Nationality*, 2nd ed. (Cambridge, Mass.: MIT Press, 1966).

[8] Statistical Office of the United Nations, *Statistical Yearbook 1972*, pp. 90–93.

southern regions, where standards are at Middle-Eastern levels. It further shows the decentralized nature of Yugoslavia's brand of socialism, which is not able to direct as much investment in hospitals and medical personnel into her backward areas as are the more coercive Communist regimes.

In sum, then, the five nations studied in this book extend both below (Spain, Italy, and Yugoslavia) and above (Sweden) the more often studied systems of Britain, France, West Germany, and the Soviet Union. In considering these five countries we expand considerably our knowledge of the range of development in Europe.

SWEDEN
2

For a small, out-of-the-way country that has not been at war with anyone since Napoleon, Sweden can still provoke strong feelings. President Eisenhower, for example, implied that Sweden showed how an "experiment of almost complete paternalism" resulted in high suicide and alcoholism rates.[1] A British journalist claims Sweden is actually a "new totalitarianism," all the more insidious because it is voluntary.[2] Conservatives tend to dislike Sweden as an example of, in Eisenhower's words again, "creeping socialism." Liberals and leftists, on the other hand, tend to like Sweden, and see it as a model of what an enlightened system can do to promote the general welfare. Swedes themselves tend to close ranks before foreigners and minimize the problems their system faces. A vigorous Swedish information service proudly promotes Swedish achievements abroad.

People see the Sweden they want to see. Before we can either denounce or imitate the Swedish system, however, we should be aware of its setting. Swedish circumstances may be unique so that Swedish institutions cannot be transplanted elsewhere. Swedes as a whole are so orderly, law-abiding, diligent, and civil that their institutions, however excellent, might not function the same way among other peoples. Let us consider the exceptional elements of Swedish history.

[1] *New York Times*, July 28, 1960, p. 1. Suicide figures are not good indicators of much. They have more to do with culture and character than with sociopolitical system. Sweden's suicide rate is high, but so are Austria's and West Germany's.

[2] Roland Huntford, *The New Totalitarians* (New York: Stein and Day, 1972). Even Swedish conservatives think this provocative book is an exaggeration.

**THE IMPACT
OF THE PAST**

GEOGRAPHY

Sweden is removed geographically from the European mainstream, far to the north, across the Baltic from Denmark and Germany. The Romans never got to Sweden, a fact that kept Sweden outside one of the rest of Europe's major unifying cultural and linguistic influences. For the same geographical reason, Sweden has been able to stay clear of the European wars of this century.

Unlike the fantastic mixture that makes up the people of Spain or Yugoslavia, the Swedes are ethnically and linguistically one people, which has made Sweden easier to unite and to govern. Regional dialects of Swedish are not very distinctive compared, say, to German and Italian dialects; thus, one of the problems that bedevils many other countries—ethnic, regional, or linguistic divisions—is absent in Sweden. Exceptions to the homogeneous population are the several thousand Lapps in the very north of Sweden, and the close to half a million foreigners (especially Finns) who, since World War II, have come to Sweden for jobs and high pay.

This geographical position and ethnic homogeniety made the founding of a unified Swedish state rather easy. During the twelfth and thirteenth centuries a state emerged at Uppsala, north of present-day Stockholm, named after the inhabitants of the area, the *Svear*. The kingdom of Svear, *Svea rike*, turned into *Sverige*, Sweden.

RELIGION

Sweden was one of the last European countries to accept Christianity; paganism fought a long rearguard action and was not suppressed until the twelfth century. Some say the Swedes were never as deeply Christianized as the Italians, French, or Spanish. Today, although virtually all Swedes are nominal Lutherans, church attendance is low (around 3 percent), and many Swedes are indifferent to religion.[3]

Elsewhere in Europe there was considerable conflict between Church and state. This was resolved early in Sweden: The state won and turned the Church into an arm of government. Churchmen operated in effect as civil servants, promulgating the government writ and recording births, deaths, and marriages in their parishes. No conflict between Church and state developed because the state was always stronger. Elsewhere in Europe anticlericalism has been a political issue; it never was in Sweden.

[3] Richard F. Tomasson, *Sweden: Prototype of Modern Society* (New York: Random House, 1970), pp. 75–79.

Furthermore, Sweden never had a Catholic-Protestant conflict. Gustav Vasa, the founder of modern Sweden, severed ties with Rome in the 1520s and proclaimed Lutheranism as the state religion with no domestic opposition. There were no wars of religion—and few other wars—on Swedish soil, although a powerful Swedish army roamed Europe in the Thirty Years' War.

IMPERIAL SWEDEN

Although only recent converts themselves, Swedes Christianized neighboring Finland by the sword and then stayed. Sweden ran Finland as a sort of colony from the twelfth century until 1809, when she surrendered it to Russia. By losing Finland early, Sweden missed one of the great scourges of other European governments: maddening colonial wars, such as those in Ireland and Algeria. To make up for the loss of Finland, Sweden forced Norway into a union in 1814. The Norwegians were never happy with this union and dissolved it unilaterally in 1905. Again, no colonial war.

Under Gustavus Adolphus (who ruled from 1611 to 1632), Sweden became the greatest Protestant power in Europe, turning the Baltic into a Swedish lake. Sweden's Baltic empire lasted only about a century, though. Under Charles XII, Sweden fought Poland, Russia, and Denmark in an effort to retain Swedish hegemony in the Baltic. Ultimately, she failed. Penetrating deep into Russia and suffering the Russian winter and scorched-earth tactics as Napoleon and Hitler later did, Charles XII's army capitulated to the Russians at Poltava in 1709. Aside from minor participation against Napoleon a century later, Sweden went back home and stayed there, practicing armed neutrality.

Sweden suffered defeats elsewhere in Europe but was never conquered at home or occupied by a foreign army. It fought Denmark for centuries over Sweden's southern provinces, but aside from that Sweden has always been run by, and her institutions developed by, her own people. Foreign occupation had terrible political effects on Spain, Italy, and Yugoslavia, problems that Sweden missed.

EARLY MODERNIZATION

Sweden's great modernizer, Gustav Vasa, began centralizing administration in the 1530s by replacing local nobles with his own bailiffs as district administrators. To monitor the bailiffs' collection of taxes, he set up a powerful exchequer. Thus Sweden's centralization and ability to collect taxes took solid form in the sixteenth century, earlier than most other European countries.

Modernization continued under Gustavus Adolphus in the seventeenth century. While the king was busy fighting in Germany (where he was killed), his chancellor, the nobleman Axel Oxenstierna, actually ran things, setting up a bureaucracy that was heavily staffed by aristocrats and quite efficient for its day. Because of its ties to aristocracy, the Swedish bureaucracy was admired and respected, and considered a fine calling for the talented. Bureaucracy elsewhere became associated with patronage, corruption, and personal gain, not the case in Sweden. Thus Oxenstierna's founding of a strong, efficient bureaucracy laid the groundwork for modern Sweden's large welfare bureaucracy.

Another point that aided Sweden's early centralization was that classic European feudalism, based on landed estates under autonomous lords, did not fully develop in Sweden. Perhaps half the farmland belonged to freeholding farmers. Instead of running estates, the Swedish nobility tended to take jobs in the royal bureaucracy. In England the feudal system diffused power throughout the realm, while in Sweden the throne tended to centralize it in Stockholm. By the middle of the fourteenth century, for example, provincial laws in Sweden had already been superseded by a national code of laws.

To firm up popular support, Sweden's monarchs took to calling national assemblies, the *Riksdag* (like the German word *Reichstag*). The Riksdag first met in 1435 and by the early 1600s was meeting annually. An interesting feature of the Swedish assembly, compared to others, was that it was composed of four estates instead of the usual three. In addition to the conventional estates of nobles, clergy, and burghers, Sweden had farmers as one estate of its Riksdag. This four-estate Riksdag lasted until 1866. The long history of representation by social category may have fostered what some claim is the Swedish tendency toward "corporatism," the functional representation of interest groups in legislatures.

THE RISE OF THE SOCIAL DEMOCRATS

Politically Sweden was ahead of most other European states. She developed a good bureaucracy, a central administration, a parliament, and a national consciousness and legitimacy early. Economically, though, Sweden was still a backward farming country until the late 1800s. Unable to provide food and jobs when the population increased in the nineteenth century, over a million Swedes emigrated to the United States. By 1910, one Swede in five lived in America.

Sweden industrialized late, starting in the 1880s, but fast: in one generation she went from an agricultural to an industrial society. Some scholars believe that rapid industrialization produces a militant labor movement. The uprooting of peasants from land to factory, the economic gap between owners and workers, and the wretched conditions make for class resentment. At this same time, socialist ideas from Germany were in their heyday, and the early Swedish socialists borrowed from them heavily. Socialist papers began appearing in the 1880s and in 1889 the Social Democratic Labor party was founded. By 1917 the Social Democrats got the largest vote of any party, and in 1932 they came to power to stay.

How could the Swedish Social Democrats have come to power so early and so durably? In Britain, France, and Germany the socialists were rarely strong enough to form a government until after World War II, and even then they were shaky. One factor may have been the relative weakness of the Swedish Liberal party, which was getting organized about the same time as the Social Democrats. Swedish workers were little attracted to the Liberal or other middle-of-the-road parties because the Social Democrats had reached them first. Thus the Swedish working-class vote went where it was "supposed" to go, to the working-class party, the Social Democrats, rather than getting siphoned off into the center parties.

Another factor contributing to the Social Democrats' success was their close tie to labor unions, even closer than in Britain. In 1898 one of Sweden's most important organizations was formed, the Confederation of Trade Unions, or *Landsorganisationen*, popularly known by its initials as LO. Stressing worker education, the LO organized study circles (and still runs them) to promote militancy and the vision of a good, socialist, egalitarian society. The payoff was big: Swedish workers are more loyal to the Social Democrats than British workers are to the Labor party.

As in other countries, the transition from a conservative agricultural society to a modern industrial one brought violence. Troops were called out to crush Swedish strikes—soldiers shot five workers dead in 1931—and workers some-times turned to violence against strike breakers. But the Swedes put labor violence behind them with the remarkable 1938 Saltsjöbaden Agreement be-tween the LO and the SAF (Swedish Federation of Employers). Their agree-ment, which still forms the basis for Swedish labor-management relations, was a sort of peace treaty in which both sides pledged themselves to negotiate indus-trywide contracts and stick to them without strikes or lockouts. Sweden has enjoyed relative labor peace ever since, in contrast to most of the rest of Europe.

Sweden's past has contributed patterns of centralization, bureaucratiza-tion, and moderation of conflicts. Few other countries have evolved similar patterns, a point to keep in mind in considering Sweden's institutions and their operation. What works well in Sweden may work badly elsewhere.

THE KEY
INSTITUTIONS

MONARCHY

Curiously, Sweden, considered one of the most democratic countries in the world, is a monarchy. By the early nineteenth century, however, the Swedish king—no queens are allowed under Swedish (or Spanish) law—was no longer very important. Power shifted to the cabinet which, although nominally at the king's service, actually represented the old four-estate Riksdag. The present royal line goes back to Jean-Baptiste Bernadotte, a French marshal under Napoleon, whom the Riksdag named king in 1810 when the old dynasty had run out of male heirs. The kings of the House of Bernadotte are long-lived; Gustav VI Adolf died in 1973 at age ninety. A scholarly archeologist much liked for his democratic ways, he used to carry his own bags and hail taxis himself. His grandson, Karl XVI Gustav, became king at twenty-seven, but was stripped of the last vestiges of political power. He was even more of a figurehead than the British monarch. About one-third of the Swedish people would abolish the monarchy in favor of a republic, but even many of them were sentimental over old Gustav Adolf, who used to chuckle, "Let them see how expensive it is with a president."

RIKSDAG

If the Swedish monarch has no power, who has? The most obvious answer is the Riksdag, although we will have to modify this statement later. In 1971, as part of a constitutional reform, a new, 350-member unicameral Riksdag was initiated. (The number was subsequently modified to 349 seats, to avoid the sort of 175–175 deadlock that grew out of the 1973 elections.) The previous legislative system, set up in 1866, was bicameral. Its 233-member lower house was elected by proportional representation for four years, while its upper house had 151 members elected indirectly by city and county councils for eight years.

Elections for the new Riksdag are held every three years in twenty-eight constituencies (mostly counties). The new Swedish electoral system is interesting, for it combines aspects of both constituency districts and proportional representation. In each constituency the parties put up slates of candidates who win in proportion to the vote for their party. Because it is impossible to send a fraction of a person to parliament, rounding off produces results that are not exactly proportional to the percentage vote in each constituency. This discrepancy between percentage vote and declared winners can get bothersome when the discrepancies of all the constituencies are added together. The representation might not be proportional to the parties' strengths nationwide. The Swedes adjust for this. Only 310 of the Riksdag's 349 seats are parceled out to the constituencies. The remaining 39 seats are reserved to see how the national vote went; then they are parceled out to rectify any variances from the parties' national percentages.

The Swedish electoral system tries to solve two longstanding problems. A pure proportional representation (PR) system that treats the entire country as one district (as in Holland, Israel, and Weimar Germany) tends to make members of parliament rootless, because they have no particular constituency. On the other hand, straight single-member districts (as in Britain and the United States), where the winner of a mere plurality takes all, can lead to legislatures that do not accurately reflect the parties' strengths nationwide. The new Swedish system uses constituencies and then evens things up with the thirty-nine "compensatory" seats. It is a PR system, but a modified one. To knock out splinter groups, a party must get at least 4 percent nationwide or 12 percent in one district to qualify for a Riskdag seat. This "threshold clause" was borrowed from the West German constitution, which requires a 5 percent minimum.

Since suffrage was expanded early this century, five parties have competed in the Riksdag:

Social Democratic Labor Party (Socialdemokratiska Arbetarpartiet)   Starting from classic Marxism, the Social Democrats soon abandoned revolution for reform via the ballot box. They also discarded nationalization of industry in favor of welfare provisions. Heavily supported by blue- and white-collar workers plus some intellectuals, the Social Democrats usually receive a little under half of the Swedish vote.

Center Party (Centerpartiet)   Called the Farmers' party until 1958, the Center party forged a new identity in opposing high taxes, bureaucracy, and nuclear power stations. In the 1970s, its share of the vote nearly doubled to one-quarter. Its leader, plain-spoken sheep farmer Thorbjörn Fälldin, capitalizing on nostalgia for a simpler rural life, became prime minister in 1976.

Conservative Party (Moderata Samlingspartiet, or Moderate Unity Party)   Although they have been in slow decline over the decades, the Conservatives still get close to 15 percent of the vote, mostly from higher-income people fighting to maintain their status in the face of egalitarianism. The Conservative party has warm ties with large businesses.

Liberal Party (Folkpartiet, or People's Party) Winning about one Swedish vote in ten, the Liberals have been struggling to find a new image to retain their middle-class and intellectual constituency. Earlier in the century the Liberals were allied with the Social Democrats, later moved into opposition, and in 1976 joined the nonsocialist government.

Communist Party (Vänsterpartiet-Kommunisterna, or Left Party–Communist)   A 1917 offshoot of the Social Democrats, the Communists still believe in nationalizing industry and erasing all class differences. With scattered votes among dissident workers, the Communists have declined from 10 percent in 1944 to just a little over the 4 percent threshold. Relatively independent of Moscow, the Swedish Communists take a moderate line, similar to that of the Italian Communists.

The Social Democrats won an absolute majority of votes only twice, in 1940 and 1968, but were in power 44 years, from 1932 to 1976. How did they do it? In earlier decades they did it by means of coalition with the Farmers' party, more recently by Communist support in key Riksdag decisions. But more basically the Social Democrats clung to power simply because nothing was able to replace them, the same situation that kept the Italian Christian Democrats in power. Sweden's three "bourgeois" parties—Center, Liberal, and Conservative—until 1976 were either not able to win a majority of Riksdag seats or to cooperate among themselves to form a coalition.

In addition to a lack of alternatives, the Social Democratic tenure can be explained in part by the high degree of civility and pragmatism in Swedish politics, a subject we shall explore later. Swedish politicians, unlike those of Italy and Fourth Republic France, do not bring down governments when they know they can't replace them.

But in 1976, about one and a half percent of the Swedish electorate switched from Left to Right, producing a Riksdag with 180 seats for the three nonsocialist parties and 169 seats for the Social Democrats and Communists. This time the three opposition parties—Center, Liberal, and Conservative —agreed to stick together, forming a coalition government with Center party chief Thorbjörn Fälldin as prime minister. The shift did not mean an end to the Swedish welfare state, but rather to a leveling off of new programs and taxes. Some voters thought it was simply time for a change.

The Riksdag is housed in a new, ultramodern building in downtown Stockholm. It is equipped with a Buck Rogers electronic voting system. But is it the real center of power? Not really. There is seldom doubt about how a division of the house will go before the Riksdag members press the *ja* or *nej* buttons on their desk. The issue has usually been hammered out elsewhere and is merely ratified on the Riksdag floor. The standing committees of the Riksdag, the cabinet, and the behind-the-scenes activities of the parties and interest groups are actually where most legislation is drafted.

Riksdag Committees   Sweden's parliament has at least 16 standing committees. Other standing committees may also be set up, and special committees can be formed as needed. Each committee has at least 15 members; thus there are at least 240 regular committee members. The standing committees are

Constitution (covers basic laws and freedoms)

Supply (equivalent to Ways and Means)

Taxation

Justice (courts, police, correctional facilities)

Laws (ordinary commercial, property, and family statutes)

Foreign Affairs

Defense

Social Insurance (national insurance plans)

Welfare (public assistance to the needy)

Culture

Education

Transportation (includes post and telephone)

Agriculture

Industry

Domestic Affairs (includes labor and employment)

Civil Affairs (includes housing and land use)

Considerable specialization is permitted; an individual Riksdag member, with a three-year term, can become fairly expert in his or her committee area. Indeed, many members are assigned to committees related to their profession.

Everything in the domain of a committee, whether new laws, appropriations, or simply reports, is handled by that committee alone. This eliminates the problem of having appropriations in the hands of a separate supercommittee, as in the United States. Another interesting point is that a Riksdag committee *must* report out all matters referred to it. Legislation cannot be put to sleep in committee by, for example, the maneuvers of a powerful chairman. Committees may initiate bills, but most are proposals from the cabinet, which in turn reflect the input of interest groups and the bureaucracy. Swedish legislative committees, although streamlined and smoothly working, are not the real centers of power.

CABINET

Originally a staff to serve and advise the king, early in this century the cabinet became answerable to the parliament alone, like cabinets in most European systems. The cabinet need not be approved by Riksdag vote but can be voted out. Most cabinet ministers are Riksdag members, but they do not have to be. The prime minister names the cabinet ministers.

As in most of Europe, the terms "cabinet" and "government" are interchangeable. The Swedish word for cabinet, *regering* (like the German *Regierung*) also translates as government. In the mid-1970s the Swedish cabinet was composed of nineteen ministers (three of them women), all of them Social Democratic politicians. As noted above, the small Swedish Communist party sometimes supported the minority Social Democratic government to keep it in power, but the Communists were not invited into the government and got no cabinet portfolios. There are thirteen ministries:

Justice

Foreign Affairs

Defense

Health and Social Affairs

Transportation
Finance
Education and Culture
Agriculture
Commerce
Labor
Housing and Physical Planning
Local Government
Industry

Five ministers were "without portfolio," that is, they were assigned to special, ad hoc tasks outside of the normal ministries.

A typical Swedish ministry, or *departement*, is quite small, usually numbering no more than a hundred people, including secretaries. Such a small group does not, of course, run much daily business. It is, rather, a leadership team that sets guidelines for numerous autonomous boards and, most important, drafts legislation and prepares budgets that the government submits to the Riksdag. The Swedish "ministry," then, corresponds to the layer of political appointees a U.S. president names to the top positions of a department. In both cases, there is an attempt by the "politicians" to control the civil servants.

As in Britain, the Swedish cabinet practices "collective responsibility"; that is, decisions are reached and supported by all the ministers, not just the one whose department is concerned. To reach these decisions, the whole cabinet meets once, twice, and even three times a week, sometimes over lunch in a private dining room in the chancery. Ministers may be called upon to defend cabinet decisions before the Riksdag, so the Swedish cabinet must practice a high degree of teamwork, unlike the American cabinet.

PARTY GOVERNMENT

The key element, or "cement," holding the system together is the party, specifically the Social Democratic party, which has ruled Sweden for more than four decades. Indeed, the Social Democrats loom so large that at times Sweden's multiparty system seems to coalesce, in Donald Hancock's words, into a two-bloc "Socialist versus nonsocialist alignment."[4]

In Sweden, as in most European political systems, the party serves as the bridge between executive and legislative, which are not seen as opposing or balancing branches as in the United States. In European theory, the cabinet is just a branch of parliament that directs the machinery of government where the

---

[4] M. Donald Hancock, *Sweden: The Politics of Postindustrial Change* (Hinsdale, Ill.: Dryden Press, 1972), pp. 111–12.

parliament chooses. In actual practice, of course, things are not that simple, for the cabinet and bureaucracy take on lives of their own. In Sweden (and most of Europe), there can be little conflict between executive and legislative for the dominant party has the say in both. In PR systems, members of parliament are elected not as individual candidates, but as names on a party list submitted to voters in each constituency. Aspirants to parliament must first work within their parties to get into the lists. The party decides whom they will enter and how high up on the list the name is to be placed. The higher up the name, the better the candidate's chance of being elected as part of his or her party's percentage of the votes. Parties in PR systems are consequently rather disciplined, unlike U.S. parties. A politician in Sweden who is at odds with his or her party may be dropped from the party list at the next election, a practice that gives relative uniformity of purpose to the parties both in parliament and the cabinet. Programs are generally adhered to and voters have a fairly clear idea of where each party stands ideologically.

Such a system places a premium on organization, and the Social Democrats are the best organized of all the Swedish parties. Over 950,000 Swedes are actual members of the Social Democratic party, more than 11 percent of Sweden's population. Some of this membership, however, is automatic through one's membership in an LO union. These members are organized into some 2,500 "workers' communes" in party districts that correspond to the constituencies.[5] A party congress of 350 members meets every three years to chart the Social Democrats' general course and choose the party's 28-member executive, its chairman, and its secretary. This executive in turn is steered by a 7-member executive committee. The student may notice here the strong similarity in organization between the Swedish Social Democrats and the Soviet or East German Communists. The similarity is not completely coincidental, for both the Social Democrats and Communists grew out of the working-class movements of the turn of the century, and both built "democratic centralism" into their structures for purposes of political combat. The difference that evolved over the decades is that the Social Democrats came to stress the democratic aspects while the Communists opted for strict centralism. The Swedish Social Democratic party contains many viewpoints and factions; unlike the Communist party, it is not a monolithic organization and does not try to be.

The Social Democrats lend great coherence to the Swedish system. Their rather mild, reformist programs have slowly turned Sweden into a model welfare state. The Social Democratic viewpoint suffused both legislative and executive. One may dispute this viewpoint, but it does give the other parties something to react against. The Social Democrats generally have the initiative, proposing welfare measures to which the "bourgeois" parties react. Even when the Social

[5] Joseph B. Board, Jr., *The Government and Politics of Sweden* (Boston: Houghton Mifflin, 1970), p. 95.

Democrats were voted out of power in 1976, they still continued to be one of Sweden's key institutions.

SWEDISH
POLITICAL
ATTITUDES

THE VERY CIVIL SOCIETY

Much of the working of the Swedish system depends on the attitudes of its participants rather than on unique, specifically Swedish institutions. On paper, Swedish governmental institutions are not all that different from several other European systems. The Swedish system, for example, if transposed to Italy, would overnight cease to be Swedish. The Italians would sabotage it by not paying their taxes, ignoring labor-management agreements, quarreling in parliament, and so forth. The Italian system, if transposed to Sweden, would probably work rather well, much better than in Italy. Swedes would immediately organize a series of Royal Commissions and recommend changes in the new system, and soon it would be like the Swedish system again. A key variable, then, is the political culture.

Political culture is, simply put, the psychology of the nation in regard to politics. As with Swedish history, Swedish political culture may be sufficiently unique to make the transfer of all or part of the Swedish system difficult or impossible.

Let us take one example of Swedish political culture, which the author experienced personally. On a Saturday morning in the university city of Uppsala, on a pedestrian mall in front of a modern supermarket (actually a consumers' cooperative), gather students of the major political persuasions plus adherents to half a dozen ultraleft grouplets. They hold up banners and placards, distribute leaflets, and sell party newspapers. Three young Conservatives take turns speaking through a small public address system they have set up, explaining that they are not reactionaries (indeed, they call themselves "moderates"), but that taxes, centralization, and planning have gone too far in Sweden and are driving out individual initiative and freedom. Facing them are the banners of Trotskyists and Maoists, demanding a total reconstruction of Swedish society. The Conservatives finish speaking, there is scattered applause (not, of course, from the Trotskyists and Maoists). There are no catcalls, no attempts to interrupt, and nothing is thrown. Instead, the members of the various groups circulate politely, passing out their literature, and occasionally explain what they stand for. The visiting American, familiar with other parts of Europe and with U.S. campuses in the late 1960s and early 1970s, is slightly amazed. Why aren't they hitting each other, shouting down their opponents, heckling the speakers? Why aren't police patrolling the area? The answer is simple: such is not the Swedish way. Swedes are so thoroughly civil that even when they disagree with each other—and their disagreements are serious—they stick to the norms of polite society. Violence is out of the question.

SWEDISH RATIONALITY

Swedish civility is the natural consequence of qualities that virtually all observers agree upon: Swedes are reserved, conformist, unemotional, and formal. Some Swedes even admit that as a people they are dull. American draft resisters and deserters who got political asylum in Sweden during the Vietnam war often experienced difficulty in adjusting to Swedish life. Some had come with an overly idealized picture of Sweden, thinking that welfare also guaranteed human warmth and happiness. To the contrary, film director Ingmar Bergman has made an international reputation dissecting the Swede's inability to love and be loved. Some viewers take his films as a statement of the human condition in general, but they are first and foremost a statement of the Swedish condition. (In the same sense, Sartre's dictum that "Hell is other people" can be more accurately read, "Hell is other Frenchmen.")

The very qualities that make life in Sweden rather dull are precisely those that make Swedes so governable and their society so open to rational change. If Swedes are overly formal, they are also committed to law and procedure. If they are unemotional, they are also committed to reason, pragmatism, and compromise. If they are reserved they also do not try to impose their viewpoints on others. What the Swedes forsake in passion they gain in the workability of their system.

Sociologist Richard Tomasson believes that the Swedish value system makes Sweden more "modern" than the United States. One of the key values, says Tomasson, is the Swedish view of institutions as malleable.[6] The Swedes do not worship existing institutions the way many Americans do—consider the awe surrounding the presidency—but rather Swedes examine how well institutions work and change them without shedding many tears for tradition. The unicameral Riksdag of 1970 is a case in point. Its inauguration was preceded by several years of calm, reasoned debate, and then the constitution was reformed, the old Riksdag building abandoned, and the new edifice swung into operation. Could that happen in Washington?

Rationality is highly prized in Swedish thinking, as it is in French thinking. The difference is that the French celebrate an abstract, Cartesian, deductive kind of rationality and then deplore reality for not living up to theory. The Swedes use an empirical, Lockean, inductive kind of rationality and do not pay too much attention to theory or ideological purity. The British and Americans

---

[6] Tomasson, *Sweden: Prototype of Modern Society*, pp. 274–75.

also pride themselves on this latter approach, but the Swedes have incorporated it more thoroughly into their political style.

The pragmatism that deeply influences Swedish politics, is not a fight over great principles, as in France and Italy, but rather a search for compromise between those who want a little more and those who want a little less. Indeed, one well-known study of Swedish government was titled *The Politics of Compromise*. [7] This is not to say that the parties agree on basic issues. Indeed, the electoral propaganda of the Social Democrats in the 1970s sounded as if the class war were alive and well. Prime Minister Olof Palme denounced the wily machinations of the "bourgeoisie" in trying to roll back the clock of social progress. The Center, Liberal, and Conservative parties saw economic ruin and the extinction of liberty if the Social Democrats continued in office. They were not faking their views (although they may have exaggerated them a bit for the campaign). But when these same antagonists meet privately in Riksdag committees or ad hoc Royal Commissions to wrestle with a concrete problem, compromise solutions invariably emerge. This situation has led some Swedes to feel they are being given a public show of fiery rhetoric while the real business of governing is conducted behind closed doors by bureaucratic and financial elites who scratch each others' backs.

OCCUPATIONAL VOTING

Swedes are interested in politics; about 90 percent turn out for elections. Furthermore, the Swedish vote follows occupational patterns: 39 percent of big businessmen, professionals, and highly-paid employees voted Conservative in 1968, while 75 percent of blue-collar workers and 71 percent of foremen voted Social Democratic. [8] This highly rational type of voting contrasts with the American pattern where many workingpeople are persuaded by Republicans to ignore the pro-labor Democrats and vote on noneconomic issues such as patriotism, law and order, and peace with honor. Many British workers vote Tory for similar reasons.

The explanation for both high turnout and economic-interest voting in Sweden lies in the strong, unified, and politically aware Swedish labor movement, the LO, which teaches the working people where their interests lie and schools them to support the Social Democrats. The other sections of Swedish society copied the Social Democrats and mobilized their own people into parties that suited their economic interests. Thus the Swedish Social Democrats' strong organization lends great rationality to the Swedish system as a whole, engender-

[7] Dankwart A. Rustow, *The Politics of Compromise: A Study of Parties and Cabinet Government in Sweden* (New York: Greenwood Press, 1955). See especially chapter 8.

[8] Bo Särlvik, "Voting Behavior in Shifting Election Winds," in *Scandinavian Political Studies 1970* vol. 5, ed. Olof Ruin (New York: Columbia University Press, 1970), p. 278.

ing high participation and strong issue-orientation, particularly on economic issues.

PATTERNS
OF INTERACTION

"ORGANIZATION SWEDEN"

As we discussed above, Swedes are organized into powerful interest groups that are part of the political process, sometimes more important than formal institutions of government. As Swedish political scientist Gunnar Heckscher put it, in Sweden "no important groups exist without formal organization."[9] Here are the more important "peak" or "roof" organizations that group together smaller constituent interest groups:

Employees' organizations
    LO, representing two dozen mostly blue-collar unions.
    TCO, representing two dozen white-collar unions.
    SACO, grouping three dozen professional organizations.
    SR, grouping organizations of middle and higher civil servants.
Management organizations
    SAF, representing employers vis-à-vis LO.
    Association of Swedish Industries
    Export Association of Sweden
    SHIO, representing smaller enterprises.
Farm organization
    LRF, representing farmers' associations.
Cooperatives
    KF, runs member-owned supermarkets and department stores.

In addition, there are organizations for high school students, temperance societies (large and important in Sweden, where alcoholism was once a major problem), landlords, renters, sports federations, and study circles.

LABOR-MANAGEMENT PEACE TREATY

Politically, the most important of these organizations are the LO and SAF. It is they who meet to set wages, hours, fringe benefits, and working conditions in industrywide contracts. It is important to note that neither in the original 1938 Saltsjöbaden Agreement nor in present negotiations does the government inter-

---

[9] Gunnar Heckscher, "Interest Groups in Sweden: Their Political Role," in *Interest Groups on Four Continents*, ed. Henry W. Ehrmann (Pittsburgh: University of Pittsburgh Press, 1958), p. 154.

fere. Indeed, part of the reason that Swedish management, represented by the SAF, consented to such sweeping arrangements was to head off possible government intervention during the worldwide depression of the 1930s, when the Social Democrats took power. Thus one of the foundation stones of Sweden's orderly progress, high standard of living, and so-called "socialism" is not a government matter, but a bargain struck privately by two powerful organizations. The process, then, falls outside of the strictly governmental sphere but is very much within the overall political system.

There is little analogous to this arrangement outside of Scandinavia. In comparison, the American equivalents are pale reflections. The AFL-CIO speaks for only a minority of the American wage workers; the LO speaks for a big majority (perhaps 95 percent) of Swedish wage workers. The American labor movement is splintered—important components such as the auto workers, teamsters, and miners are not affiliated with the AFL-CIO; the LO essentially has no competition in Sweden among blue-collar workers, although white-collar unions have their own peak organization, the TCO. On the management side there is even less to compare. In the United States the National Association of Manufacturers attempts to speak for big business on Capitol Hill and in the executive departments, but it has no authority (or even interest) in negotiating with unions. Compared to the SAF, the NAM is little more than a discussion and lobbying group. The labor movements of Britain and West Germany are more cohesive than the American, but again British and German management have nothing like the SAF to negotiate contracts industrywide (instead of one firm at a time).

Founded in 1898, the *Landsorganisationen i Sverige*, the National Organization in Sweden, now speaks for more than 1.9 million wage earners, including virtually all industrial workers. The LO itself is composed of three dozen unions ranging from the massive metal workers' to the tiny chimney sweeps' unions, all of which are required to support the Social Democrats. Many unions confer automatic Social Democratic membership on their rank and file, one reason why that party has so many members enrolled. The other employees' peak organizations, the TCO, SACO, and SR, have no party affiliations. Indeed, because SACO aims to preserve income differentials for its university-trained members, it generally opposes the leveling efforts of the Social Democrats.

The Swedish Employers' Confederation (*Svenska Arbetsgivareföreningen*) was founded in 1902 in large measure as a response to the LO. Business wanted to close ranks in the face of the growing power of organized labor. Now over 40 employer associations belong to the SAF, representing some 25,000 firms with over 1.2 million employees.[10] The SAF's largest component, like the LO's, is the metal-working industry. The SAF and LO are in many respects mirror images of each other.

---

[10] Martin Schnitzer, *The Economy of Sweden* (New York: Praeger, 1970), p. 192.

Central wage negotiations in Sweden go back to 1908 and even survived the disastrous (for labor) 1909 general strike. Still, the late 1920s and early 1930s was a time of labor turmoil; strikes and lockouts were commonplace. The worst came in 1931 with the shooting of five strikers by government troops. Labor bloodshed had been rare in Sweden, and the incident shocked Swedes on both the labor and management sides of the fence. With the Social Democrats coming to power the following year, the situation was ripe for some kind of labor-management "peace treaty."

Meeting irregularly for some years at the seaside resort of Saltsjöbaden near Stockholm, representatives of the LO and SAF hammered out a Basic Agreement that includes the following points:

1. No strikes are allowed while a contract is in effect; they can be called only after it has expired.
2. Wildcat strikes are illegal, and those who engage in them are liable to civil (but not criminal) penalties.
3. Labor and management *must* negotiate their disputes; a detailed outline for procedure is included.
4. Management lockouts of workers are prohibited.
5. Secondary boycotts are severely limited.
6. Both sides must live up to their contracts, no matter for how long a term they run.
7. Whole industries come under one contract.
8. The unions cannot block industrial modernization and the replacing of men by machinery.

Later a Labor Court, staffed in part by LO and SAF appointees, was set up to interpret disputed contracts. At first glance it may seem as if management got the better end of the bargain; for example, the restrictions on strikes and no opposition to mechanization; but labor got the key concessions of binding, long-term, industrywide collective agreements. It was a compromise, and it has worked quite well.

The Saltsjöbaden Agreement is one of Sweden's more attractive institutions, one that might seem worth duplicating in other countries. But in how many countries are both labor and management cohesive enough to make such an agreement stick? The demands of Swedish unions must first be cleared with the LO, which, as its part of the treaty, cracks down on wildcat strikes. Few union confederations are that strong elsewhere. On the other side, few countries have managers willing to lock themselves into industrywide contracts. Saltsjöbaden took the twin Swedish characteristics of organization (of both labor and management) and compromise, items in short supply elsewhere.

The Saltsjöbaden pattern has continued. Sweden has lost far fewer working days to strikes than most industrialized countries. Only West Germany and Switzerland have fewer strikes, while Italy and Britain are often paralyzed by walkouts. In Sweden the two great antagonists of modern society, labor and management, have learned to cooperate and to moderate and institutionalize their struggle. Swedish labor does not try to bring the country to a halt and Swedish management does not try to sweat workers.

CORPORATISM

Some observers find Swedish interest associations so strong and their influence in governmental decision making so pervasive that they offer Sweden as an example of "corporatism." Swedophobe Roland Huntford, for example, claims, "Like Fascist Italy, Sweden is today a corporate State."[11]

Just what is "corporatism" and how did it acquire such a pejorative connotation? The term will come up in relation to all five of the countries we consider in this book. Some, namely Italy and Spain, have at one time tried to build corporate states. Others, Yugoslavia and East Germany, have set up bodies to represent workers based on their place of work, although since they are Marxist these regimes would deny practicing corporatism. And Sweden is sometimes accused of being a corporate state. Is the charge a fair one?

The theory of corporatism harks back to the Middle Ages, when guilds of craftsmen and traders controlled much of the economic life. In these guilds there was neither "labor" nor "management" but, it has been theorized, what seems to have been one happy family all plying the same trade. Sometimes representatives of the guilds would have a say in governing the town. With the later industrialization of the nineteenth century, some thinkers, particularly Catholic thinkers, became alarmed at the bitterness of labor-capital strife and suggested the old guilds as an alternate model of economic organization, one in which workers and bosses would be on the same team, not at each others' throats. An outgrowth of this idea was the concept of representation not by geographic district or proportional party vote, but by branch of industry.

Fascist thinkers in Spain and Italy saw this concept as a way to abolish political parties and all the fractiousness that goes with them and still give people some representation in government. Instead of allowing clashes of interests, for example those of blue-collar workers against those of factory owners, the corporate state would emphasize the two groups' common interest, that is, the promotion of that branch of industry. Unity, not conflict, was the theme, and both labor and management were to be adequately represented by the same man.[12] Corporatism ranked as only a minor European ideology until Mussolini used it as one rationale for his Fascist order. In practice, of course, the corporations were used mainly to control workers and give managers the upper hand.

---

[11] Huntford, *The New Totalitarians*, p. 86.

[12] Slight tinges of corporatism can be found in the United States, where one senator garners support from both labor and management of the same industry. Henry Jackson, for example, has been called "the Senator from Boeing."

Mussolini's "Corporate State" was a sham, all theory and no practice, and with the *Duce*'s demise corporatism returned to deserved obscurity, but now with a derogatory connotation for its supporting role in Fascism.

Now, seen in this light, is Sweden a corporate state? In terms of governmental structure, definitely not. Sweden has no equivalent to Mussolini's National Council of Corporations or Yugoslavia's Federal Chamber, which is elected from "self-managing organizations." On the unofficial level, ties between interest groups and government are indeed close in Sweden but probably would not fall under the above description of corporatism. When Swedish interest groups meet with each other and with organs of government (in ways described below), they do so not as representatives of a whole branch of industry, but generally as representatives of labor or of management and, as such, they meet in a context of conflict rather than of the fake unity that Mussolini's corporatism tried to impose. Whereas the corporate state attempted to erase distinctions between workers and capital, the Swedish system starts with the premise that such conflict is natural but can be handled by reason and compromise.

Rather than corporatism, then, Sweden has a highly evolved and institutionalized form of bargaining among interest groups.

Let us now consider how Swedish interest groups make their voices felt in the process of turning an idea into a law.

1. Commissions   Commissions are one of the great avenues for starting legislation in Sweden. The government (i.e., the cabinet) names a Royal Commission to study a current problem. Perhaps half of the people named to sit on this commission are from well-known interest associations. This is done deliberately, to give the groups a chance to state their viewpoint at the very beginning. Experts from the groups often appear as witnesses before the panel; they are important data sources.

2. Remiss   *Remiss* is the name given to the circulation of the commission's final report to the interest associations and their sending it back with comments. The relevant ministry then summarizes the various groups' comments and sends the whole package to the Riksdag along with the government's draft of a bill. Even if the group was not represented on the commission, or its experts not called as witnesses, the *remiss* stage gives it an important chance to make its views known.

3. Riksdag deliberations   These can be another point of input, because many deputies are also active in various interest groups, particularly LO officials serving as Social Democratic members of parliament. Influence here is no longer direct, for Riksdag committees meet behind closed doors and call no witnesses; data gathering has already been done in steps 1 and 2.

4. Application Application, on the so-called "output" side of the process, is another area of group influence. Since the daily administration of a ministry is in the hands of bureaucrats, the interest associations take pains to establish good working relations with civil servants who often have considerable discretionary power over the details of applying a law. In addition, some government programs are actually administered by interest associations. For example, unemployment insurance is run by the LO and certain agricultural benefits are handled by farmers' associations.

The first two steps of the above process may be seen as a kind of legalized and formalized lobbying. Instead of making campaign contributions to individual parliamentarians (which would do them no good in Sweden since they are elected on party slates), groups put their interests right out on the table and discuss them openly. Lobbying by payoff, Washington-style, is unnecessary in Sweden.

THE BUREAUCRACY

As in most modern countries, the Swedish bureaucracy, long a model of efficiency, has taken on a life of its own. No longer the passive recipient of decisions made by the process described above, the Swedish bureaucracy increasingly jumps into the process as a highly knowledgeable interest group in its own right. Swedish political scientist Nils Elvander notes that in recent years the strength of interest groups on the important study commissions is on the wane, and more and more influence comes from the governmental bureaucracy itself.[13] Now, when a Royal Commission is set up to study something, chances are that government experts will be the largest group on the commission.

The Swedish bureaucracy is powerful and respected. Owing to its long connection with aristocracy, the Swedish civil service generally has high status. Corruption is unknown. As noted earlier, most Swedish civil servants do not work directly for ministries, which are mostly just small planning staffs; instead, boards and agencies handle most of the daily work, and they have considerable autonomy. Although the several dozen boards and agencies have standardized salary scales and regulations, they by and large recruit their own people. Among the higher-level civil servants, the traditional educational background has been a law degree, although recently more positions have opened up for liberal arts and social science graduates.[14]

As mentioned earlier, interest groups try to work closely with boards and agencies. As Elvander observes, this closeness may even turn into a "client relationship" between interest group and bureaucrat of the sort we will discuss

---

[13] Nils Elvander, "Interest Groups in Sweden," *The Annals of the American Academy of Political and Social Science*, 413 (May 1974), 34.

[14] For an overview of the Swedish civil service, see Neil Elder, *Government in Sweden: The Executive at Work* (Oxford: Pergamon Press, 1970), chap. 4.

in relation to Italy.[15] In sum, the Swedish civil service has great influence on both the "input" side of government, on the commissions, and on the "output" side, as administrators. This situation is not without its critics.

"Harpsund democracy" is one term used to criticize behind-the-scenes decision making in Sweden. Harpsund is the location of the prime minister's country home, and there, from 1955 to 1963, ministers and interest-group representatives met twice a year. Included were representatives of such peak organizations as the LO, SAF, TCO, and KF. Objecting to this too-cozy arrangement, which bypassed the Riksdag altogether, was the leader of the opposition Liberal party, Bertil Ohlin, who coined the phrase "Harpsund democracy" to mean "an overpowerful government, a powerless parliament and unjustifiably strong associations, which directly influenced the government."[16]

Ohlin's appellation stung, and the regular Harpsund meetings were discontinued, although representatives of groups still meet there sometimes. Was Ohlin right? Is such an arrangement an end run around representative democracy? If so, then the charge of Swedish corporatism is perhaps partially accurate.

The problem—a generic one of modern governments—is the weakness of the parliament vis-à-vis the executive. Elected on the basis of party lists and hence subject to tight party discipline (lest they be left off the list at the next election), members of parliament have little to do but follow their parties' instructions and vote either for or against the government. Indeed, for most debates on the Riksdag floor the parliamentarians do not have to be present —and they aren't. The chamber is nearly empty as the perfunctory debate drones on. When the question is called, the members are summoned electronically from all over the new *Riksdaghusset*—offices, committee rooms, the gymnasium—and informed which question is up on a gigantic screen overlooking the chamber. At a signal they press their buttons for a yes or a no vote. Colored lights flash on the screen, indicating who voted what (green for yes, red for no). Then a computer prints out on the screen how the vote went, and the deputies quickly leave the chamber and go back to doing what they were doing before.

There is no point in fiery debate, which is not the Swedish style anyway, because the question has been settled in advance by compromise among the interest groups during the commission, *remiss*, and committee stages. Breaches of party discipline are rare, so votes generally can be closely predicted by adding up which parties are for and which against a measure. A Riksdag speech changes no one's vote.

---

[15] Elvander, *Annals,* p. 38.

[16] Elvander, *Annals,* p. 37.

"Harpsund democracy" or something like it is the logical outgrowth of a cut-and-dried parliament. If parliament does not originate laws, someone else will. For the locus of decision making to shift back to the Riksdag it would be necessary to give that body at least some power independent of the executive. If Riksdag votes were uncertain, if deputies could vote as they personally wished, the Riksdag would get some "action." As it is now structured, the Riksdag serves largely to confirm decisions made elsewhere. In a sense, the critics of "Harpsund democracy" should be grateful: at least *someone* is legislating, even if it is not parliament. And, in defense of the Swedish system, it must be said that various viewpoints do get a hearing in the lawmaking process.

GOVERNMENT BY THE FEW?

The danger in Sweden and in many other societies, is that the direction of society is charted by a relative handful of people, an establishment club, rather than by the body politic as a whole. The leading personalities of Sweden's peak organizations all know each other personally. They meet together privately and compromise issues out of public sight. Increasingly Swedes feel they are being ruled by a group of experts, "technocrats," who paternalistically decide what is good for the population.

This, then, is the negative side of Swedish organization and concentration. The peak organizations have gradually been consolidating their positions (usually via merger), becoming bigger and fewer. Such consolidation makes them more rational and effective, but it also risks making a mockery of democratic participation and alienating rank-and-file members. Presumably, everyone's interest is spoken for when the "big boys" meet because everyone is in one interest association or another. But the distance between member and leader becomes so great that the member feels the decision is not *his* or *her* decision. A further problem may arise, as Karl Deutsch put it, "if most interest groups are organized, heaven help the residual groups that are not."[17]

The Swedish system sometimes rides roughshod over individuals. In 1976 famed director Ingmar Bergman was rudely arrested and grilled about alleged income tax violations. Charges were dropped, but Bergman suffered a nervous collapse and left Sweden, disgusted with the bureaucracy. The Swedish system, however, has at least two safeguards for such problems: the ombudsman and a critical press.

The Ombudsman   The ombudsman is Sweden's best-known contribution to the art of governing. Basically, the ombudsman is a government lawyer who hassles the government on behalf of the citizen. More

---

[17] Karl W. Deutsch, *Politics and Government: How People Decide Their Fate*, 2nd ed. (Boston: Houghton Mifflin, 1974), p. 61.

precisely, he or she is named and paid by the Riksdag (not by the cabinet or the bureaucracy) to receive and consider complaints on governmental misdeeds and injustices. Originally set up by the 1809 constitution, the *Justitieombudsman* (literally, agent of justice) now consists of three ombudsmen with assistants and a small staff. They can subpoena government documents and officials must comply. They get their leads from individual complaints (everyone knows where the Stockholm office is and no lawyer is required to draft the letter) and newspaper stories.

Swedes are supposed to exhaust other legal remedies for their problem before turning to the ombudsman. Most cases are not pursued, but some 20 percent of them lead to action, usually the simple reprimanding of the erring official. Only about six cases a year are actually prosecuted.[18]

As Joseph Board points out, the ombudsman's effectiveness depends heavily on the Swedish context of respect for facts and a political and moral climate in which a simple reprimand is in most cases enough to produce speedy rectification.[19] Denmark, Norway, Britain, and New Zealand, all nations with a tradition of respect for law, have set up similar institutions, and from time to time there are suggestions that the United States inaugurate such an office. The American context, though, is considerably "wilder" than the Swedish. Would an ombudsman function effectively in the United States?

The Press   The press is one important area of Swedish political life in which the LO and Social Democrats are not at all dominant. Swedes read more newspapers than anyone else (even more than the British or Japanese), and most of these papers are connected with parties who oppose the Social Democrats. In 1970 the percentage breakdown of the circulation of Swedish dailies by political affiliation was

Conservative	17.8
Liberal	53.8
Center	3.0
Social Democrat	21.0
Other	4.4

The press is an important power to countervail that of the ruling party: More than half the papers printed are Liberal. While the opposition papers are not usually out for blood, they can be highly critical of Social Democratic policy. Curiously, while some 45 percent of Swedes vote Social Democratic, about three-quarters of Swedes read papers with a more conservative viewpoint. We see here, as in the United States, that newspaper readers do not necessarily vote

---

[18] Hancock, *Sweden: The Politics of Postindustrial Society*, p. 237.

[19] Board, *The Government and Politics of Sweden*, p. 185.

the way their papers suggest. U.S. newspapers are overwhelmingly Republican, but more Americans register Democratic than Republican.

Sweden's 1949 Freedom of the Press Act guarantees freedom from censorship, protects anonymity of sources (a current issue in the United States), makes one person responsible for a newspaper's contents, and grants sweeping access to public documents. The Swedish press is thus one of the freest in the world. To guard against abuse of this freedom, the Swedish National Press Club polices its own members (an example of quasicorporatism) by making them adhere to a Code of Professional Ethics covering unfair practices. Anyone who feels he or she has been mistreated by a newspaper can turn to an industry-appointed "press ombudsman" who can take the matter to the Press Council, composed of leading jurists, who in turn can fine a paper up to $600.

The government even subsidizes newspapers, but indirectly, through their parent political parties. Each party in the Riksdag gets an amount proportional to the number of seats it holds, intended (but not always used) for the party's newspapers. The obvious winners from this arrangement are the Social Democrats; the losers are those groups too small to surmount the 4 percent threshold necessary for any Riksdag seats. The subsidy began in 1966 with a total fund of $5.5 million. Because the parties can spend the money as they wish, the sums are in effect a subsidy of the parties themselves. This sort of thing is not unique; West Germany has subsidized its parties' election campaigns since 1967.

The Swedish radio and television industry is not state owned, but rather, like the West German system, it is a nonprofit public corporation financed by compulsory annual fees from radio owners ($11) and television owners ($50). There is no advertising. *Sveriges Radio/TV* is guided by a board half of whose members are named by the government (but are not necessarily bureaucrats), and half by the shareholders who include members of industries, the press, and associations. By law, radio and television news coverage is to be "factual" and "impartial," and a Radio Council monitors this mandate. Swedish radio and television are therefore more or less politically neutral; no party can control their programming. By the same token, they cannot serve to counterbalance and criticize the power of the government.

Is Sweden too much of an elite society? It certainly did not start out earlier in this century to become an elite society. The unions, interest associations, and Social Democrat and Liberal parties struggled to open up, to democratize, a Sweden that was largely run by a conservative establishment. The irony is that in order to democratize, they perfected the weapon of organization to the point where in some cases it has created new elites at the tops of the various associations. Governance then can turn into an establishment tea party, a "Harpsund democracy," leaving the common person out.

This pattern, to be sure, may be unavoidable. It is precisely what Robert Michels had in mind with his "Iron Law of Oligarchy": The many cannot rule; power tends to gravitate into the hands of a few. The Swedes, to their credit, have recognized the problem—which is built into any modern, efficient society—earlier than most and are considering ways to insure fuller popular participation. In any case, Sweden's pattern of elite interaction has produced a remarkable system, which we shall turn to next.

WHAT THE
SWEDISH SYSTEM
PRODUCES

IS SWEDEN SOCIALIST?

Many Americans call Sweden a socialist country because, allegedly, "They take care of everything for you over there." Americans have tended to equate socialism with welfare, partly because of the American Medical Association's publicity against "socialized medicine." True, Swedes get a lot of welfare benefits, although describing them as "cradle to grave" may be a bit of an overstatement.

On the other hand, little of Sweden's economy is state-owned, which some (including Communists) believe is the real definition of socialism. Over 90 percent of Sweden's labor force work for private firms. Cooperatives employ another 4 percent, and the remaining 5 or 6 percent work for the government. In addition to infrastructure items like railroads, telephone, and electric power (which are state-owned throughout Europe), Sweden has an important iron mine, a wood and pulp operation, and a shipyard under government control, as well as a few other enterprises. Curiously, most of the nationalization in Sweden took place under nonsocialist governments, before the Social Democrats took power in 1932. Since then takeovers have been rare and confined mostly to the lagging northern part of the country where the government has occasionally been forced to step in to prevent a firm from closing and laying off its workers. Unemployment, not ideology, has been the reason.

There are even millionaire dynasties in Sweden; the Wallenberg family in particular steers much of Sweden's industry and banking. Far from squeezing business dry, the Social Democratic governments have developed generous tax policies to encourage reinvestment and growth. As in the United States, better-off persons take advantage of tax deductions; some do not even pay as high a percentage as wage and salary workers who do not enjoy loopholes for their incomes. The rich do not suffer too badly in "socialist" Sweden.

Although they were rather doctrinaire Marxists before the turn of the century, the Swedish Social Democrats gradually adopted the view that private capital is not inherently evil, so long as it can be directed for the common good. This includes economic growth and equitable wages and benefits. The Swedes are pragmatists: if private ownership works, why discard it? Accordingly, private economic growth and expansion of welfare have gone hand in hand. As Prime

Minister Olof Palme put it, "If industry's primary purpose is to expand its production, to succeed in new markets, to provide good jobs for their employees, they need have no fears. Swedish industry has never expanded so rapidly as during these years of Social Democratic rule."[20]

Another test for "socialism" is equality of incomes. Sweden's income distribution is actually about the same as the United States'—before taxes, that is. By the time taxes are deducted and income redistributed, Swedish income is more equal than American. Taxes are among the world's highest and steeply progressive. While Swedes on the average pay over 40 percent of their income in national and local taxes, Swedes earning $50,000 a year may have to pay as much as two-thirds of it in taxes, although loopholes help cushion this bite. Swedes also pay inheritance taxes and even taxes on wealth (as opposed to income). When an individual's wealth totals $31,000 he or she pays 1 percent as a net wealth tax. When net wealth tops $208,000, the Swede pays 2.5 percent. But these are just the direct taxes Swedes pay. They also get hit with an indirect "value-added" tax, a sort of hidden sales tax of 17.65 percent of the value of a purchase.

In comparison with some other industrialized countries, in 1969 total taxation as a percentage of GNP went like this:[21]

Sweden	41.7%
Norway	39.9
France	37.2
West Germany	35.9
Britain	35.9
Italy	30.5
United States	29.9

Only Israel, constantly geared for war, pays a higher portion of GNP in taxes than Sweden. But what do Swedes get for their heavy tax burden?

THE WELFARE FLOOR

There is no grinding poverty in Sweden, no slums, no hunger, no untended old people, and no destitution from disability. There are some people whose various forms of assistance have failed to keep pace with inflation. These "newly poor," as they are called, get by, but not much above the poverty line. It must be conceded, however, that there are probably no Swedes who go without decent food, housing, and medical care.

[20] Quoted by Ruth Link, *Taking Part: The Power and the People in Sweden* (Stockholm: Ingenjörsförlaget, 1973), p. 119.

[21] Skandinaviska Enskilda Banken, *Some Data About Sweden* (Stockholm: Skandinaviska Enskilda Banken, 1972), p. 76.

Swedish assistance includes paid maternity leaves, child allowances, rent supplements, unemployment insurance, and pensions that pay two-thirds of the average of the individual's fifteen highest earning years. But Sweden is most renowned for its public medical program, which alone accounts for 10 percent of its GNP. In comparison, medical expenses account for 8.3 percent of the U.S. GNP. Swedish medical care is handled largely at the county level; local governments collect appreciable income taxes, some 80 percent of which goes for health care. Public health (a less propagandistic word than "socialized medicine") did not come to Sweden all at once. The Riksdag instituted it one step at a time over the decades, never letting it get ahead of what the economy could afford—again, Swedish pragmatism at work. For example, national dental insurance did not take effect until 1974.

A Swede pays only $4.50 a day for hospital treatment, $3.50 for a visit to an outpatient clinic. Patients are free to choose their own doctors, public or private. The new dental insurance pays for half of any dental treatment. In addition, everyone can get home nursing care, travel expenses to a hospital, and special coverage for industrial injuries. Public health, then, does not mean totally free medical care, but ample assistance to make it available to all.

The net effect of Sweden's welfarism is to redistribute incomes so as to place a floor, a minimum standard, under each citizen. Does this lead to laziness, to abuses, to freeloading, as critics of welfare often charge? Not in Sweden. In the first place, even if a freeloader could take advantage of all possible benefits, he or she could not live very well. There is little cheating in Sweden; neither citizens nor administrators stand for it. Swedes feel compelled to work diligently; theirs is not a lazy culture. Some think that steeply progressive taxation, as in Sweden, discourages people from trying to earn more money. Indeed, half of Swedish wage increases disappear in taxes. But that doesn't seem to stop the Swedes from working; they still want (and need) the additional income. Sweden has the highest percentage of people employed (47 percent) of any Western nation, chiefly because most wives work. If the welfare floor is a disincentive in some countries, it is not in Sweden.

THE HIGH POINT OF WELFARISM?

Is Sweden settled into a permanent pattern, or can we expect some changes? Drastic upheavals are out of the question; neither Swedish history nor Swedish character has favored sweeping, revolutionary changes. The 1976 election, however, showed that some changes may be due in the Swedish system. Two forces seem to be growing: a taxpayers' revolt (or, at any rate, dissatisfaction) and a certain disenchantment with the Social Democrats. The two are closely related.

The average Swede pays over 40 percent of his or her income in taxes. Above a level of about $6,500 a year, of every additional dollar he or she earns, around 65 cents of it go to taxes. The welfare benefits are extensive, and Swedes like them, even the conservatives. But increasingly they feel that their income is no longer theirs. Even some better-paid workers grumble that taxes are too high, and workers are the backbone of Social Democratic rule. Intellectuals who favor a social democracy on the theoretical level sometimes admit that they also find the tax bite too big. Many Swedes say they are *skattetrott*, "tax-tired."

Matters came to a head in the 1976 election, which ousted the Social Democrats after more than four decades of rule. The issues of high taxes and too much bureaucracy made inroads into their strength. New issues appeared: nuclear power plants and a plan to let trade unions take over industry. Both issues hurt the Social Democrats who apparently misjudged public opinion on these questions. The Social Democratic government was firmly committed to developing nuclear power-generating plants—five were in operation and another eight planned. The Center party turned nuclear plants into a major issue, stressing the potential dangers of these plants and their radioactive wastes. Among ecology-minded younger Swedes especially the issue caught on. The Social Democrats and their LO supporters also backed a controversial plan to gradually let unions take over majority stock control of companies, thus producing a more East European type of socialism.

The voters said no. The Social Democrats dropped to 43 percent of the popular vote, their worst showing in four decades. Together with the Communists they lost six seats in the Riksdag; their nonsocialist opponents gained five seats. What happened to the remaining seat? It simply disappeared, for the Riksdag was reduced from 350 members to 349 to avoid the 175-175 deadlock that came with the 1973 elections. Thus in the 1976 Riksdag the socialist parties held 169 seats while the nonsocialist parties held 180, a major upset in Swedish terms. A coalition of the Center, Liberal, and Conservative parties took power.

This situation was duplicated in 1973 in both Norway and Denmark. Their respective Social Democratic parties lost seats and depended on parliamentary support from small leftist groups. In Norway and Denmark the tax-revolt pattern was more pronounced than in Sweden; antitax parties sprang up in the two former countries and did surprisingly well in elections. The name of the new Norwegian party was highly personal: Anders Lange's Party for the Reduction of Taxes and Other Duties and Government Interference. The head of the Danish party was a wealthy tax lawyer who prided himself on his use of tax loopholes for his clients and himself.

The Swedes have less whimsey than their Norwegian and Danish neighbors. Instead of forming a new party, it appears that tax-tired Swedes shifted some of their votes to the big gainer of the 1970s, the Center party, which climbed to one-fourth of the Riksdag seats.

Does this activity indicate that the three Scandinavian societies, where taxes take about the same 40 percent of income, have reached a kind of "ouch point" at which traditional Social Democratic voters start deserting their party? If so, it would mark the high point of welfarism and the maximum share of income that Scandinavians are willing to have taxed away, regardless of how much they appreciate welfare benefits.

Sweden's Prime Minister Olof Palme, who served from 1969 to 1976, was, however, convinced that Sweden needed more, not less, welfare. "Society is about homes, people, their loneliness and their need of community with others," he said. "The trouble is we have still too little welfare permeating society. We must go more deeply with the welfare state."[22] Palme's strong ideological commitments seem to have put him out of touch with Swedish voting trends. Palme became prime minister at age forty-two with a somewhat radical reputation. Scion of an elite Swedish family, Palme had been a cavalry officer; his wife is a countess. But after he took his bachelor's degree in Ohio (at Kenyon College, where he got straight A's) in 1948, he hitchhiked around the United States and was so appalled by American poverty and inequality that he became a dedicated socialist.

Swedish-American relations chilled in the early 1970s when Palme voiced strong opposition to the American war in Vietnam. Not only was he personally committed on Vietnam, but he found that demonstrating against the war helped cement relations with radical younger Swedes. They needed a bit of cementing, for Palme faced the danger of defection not only on his party's right, but on its left as well. For some of the radicals, the Social Democratic party had awakened the expectation and vision of complete equality, worker control of industry, and the end of bourgeois cultural norms—but the party was not now trying to reach them. The Social Democrats' quasi-revolutionary campaign rhetoric contrasted with their pragmatic, compromising performance in government. Palme's Social Democrats faced the same dilemma as Brandt and Schmidt did with the German Social Democrats in the late 1960s and early 1970s. The German Young Socialist (*Jusos*) wing of the party tugged leftward, but to follow them could spell electoral disaster just as the SPD was making inroads into the German middle class by means of a moderate platform. Viewed in this way, Palme's anti-American statements and trip to Cuba were a politician's effort to hang on to his party's youth wing, lest they defect either to the Communists or to an ultraleft splinter group.

The Social Democrats had done a remarkable job in gently guiding Sweden through difficult times and turning it into a society that many regard as the world's most modern. But on the way, they also created new problems. Housing, as in most of Europe, was difficult to find and expensive. With the growth of the welfare state came the large Swedish bureaucracy and its attendant problems.

[22] Henry Kamm, "Scandinavia Tightens Hold on Welfare Costs," *New York Times*, March 22, 1974, p. 3.

The smooth surface of Swedish politics concealed a too-cozy arrangement whereby the gigantic interest associations steered Swedish society with little democratic input. And finally, the very success of the Swedish system produced a certain amount of boredom. The most exciting political disputes concerned such things as a little more or a little less government subsidy for the national dental program. Some observers suggest this ennui is why Swedes turn outward and make distant causes, such as South Africa or Vietnam, their own. Let us now turn to countries in the South of Europe where boredom is hardly a threat.

SPAIN
3

Great hopes emerged with the death of Francisco Franco in late 1975. Most observers breathed a sigh of relief that *El Caudillo* (The Leader) had finally left the scene a few days short of his eighty-third birthday, after ruling Spain for thirty-six years. At long last Spain, frozen in its political development under Franco's ultraconservative regime, could rapidly progress in a democratic direction and become a "normal" West European country.

But were things that simple? Had Franco been the only block to Spain's progress? Was orderly reform assured in the post-Franco era? Or was Franco merely the thumb on the champagne cork which, when it blew, would release anew social and political violence like that of the 1936–39 Civil War?

The point is that we know little about contemporary Spain. We have lots of books on Spanish history and some biographies of Franco.[1] But in the main, serious inquiry stopped with the Spanish Civil War, which has been studied in almost morbid detail. Relatively little scholarly work has been done on the Spain of today. This has left a curious gap. While American high school and college students have made Spanish the most-studied foreign idiom in the United States, they learn little of the country whence the tongue sprang. While American and West European visitors have made Spain the world's number-one tourist country, they know little or nothing of Spanish political life. Let us try, in a small way, to heal this breach.

THE IMPACT OF THE PAST

Spaniards have made a small industry out of the study of their own history. Particularly since the humiliating defeat in the Spanish-American War they have combed Spanish history to find out why Spaniards are so disunited, so passionate about causes, so frac-

---

[1] The best is probably J. W. D. Trythall, *El Caudillo: A Political Biography of Franco* (New York: McGraw-Hill, 1970).

tious—in a word, so Spanish. While Swedish history is marked by early unification and efficient centralized administration undisturbed by civil violence, Spain has suffered from precisely the opposite. Several reasons have been advanced to explain the Spanish disunity and internal conflict.

IS SPAIN ISOLATED?

"Europe ends at the Pyrenees," people used to say, implying that south of these mountains Africa begins. But the rocky spine that forms Spain's frontier with France never pushed Spain out of the European mainstream. There have been kingdoms that covered both sides of the Pyrenees without undue difficulty. As George Hills points out, "the Pyrenees were no barrier to men or ideas at any time during the Middle Ages."[2] Too much has been made of Spain's alleged isolation from the rest of Europe. Geographically Spain is no more isolated from Europe than is Italy, its sister Mediterranean peninsula, which also has a mountain barrier on its north. Spain became a European backwater out of political, cultural, and economic grounds, not geographical.

Internally, however, geography does play a role. Iberia consists of a narrow coastal belt somewhat cut off from the upland mountainous interior. Some Spanish coastal regions, both because they were better watered and because they had immediate access to the sea, became more prosperous than the dry and isolated interior. Further, they have spawned non-Castilian groups (the Portuguese, Gallegans, Basques, and Catalans) that have repeatedly tended toward autonomy or even independence in their relations with the center. Center-periphery tension, long one of Spain's political headaches, grows out of her geography. In terms of internal communication, Spain offered no easy passage through its mountainous interior. Geographically, Spain was harder to unify than France.[3]

A MAD ETHNIC MIXTURE

In terms of the peoples who have made up the Spanish ethnic stock, Spain is one of the most complex nations of Europe. On top of the original Iberians washed waves of Celts, Phoenicians, Greeks and Carthaginians in the first millennium B.C. The Romans came in 211 B.C. as part of their war against Carthage. Spain was an important part of the Roman Empire for six centuries, and Roman influence looms large. The several languages of Iberia are all (with the exception of Basque) variations of vulgar Latin. Many place names, much architecture, the legal system, and, in the fourth century, Christianity came from Rome.

[2] George Hills, *Spain* (New York: Praeger, 1970), p. 40.

[3] See W. B. Fisher and H. Bowen-Jones, *Spain: An Introductory Geography* (New York: Praeger, 1966).

The waves of immigration did not stop. The Romans sent to Spain tens of thousands of Jewish slaves (with Christians among them) following the destruction of Jerusalem in A.D. 70. Starting in A.D. 406, wandering Germanic tribes began crossing the Pyrenees. Alani, Suevi, Vandals (who gave their name to Andalusia), and Visigoths arrived in quick succession. The Visigoths ruled Spain for three centuries and in 586 made Roman Catholicism the state religion.

From at least that time Spanish Catholicism has been a special breed: fanatic, intolerant, and closely identified with the Spanish government. The Visigoths, for example, started a persecution of the Jews that lasted through the Spanish Inquisition. To be Spanish meant to be Catholic, for there were no ethnic criteria to define what "Spanish" meant.

THE MOSLEM CONQUEST

Another Spanish pattern appeared under the Visigoths: political fractiousness. By 710 there was full-scale civil war over who should accede to the throne. In 711, taking advantage of the internal strife, an army under Tarik ibn Zeyad crossed from North Africa, beginning the Moorish conquest of Spain. Tarik's name is still with us in the rock near where he landed: Gibraltar, from the Arabic *gib al-Tarik*, "the mountain of Tarik." Tarik was actually invited by dissident Christians to help in the civil war. In his first battle, two wings of the Visigoth army actually went over to the invaders. It was not the last time that dissident Spaniards would turn to outside help for their political quarrels.

The Moorish conquest of Spain was easy; by 716 all but the northwest Atlantic corner of the peninsula, shielded by the Cantabrian Mountains, was under Moslem rule. Unlike the Christians, the Moslems were not fanatics about religion; for the most part they practiced a live-and-let-live attitude toward Christians and Jews, who, as fraternal "people of the book," were not to be forcibly converted or persecuted. The Moorish conquest gave rise to a cultural highpoint for Spain. While the rest of Europe wallowed in the Dark Ages, Arabic culture made Spain the most advanced civilization of the continent. From Greek philosophy (Aristotle spread to Europe through Arab translations from Spain), to medicine, architecture, agriculture, and handicrafts (Toledan steel, Cordovan leather), Spain and its products awed the rest of Europe.

The Moors, however, like the Visigoths, did not excel at the art of governing. They too were incurably fractious, and their empire repeatedly splintered into local principalities, some Moslem-ruled, some Christian-ruled. Many observers of Spain hold that the centuries of Moorish rule bequeathed to Spain its political instability and fragmentation. Furthermore, the pattern of Christian reconquest was drawn out, intermittent, and local, so that feelings of national unity failed to develop. On balance, the Moorish interlude delayed Spain's internal development compared with lands north of the Pyrenees.

The Christian *Reconquista* began immediately after the Moorish conquest, but it took nearly eight centuries to complete. Gradually pushing out of their northwest corner, Christians over the centuries drove the Moors southward until, by 1250, all but a portion of the Moslems' beloved *al-Andalus* (Andalusia) had been retaken. Finally, in 1492, the last Moorish capital—Granada, with its magnificent Alhambra—fell. Moslems and Jews were given the choice of conversion to Catholicism or expulsion.

The curious thing about the Reconquista is that it was not a unified, centralized effort on the part of either Christians or Moors. Often Christian counts sided with Moslem chiefs and vice versa in essentially local squabbles. The Spanish hero El Cid (from the Arabic *al-sayyid*, lord), for example, spent most of his years fighting in the service of Moors. A more accurate image of the reconquest is that of a growing northern belt of several Christian principalities, a shrinking southern belt of several Moslem kingdoms, and between them an irregular belt of anarchy that slowly moved south. The Christian reconquerers, in order to gain supporters, granted numerous local rights to nobles, cities, and regions. These *fueros,* as they were called, permitted autonomous governing and taxation and were highly prized and jealously guarded up to recent times.

Spain's national unification was retarded. Some historians claim that the 1469 marriage of Isabelle of Castile to Ferdinand of Aragon actually makes Spain one of the earliest unified European states. But this was a dynastic marriage only; the two kingdoms were not actually merged until much later, and even then the consolidation was superficial.

Two important nationalities, for example, have resisted rule from Madrid (Spain's capital only since 1561) until the present day: the Basques and the Catalans. The Basques, an ancient people of obscure origin who speak a language related to no other, occupy the western end of the Pyrenees and part of Spain's Atlantic coast. Some 2 million Basques are in Spain, 200,000 in France. While many Basques have become culturally Spanish—indeed, some of Spain's greatest minds have been Basque—most retain a sharp sense of their difference from Spaniards and have tried, intermittently, to establish Basque autonomy or even independence. The Basques are also Spain's most devout Catholics, and their priests have often supported their separatist views. The Basque region, particularly the port of Bilbao, is one of Spain's two most industrialized areas; the other is Catalonia.

Catalonia, at the eastern end of the Pyrenees and down the Mediterranean coast a way, enjoyed at various times an independent kingdom that spilled over into France. Speaking a Romance language quite distinct from Spanish, the Catalans treasure their literature, poetry, and song. Counting the Valencian and Balearic dialects, there are an estimated four million Catalan speakers. A gifted commercial people, the Catalans have made Barcelona Spain's leading business center. Much more influenced by Europe (particularly France) than are Castillians, Catalans have tried at various times for regional autonomy within Spain. Catalonia too has contributed a disproportionate share of Spain's intellectual talent: painters Joan Miró and Salvador Dali, cellist Pablo Casals, and architect Antoni Gaudí were all Catalans.

BUSY ELSEWHERE

Another factor contributing to the unfinished character of the Spanish nation-state was its preoccupation, during the sixteenth and seventeenth centuries, with foreign areas, both in Europe and the Americas. While other European monarchies were unifying their kingdoms and laying the groundwork for modern nation-states, Spain's energies were directed outward. The 1516 accession of Charles V to the Spanish throne brought under one Hapsburg crown Austria, the Low Countries, and several parts of France in addition to Spain and its vast American colonies. It also guaranteed Spanish involvement in one European war after another.

The fantastic treasure of gold and silver from the Americas merely led to inflation. Unable to pay for its wars, the Spanish crown had to resort to extremely heavy taxation, which in turn ruined Spanish industry. The sixteenth century was a Spanish golden age, but it was economically bankrupting. With industry and agriculture in decline and able-bodied men either emigrating to the colonies or serving as soldiers in Spanish armies north of the Pyrenees, the population of Spain actually fell during this period.

THE TWO SPAINS

By the eighteenth century Spain was exhausted and under French influence. In 1808 Napoleon occupied Spain, and the Spanish people rose against the French troops in *guerrilla* (Spanish for "little war") fashion until they were expelled in 1814. Hating the French but influenced by their new ideas, Spanish liberals meeting in Cadiz in 1812 produced a remarkable constitution that would have turned Spain into a constitutional monarchy rather advanced for its day. The Cadiz constitution was probably too advanced for Spain in 1812. Two years later the reactionary Ferdinand VII returned from French sanctuary and abolished the constitution, and a large portion of the Spanish population supported him. At this point (if not before), Spain split into two societies fiercely antagonistic to each other, the so-called Two Spains. The one was liberal, anticlerical (picked up in the eighteenth century from French Voltairians), urban, progressive, and in favor of centralized government. The other Spain was absolutist, Catholic, rural, traditional, and in favor of regional fueros.[4] This polarization reached its high point in the Carlist War of the 1830s and may still not be overcome.

Foreign military misadventures contributed to Spain's slide into civil war. Humiliated by the United States in 1898, Spain lost Cuba, Puerto Rico, and the Philippines, her remaining colonies in the Western Hemisphere. This left an overlarge Spanish army with little to do. Copying France, Spain then tried to tame part of Morocco with nearly disastrous results. Fierce Berber Moslems inflicted heavy casualties in fighting that dragged on from 1909 to 1927. The impact of the Moroccan campaigns on Spain was similar to the effect of the Algerian war on France in the 1950s. Both situations were exasperating to the home populations and the armies in the field, and both led to generals assuming power.

During the nineteenth century Spanish army officers repeatedly attempted *pronunciamientos* (coups), some of them briefly successful. With the frustrations of 1898 and the Moroccan war, the overstaffed officer corps increasingly came to think of itself as the last defense of Spanish unity against incompetent, radical, or corrupt civilian politicians. In 1923, in the midst of setbacks in Morocco and turmoil at home, General Miguel Primo de Rivera "pronounced" against the civilian government and ruled Spain as dictator until 1930.

The Primo de Rivera interlude is interesting both in relation to Mussolini's Italy and to what was to follow in Spain. In many respects Primo de Rivera was the curtain-raiser for Franco's era. Like Mussolini, Primo came to power amidst fears of a socialist uprising and growing disorder. Like Mussolini and Franco after him, Primo abolished political parties and attempted to set up a single national movement, the *Unión Patriótica*. Borrowing from Italian Fascist theory, he instituted for various industries twenty-seven "corporations" in which labor and management were equally represented. Like Mussolini, Primo launched ambitious public works projects and accomplished much in irrigation and highway construction. But Primo also overextended the Spanish economy, and when the world depression hit in 1929, his support evaporated. Helping to bring him down were precisely the same forces that emerged against Franco and his successors: intellectuals, professors, students, Catalan autonomists, and the working class in general.

---

[4] The author is grateful to Madrid philosopher-historian Julián Marías for sharing his insights on the Two Spains.

THE UNWORKABLE REPUBLIC

In 1931, finding little support, King Alfonso XIII abdicated and the Spanish Republic was set up. With hindsight, many believe that the Republic was doomed from the start. Lacking a democratic consensus, it was undermined by extremists of the Right and Left. On the far Left, militant Socialists and Anarchists—Spain is the only country where mass political anarchism ever took root—burned churches, killed priests, promoted violent strikes, and tried for a revolutionary takeover. On the far Right, conservatives fearing for life, property, and the unity of the country organized fascistic youth groups. Basque and Catalonian separatists demanded far-reaching autonomy.

Meanwhile, the two largest parties, the Socialists and the Catholic CEDA, instead of cooperating to save the day, were at each other's throats. Spanish Socialists had turned radical or "maximalist" like the Italian Socialists earlier in the century. And, as in Italy, this alarmed many moderate Spaniards into moving toward the Right. The CEDA, an outgrowth of Catholic Action, might have turned into a moderate-right party like the postwar Italian Christian Democrats, who were also an outgrowth of Catholic Action. But in the polarization of the 1930s, CEDA barely cooperated with the government.[5]

In the five years of the Republic there were eighteen different governments each lasting an average of three and a half months.[6] Over thirty parties and political groups battled for power. Popular opinion and parliamentary seats shifted wildly. In the three elections of the Republic seats were distributed as follows:[7]

	1931	1933	1936
Left	299	100	280
Center	109	224	40
Right	41	145	138

Moderate government did not have much of a chance during the Spanish Republic. The Republic's last elections, in February 1936, show a country split almost down the middle:[8]

---

[5] For a review of the collapse of the Republic, see Hugh Thomas, *The Spanish Civil War* (New York: Harper & Row, 1961), Book I.

[6] Ramon Tamames, *La Republica, La Era de Franco* (Madrid: Ediciones Alfaguara, 1973), pp. 172–73.

[7] Adapted from Juan J. Linz, "The Party System of Spain," in *Party Systems and Voter Alignments,* ed. Seymour Lipset and Stein Rokkan (New York: Free Press, 1967), p. 261.

[8] Adapted from Javier Tusell, *Las Elecciones del Frente Popular* (Madrid: Edicusa, 1971), appendix I, pp. 265–97. I am grateful to Juan Linz for drawing these figures to my attention.

Left	4.5 million, 47%
Center	2.1 million, 22%
Right	3.0 million, 31%

Instead of the nice, bell-shaped curve that depicts the distribution of political views in many democracies, Spanish opinion divided into two camps, both of them hostile to democracy in our sense of the word. The Left was prepared to ride roughshod over conservatives, moderates, and Catholics to establish a "workers' state." The Right stressed order, hierarchy, and tradition and minimized demands for social and economic change. A spirit of compromise, the *sine qua non* of democracy, was absent.

Marxists contend that Spain split along class lines with proletarians joining the Socialists, Anarchists, Communists, or Trotskyists, and the middle and upper classes joining the Monarchists, Catholic Right, or Falange (a movement similar to Italian fascism). There is some truth to this class analysis, but it has been overdone. Many Spaniards were motivated by philosophical conviction rather than by objective class position: Some workers and peasants supported the Nationalists and some middle-class intellectuals the Republic. Rather than a simple showdown between the bourgeoisie and proletariat, as the Marxists would have it, in the Spanish Civil War society fractured along clerical and anticlerical lines and between the Castilian center and Basque and Catalan periphery as well. Thus the highly Catholic Basques supported the Republic not because they were leftists, but because they had been promised regional autonomy by the Republic. Some lower-class Castilians and Andalusians identified with the Franco forces simply because they felt they embodied the tradition of the Spanish state against breakaway peripheral areas.[9] A simple thing the Spanish Civil War was not.

THE CIVIL WAR

Rising against the government in July 1936, the Nationalists took with them most army officers but only three-fifths of the enlisted men. Since the political movements of the Right and Left had been organizing their own private armies, the two sides initially faced each other with a nearly identical number of troops. The military leaders of the rising had hoped for a quick takeover; instead they had to struggle for three years, until April 1939, because the two sides were too closely matched and too fiercely committed to permit a rapid victory.

Both sides killed tens of thousands of civilians on the least suspicion of disloyalty. Spain's great poet Federico Garcia Lorca was gunned down by

---

[9] The author is grateful to sociologist Juan F. Marsal of the Autonomous University of Barcelona for his description of the Spanish Civil War as actually three wars at once: upper class vs. lower class; center vs. periphery; and religious vs. nonreligious.

Nationalists. The founder of the Falange, Jose Antonio Primo de Rivera (the dictator's son), was shot in prison. Hemingway's description in *For Whom the Bell Tolls* of villagers' execution of the local gentry (by flinging them over a cliff), was apparently based on real incidents.

The two sides turned immediately to outside help, but the Nationalists were more successful. Hitler and Mussolini, recognizing the kindred spirit of the Nationalists, supplied arms, munitions, troops, and an air force. Stalin, at that time courting British and French opinion, was reluctant to commit the Soviet Union to the Republic's side. The Soviets did sell weapons and send some military advisors. They also had the Comintern recruit International Brigades to fight in Spain, making the war the twentieth century's most romantic struggle. Some 3,200 Americans fought in Spain as members of the Communist-led Abraham Lincoln Brigade; more than half perished.

But while men on both sides died for lofty ideals, Hitler and Stalin used the war for their own purposes of political manipulation and as a testing ground for their new weapons. In this respect, the Spanish Civil War was a sort of dress rehearsal for World War II. The Spanish Civil War cost a very roughly estimated 600,000 lives: some 400,000 in the war itself, perhaps 40,000 in executions after the war, and the rest from malnutrition and disease over several ghastly years following the war.[10] Spanish prisons still hold some survivors of the losing side.

The triumphant figure emerging from the Civil War was Francisco Franco, a hero of the Moroccan fighting who had been named (at age 33) Europe's youngest general. Franco, a priggish, diligent infantry officer, harbored a mystical devotion to the greatness and unity of Spain. For him, treason was anything that promoted disunity, and this the Republic supplied in plenty. Let us now turn to the Spain that Franco constructed and bequeathed to his successors.

THE KEY
INSTITUTIONS

THE MONARCHY

Although Spain's last king, Alfonso XIII, abdicated in 1931, in 1947 Franco turned his regime officially back into a monarchy but named no king. The most likely candidate for king Franco ruled out: Don Juan de Borbón, son of Alfonso XIII. Living in exile in Portugal, Don Juan angered Franco by condemning his regime and voicing support for Spanish democracy under a constitutional monarchy.

---

[10] One noted historian offers the total estimate of 580,000 deaths, but holds that 400,000 of them came as a result of Nationalist executions or of disease of their "red" prisoners during and after the war. See Gabriel Jackson, *The Spanish Republic and the Civil War, 1931–1939* (Princeton, N.J.: Princeton University Press, 1965), p. 539.

So Franco bypassed Don Juan and ruled in effect as a regent while he groomed Don Juan's son, Juan Carlos, for the throne. Born in 1938, Juan Carlos was educated in Spanish military academies under Franco's supervision. Franco thought he could mold the young prince in the Caudillo's own image as a conservative continuer of the regime. Juan Carlos was invested as king only in 1969 but given few but ceremonial duties.

The world held its breath in 1975 when King Juan Carlos I took over upon Franco's death. Would he be the "son of Franco" as intended? Would he step right into Franco's shoes? The Caudillo might have been disappointed, for the young king showed himself to be his own man. Like his father, he came out in favor of democracy under a constitutional monarchy, but one instituted gradually. Unlike Franco, he took little part in the daily affairs of state. He named a cautiously reformist cabinet but did not attend its meetings in the Franco manner, preferring to stay above the political fray.

For Juan Carlos, success would mean transition to a democracy in which he would have a largely symbolic role, more important than the figurehead British or Swedish monarchs but less important than what Franco had in mind. Failure would mean either a royal dictatorship, for which he had no taste, or the end of the monarchy and establishment of a republic.

THE COUNCIL OF THE REALM (CONSEJO DEL REINO)

Franco had no intention of leaving Juan Carlos to govern by himself. In the Organic Law (roughly speaking a constitution) of 1967, Franco designated a body to have considerable powers in relation to both king and Cortes (the national parliament). The Council of the Realm, composed of seventeen top government officials, mostly elderly, includes the chief justice of the Spanish Supreme Court, the leaders of the three military services, and ten members of the Cortes.[11] It is thus highly conservative, especially since Franco himself handpicked most of the officials who belong to the Council *ex officio.*

The Council's powers are potentially sweeping. Under Article 17 of the Organic Law, the Council of the Realm can return to the Cortes for redeliberation any bill; can dissolve the Cortes in emergencies; can dismiss top officials; can set up popular referendums; and can decree emergency measures.[12]

Another power of the Consejo del Reino is to propose three names to the king, who then picks one as head of government (i.e., premier) to serve for five years. This premier can choose his own cabinet, but it must be approved by the king. The innovation here was in the splitting apart of the offices of head of state and of government, which Franco had previously combined in himself. The 1967

---

[11] Jorge de Esteban et al., *Desarrollo Político y Constitución Española* (Barcelona: Ediciones Ariel, 1973), pp. 108–9.

[12] Ibid., pp. 112–13.

Organic Law thus returned Spain to the more normal pattern in which these two functions are quite distinct.

Franco hoped the Consejo would serve as a gerontocracy of his own type of people to supervise the young king, but within a few months of taking over Juan Carlos was able to turn the Council his way. The new king named a friend and presumed conservative to head the body so that when a new premier was needed in 1976, the three names the Consejo proposed were the three that Juan Carlos wanted. From them the king picked another close friend and moderate reformist, Adolfo Suárez Gonzalez, as his premier. The young king thus got the cabinet he wanted: young—mostly men in their forties—and with a conservative, Christian Democratic slant, open to the gradual, controlled kind of change Juan Carlos favored.

THE CORTES

Franco despised the parliamentary fragmentation and squabbling during the Republic, so when he revived the Cortes in 1942 he kept it under his personal control. Many Cortes members served by virtue of holding other appointive offices (to which Franco had appointed them); others Franco named specifically to the Cortes; none was popularly elected. The Cortes under Franco was largely a rubber stamp, refining the wording and explicating the legalism of proposals placed before it.

With the 1967 Organic Law, however, the Cortes changed somewhat. Its approximately 565 members were taken from the cabinet, the *Movimiento*, the Church, the military, universities, professional groups, *sindicatos* (see below), city and provincial councils, and a strange group called "family representatives," elected two from each province by heads of families and married women.[13]

George Hills points out that Franco still named 150 Cortes members, but this was considerably fewer than under the pre-1967 setup. Some 415 members were elected, not necessarily by popular vote, but rather by their colleagues in the unions, Movement, and professional organizations. The only popular vote was for the 108 "family representatives," and that was under a restricted franchise.[14]

We notice here that Franco's Cortes had a strong corporatist element: Over a third of the membership was reserved for the sindicatos, professional groups, and academic leaders. Among Franco's followers were admirers of Mussolini's "corporate state," which sought to structure representation according to branch of industry rather than geographic subdivision or proportional party preference. The sindicatos, for example, were supposed to represent labor and management

[13] de Esteban et al., *Desarrollo Político*, p. 231; and Hills, *Spain*, pp. 380–81.

[14] Hills, *Spain*, p. 381.

equally for two dozen branches of industry; they were not labor unions in our sense of the word but rather, on the Italian Fascist model, purported to bridge the gap between workers and bosses. The Spanish system, in claiming to represent all Spaniards, was just as phoney as the Italian system had been.

The first post-Franco Government planned sweeping reforms for the Cortes. Premier Carlos Arias Navarro in 1976 announced that a two-chamber parliament would be set up with the lower house popularly elected to be equal in power with an upper house indirectly elected and hence more conservative. Elections were to take place in 1977 between moderate political groups, but with Communists and anarchists still banned.

Half-measure though this proposal was—the upper house would not be democratically chosen—Arias faced strong opposition from the existing Cortes. Ironically the rubber stamp under Franco had, with his demise, taken on a life of its own in an effort to preserve the old system. While the cabinet appointed by Juan Carlos was mildly reformist, the Cortes stayed strongly conservative. Premier Arias was in a bind. As one commentator put it, "Mr. Arias is like a bullfighter having to face two bulls simultaneously. One is the Parliament, a stronghold of nostalgia for and fidelity to the Franco regime. The other is the Spanish public, an increasingly aggressive and articulate section of which does not want a future tied to the past."[15]

The Cortes, like the Council of the Realm, was structured to preserve Franco's rule even when he was in his tomb. If Spain was to modernize politically, the old Cortes would have to go and a new, popularly elected, liberal one would have to take its place. The transition would not be easy.

THE CABINET

Under Franco and his immediate successors, the cabinet was not "responsible" to the Cortes; that is, it was neither installed by parliamentary vote nor could it be ousted by a vote of no-confidence. Still the cabinet had a certain representational function, not of Spanish society as a whole but of the groups supporting the regime. As we will explore more fully later, Franco used to handpick his approximately nineteen-man cabinets with great care, letting no one group dominate them for too long.

In addition to the usual ministries, the Spanish cabinet had some interesting differences. The three military ministries, army, navy, and air force, were all headed by officers on active duty—no civilian control here—in a way that resembled Japanese cabinets before World War II. The National Movement, described below, was represented in the cabinet by its secretary-general, who

---

[15] Henry Giniger, "Power Blocs of Spain, Old and New," *New York Times*, February 1, 1976, p. E4.

was appointed by Franco. The corporatistic sindicatos got a Ministry of Syndical Relations. With Spain's emphasis on economic growth there was a Ministry of Development Planning.

Political scientist Charles Anderson identifies the cabinet as "the focus of coalitional politics, the place where the disparate forces supporting the regime came together to seek common ground before the Caudillo."[16] Exactly what happened in cabinet meetings we do not know. Under Franco they were held twice a month on Fridays and usually continued until dawn Saturday. Journalist Benjamin Welles described them as handling all business of government, from foreign relations to details of domestic administration. Even though the sessions lasted many hours, "Franco himself has never been known to quit a cabinet session. This is how he rules Spain. From start to dawn, he remains imperturbably in his place, attentive, seldom interrupting, unruffled even when his ministers break into angry quarrels."[17]

Juan Carlos, as noted, had a different style. He supervised the building of the cabinet, demanding (and getting) moderate liberalizers in the key ministries of interior, foreign affairs, and justice. Then the king stepped into the background, not attending cabinet meetings but conferring with individual ministers as the need arose. This was probably the safest path for Juan Carlos to follow. If the cabinet failed in leading the incredibly difficult transition to post-Franco democracy, the king's name would not be tarnished.

THE NATIONAL MOVEMENT (MOVIMIENTO NACIONAL)

Of all that Franco loathed in the Republic, political parties occupied first place. To Franco, parties were corrupt, quarrelsome, demagogic, unrepresentative of Spaniards, and, worst of all, destructive of Spain's unity. Accordingly, Franco permitted no political parties in our sense of the term. Underground parties, to be sure, flourished beneath the political surface. After Franco's death the more moderate ones operated openly but still without official sanction. The Communists stayed underground.

Franco did not even like the word "parties." Instead he promoted something called a "National Movement," which was supposed to provide adequate political representation and participation for Spaniards of all classes, regions, and viewpoints. Some observers hold that the Movimiento is a Fascist party controlling a Fascist state, the last such system in existence since the fall of Hitler and Mussolini. Indeed, the omnipresence of the Movement's symbol—the yoke and arrows—throughout Spain seems to give the impression that is quite powerful.

---

[16] Charles W. Anderson, *The Political Economy of Modern Spain: Policy-Making in an Authoritarian System* (Madison, Wis.: University of Wisconsin Press, 1970), p. 73.

[17] Benjamin Welles, *Spain: The Gentle Anarchy* (New York: Praeger, 1965), p. 33.

Its actual power is quite limited (see the section "Patterns of Interaction" below), and it is far from a unified political movement.[18]

The Movimiento is actually a merger of several different political movements, and they still coexist uneasily within its ranks. The best-known and largest component of the Movement is the *Falange* (Spanish for phalanx, Alexander the Great's infantry formations), founded in 1933 by José Antonio Primo de Rivera, son of the dictator who was in power from 1923 to 1930. A colorful speaker, José Antonio (as he was affectionately known), rallied thousands of anti-Republic youth to his cause. Imprisoned by the Republic, José Antonio was executed after the military revolt broke out.

What did the Falange stand for? Certain elements were borrowed from Italian fascism: the arm-outstretched salute, the paramilitary youth formations, and a socialist-sounding program that promised to restore and revitalize the nation. The quasi-socialist element of the Falange is especially interesting. Although extremely vague in ideology, the movement was not reactionary nor even conservative. It showed strong overtones of anticlericalism, antimonarchism, and anticapitalism, depending on which leader was speaking. The Falange did demand order, authority, and hierarchy to modernize Spain and eliminate poverty. As opposed to socialism, though, the Falange emphasized national greatness and unity and rejected the idea of class struggle. "There is only one class, Spaniards," the Falange proclaimed.[19]

Another component of the Movimiento were the Carlists, centered in Navarre in the north of Spain. Carlism is a remnant of a nineteenth-century conflict over the successor to the throne that evolved into a movement opposed to the centralizing efforts of Spanish liberals. As ideologically vague as the Falange, the Carlists hark back romantically to their medieval fueros (local rights); they sometimes go by the name of Traditionalists.

These two movements had little in common with each other. The Falange in particular was at odds with many Nationalist supporters who were pro-Church, pro-monarchy and pre- (rather than pro-) capitalist. But Franco needed a political movement to rally anti-Republic forces. The army officers around Franco had little ideology except a commitment to national unity with a conservative slant. So in 1937 Franco decreed the merger of the *Falangistas* and *Carlistas* into the *Falange Espanola Traditionalista* and made himself its head. Later he changed the name to the National Movement, which included women's sections, youth groups, and other organizations.

What does the Movimiento mean today? Very little. Although nominally claiming about one million members, only a few thousand actually bother paying

---

[18] For a detailed history of the Movement see Stanley G. Payne, *Falange: A History of Spanish Fascism* (Stanford, Calif.: Stanford University Press, 1961).

[19] Quoted by Juan J. Linz, "From Falange to Movimiento-Organizacion: The Spanish Single Party and the Franco Regime, 1936–1968," in *Authoritarian Politics in Modern Society*, ed. by Samuel P. Huntington and Clement H. Moore (New York: Basic Books, 1970), p. 137.

the token dues. Most government officials are automatically declared members of the Movement as soon as they are appointed to office. Unlike the Yugoslav Communist party, the Movimiento does not attract bright young persons, not even opportunists, for Movimiento membership confers few opportunities for personal advancement. Further, with no serious ideology or membership qualifications, the National Movement can provide little in the way of disciplined support for the regime.

FRANCO AS AN INSTITUTION

By now it will have occurred to the reader that the institutions of Spain counted for little apart from Franco. The monarchy, the Cortes, and the National Movement were largely creations of Franco. Political scientists, of course, cannot count a single individual as an institution, no matter how long he lives. And this was precisely Spain's trouble: its institutions were weak, their viability uncertain once Franco was gone. While the Yugoslav Communist party—hardly the most coherent Communist organization in the world—provided a backbone for continuity in the post-Tito era, Franco did not sufficiently institutionalize his personal power. In the phrase of the great Spanish philosopher Ortega y Gasset, Spain was still *invertebrada,* without a backbone.

SPANISH
POLITICAL
ATTITUDES

UNGOVERNABLE SPANIARDS?

"We Spaniards are really bastards to govern," one Spaniard told the American writer James Michener.[20] Others have heard similar statements from Spaniards over the years. Many observers, both Spanish and foreign, have come to accept such views as accurate: Spaniards are so passionate, so quarrelsome, and so uncompromising in their views that a representative democracy cannot possibly work in Spain. Indeed, the history of nineteenth- and twentieth-century Spain seems to underscore the impossibility of parliamentary government in that country.

Are Spaniards really so different from Europeans north of the Pyrenees? Does Spanish character cause Spanish political culture, or vice versa? This author holds the view that differences between Spanish and other European political cultures are ones of degree, not of absolute quality, and that Spain has

---

[20] James A. Michener, *Iberia: Spanish Travels and Reflections* (Greenwich, Conn.: Fawcett Crest, 1968), p. 67.

merely suffered from retarded development due to a variety of historical circumstances: the Moslem conquest, the incredibly long reconquest, and then imperial overextension and failure to integrate city and countryside and the various regions of Spain. This integration is still not fully complete, but as it becomes so, Spain becomes more and more "European." What we have in Spain is not a non-European political system and culture but simply retarded modernization lagging behind other countries of Europe by a century or more.

This debate—on whether Spaniards are somehow different in temperament from other Europeans—is not a musty, philosophical dispute but a determinant of Spanish political attitudes. One finds two broad schools of thought on this subject, and they may connote whether a Spaniard is conservative or liberal. The conservative looks at the Spanish people as quite different from Europeans, so temperamental that they can be governed only by authoritarian means. There is no point in playing around with imported notions of liberal democracy, the Spanish conservative argues, because these children will soon break their toys and Spain will be back under some kind of strict leadership again. If the Left (the Republic) had won in the Civil War, our conservative believes, it would have dealt just as harshly with the losing side as Franco did, and it would not have founded a democracy any more than Franco did.

The Spanish liberal resents being thought of as somehow inferior to other Europeans. Spaniards are just as capable of sustaining a parliamentary democracy as the French, the Italians, or the Germans, the liberal argues. The problem, our liberal holds, is that at least since the return of the reactionary King Ferdinand VII in 1814, the "natural" course of Spanish political development has been stifled by right-wing authoritarianism. The reason Spaniards have sometimes acted with passionate extremism, our liberal argues, is that they have been so long suppressed, both materially and politically. The solution is major reforms.

There is truth in both views. In reality, the conservative and liberal are looking at two sides of the same coin, or two poles of a vicious circle, in which it is impossible to determine exactly which—behavior or environment—causes which. This returns us to the original question: Does the Spanish national character create the Spanish political culture or vice versa?

PASSIONATE POLITICS

Either way, the Spanish national character is sufficiently different from, say, the Swedish as to make the two almost polar opposites. It would be hard to find two more different political psychologies on the European continent.[21] Where the Swedes are undemonstrative, the Spaniards are often profoundly emotional and

[21] For a general discussion of Spanish character see V. S. Pritchett, *The Spanish Temper* (London: Chatto & Windus, 1954).

proud of it. Where Swedes are committed to reason, pragmatism, and compromise, Spaniards tend toward passion, ideological fixedness, and inflexibility. Swedes usually listen closely to other people's arguments and accept the valid points in them. Spaniards tend to talk past each other; neither gives an inch or even pays close attention to what the other says. As Brian Crozier has observed, "often a dialogue with a Spaniard is, in fact, not a dialogue at all but two separate monologues."[22] Some observers relate this characteristic to the allegedly colossal Spanish egoism: "Only *he* exists."[23] Compromise is considered to be the basic requirement of a democratic political culture. If the Spaniards continue in their inflexible pattern, the prognosis for Spanish democracy is poor.

UNINTEGRATED SPAIN

It may be wrong to speak of one Spanish political culture or temperament, for the many regions and classes of Spain have not yet been integrated into a single entity. Like Italy, Spain suffers from an excess of localism. Poor internal communications and a stagnant economy over the centuries have contributed to an exaggerated interest in one's own *pueblo* (village or town) to the exclusion of anything outside. Spanish villages, particularly of the South and Center, tend to be quite compact, with the houses clustered closely together. Outside villages and their inhabitants are scorned as inferior.[24] Sometimes local rivalries reach silly proportions. The English anthropologist J. A. Pitt-Rivers reported that at one town festival there was an announcement reading, "A hearty welcome is extended to all outsiders with the exception of those from Logroño."[25]

Pitt-Rivers holds that Spanish anarchism grew in part from the pueblos' resentment at the penetration of state power into the hitherto autonomous life of the village. Villagers and townspeople, unaccustomed to outside authority, were easy prey for a simplified philosophy that preached the destruction of all state power. If this analysis is correct, then anarchism can be seen as an offshoot of the modernizing process and unlikely to strike new roots in the Spain of today for two reasons: the Franco regime has completed the penetration of state power into the remotest pueblos, while economic changes have eroded the old village autonomy. Similar anarchic movements characterized corresponding periods in the development of central administration in other European countries, only in Spain this movement was stronger and later, as are most movements in Spain.

Economically, Spain, like Italy, shows large North-South differences in development. Per capita income in 1971 in Spain's five leading provinces (which

---

[22] Brian Crozier, *Franco* (Boston: Little, Brown, 1967), p. 511.

[23] V. S. Pritchett quoted in Crozier, *Franco.*

[24] J. A. Pitt-Rivers, *The People of the Sierra* (New York: Criterion Books, 1954), especially Chaps. 1 and 2.

[25] Ibid., p. 11.

include Catalonia and the Basque country plus Madrid) was two and a half times that of the five poorest provinces, mostly but not exclusively in the South.[26] And the differences have tended to remain, for capital in the poor areas generally sought investments in the already industrialized regions, where it could bring a higher return. The Madrid government did little to try to reverse this flow; the Italian and Yugoslav regimes, in contrast, genuinely tried to decrease the gap between their rich Norths and poor Souths, with mixed success.

In terms of social class too, Spain has been poorly integrated. Until recent decades the bulk of the Spanish people have been peasants, mostly wretchedly poor, landless farm laborers. Such societies are usually characterized by a tiny elite of wealthy landowners, a small middle class of merchants, professionals, and better-off peasants, and a mass of destitute rural day laborers. Such was the condition of Spain until the post–World War II industrialization took hold in the 1950s and 1960s. From 1961 to 1969 more than three million Spaniards moved, chiefly from village to city and especially northward to the industrial areas of the Basque country, Catalonia, and Madrid.[27] Like the inhabitants of two other Mediterranean lands, Italy and Yugoslavia, Spaniards streamed abroad to work in France, Germany, and Switzerland. From 1960 to 1967 around two million Spaniards went north of the Pyrenees, although many returned within a few years. Still, an estimated 850,000 Spaniards are working elsewhere in Europe at any one time.[28]

This tremendous movement has helped destroy the old Spain more thoroughly than could a political revolution. In particular, the rural exodus has eliminated much of the former grinding poverty. The problem of rural poverty was not "solved" in the same sense that land reforms or government aid would have accomplished it; poor Spaniards simply abandoned the land for a much better life working in the city or abroad. Much of rural Spain has lost its population, and whole villages have been deserted.

Major social inequality still exists in Spain. The very top of the pyramid is still reserved for some 2,000 titled Spaniards.[29] Near them are the financial and industrial elite and top professionals and civil servants of bourgeois origin. Below this level there has been considerable social mobility—particularly between generations—and the formation, for the first time in Spanish history, of a substantial middle class. Spanish sociologists draw the following picture of Spain's social pyramid:[30]

---

[26] Banco de Bilbao, *Renta Nacional de España y Su Distribución Provincial, 1971* (Madrid: Banco de Bilbao, 1973), pp. 20, 21.

[27] Amando de Miguel et al., *Sintesis del Informe Sociologico sobre la Situacion Social de Espana 1970*, 4th ed. (Madrid: Fundacion FOESSA, 1972), p. 158.

[28] Ibid., p. 155.

[29] See Tad Szulc, *Portrait of Spain* (New York: American Heritage Press, 1972), pp. 225–27.

[30] Amando de Miguel et al., *Sintesis*, p. 175.

Upper	less than 0.5%
Upper Middle	6
Middle Middle	31
Lower Middle	18
Working	32
Poor	13

A lot depends, of course, on how one defines classes, but, if this breakdown is accurate, a majority of Spaniards (55 percent) would be in the middle class. The distribution of Spain's national income is somewhat less equal than it is in the rest of Western Europe, but far more equal than that in Third World countries.[31]

The irony of the Franco era, since the 1950s at any rate, is that backward Spain, under the thumb of an archconservative, almost totally changed its social basis. Near destitution still exists in rural pockets, but Spanish workers increasingly own their own apartments and small cars. The situation in Spain is not what it once was—a permanent civil war between social classes. Indeed, the profound social and economic changes of the 1950s and 1960s are the best impediment to a renewal of the Civil War. A worker with some property has a stake in the system; he thinks twice about trying to overthrow it.

A BASIS FOR DEMOCRACY?

Under Franco, apathy toward politics appeared to be high. Spaniards were simply discouraged from taking a great interest in politics; they were afforded little opportunity to participate politically and were aware that serious opposition could land one in jail. Memory of the tens of thousands executed in the 1940s made people cautious in their public (but not necessarily private) utterances. Much of Spain's political apathy was enforced. We must take Spanish public opinion data with a grain of salt: a Spanish respondent may not tell a questioner exactly what he thinks.

University students emerge as the most political and the most radical Spanish group in surveys. The least political and most authoritarian group are the workers. A 1969 poll asked Madrid residents how often they spoke about politics. The results are shown in Table 3–1.

Political information follows a similar pattern. Asked to name six key cabinet ministers, 44 percent of university students and 50 percent of lawyers could; only 4 percent of blue-collar workers and only 2 percent of the most general category, "heads of household," could name six. Of this last category, heads of household, 51 percent could name none. Thus the group that the Franco regime singled out to participate in elections, "family representatives," seemed

[31] Ibid., p. 146.

Table 3–1   Spaniards Speak About Politics

	High School Students	University Students	Lawyers	Doctors	White-Collar Workers	Blue-Collar Workers
Much	18%	26%	26%	19%	14%	8%
Some	30	50	32	25	20	10
Occasionally	34	17	25	25	25	14
Never	19	8	16	32	41	68

Source: Amando de Miguel et al., Vida Politica y Asociativa (Madrid, 1970), p. 58. This work is a political story itself. Intended as a chapter in a much larger study of Spain, it was scissored out at the last minute by Spanish censors—but is still listed in the table of contents! It was later mimeographed privately and is the source of the data presented here.

to be the least informed on political questions, which, of course, may have been precisely Franco's intention: to leap over the heads of informed, critical intellectuals and go directly to the more traditional and obedient masses.

Older Spaniards are more conservative. Madrid professional people under thirty-five gave less importance to "order and peace" and "discipline," items that were more favored by those thirty-six to fifty and even more strongly favored by those over fifty. The younger group also agreed with liberal ideas like "changing a lot of things" and "there is misery and exploitation of the lower classes;" their elders agreed with them less.

This same scale of liberalism–conservatism also showed interesting differences between social classes. The most liberal groups were university students, lawyers, and doctors, testimony that higher education is indeed a liberalizing experience. The workers, on the other hand, agreed most strongly that "there is misery and exploitation of the lower classes" (88 percent), but they were less interested than the higher classes in the right to think as one wishes.

This pattern of "working-class authoritarianism"[32] is more pronounced in response to the question of "which political system you prefer for the country." Only 1 percent of university students wanted a system "like now," but a full 55 percent of blue-collar workers did. Conversely, 76 percent of university students preferred a republic while only 30 percent of blue-collar workers did. Interestingly, lawyers were the group with the highest percentage of monarchists (23 percent) of all groups interviewed. Here again age mattered: younger Spaniards tended most strongly toward a republic. Further, as one ascends the social scale there are more who favor a republic.

In this same pattern, blue-collar workers most strongly favored having no political parties (31 percent), while university students most strongly preferred

---

[32] For a discussion of working-class authoritarianism in general see Seymour Martin Lipset, *Political Man: The Social Bases of Politics* (Garden City, N.Y.: Anchor Books, 1963), Chap. 4.

having more than two political parties (61 percent). On the question of how they would vote if parties were permitted, *Madrileños'* responses are shown in Table 3–2.

Table 3–2   Spaniards Pick Parties

	High School Students	University Students	Lawyers	Doctors	White-Collar Workers	Blue-Collar Workers
Traditionalist	5%	4%	1%	—	2%	—
Falange	7	2	9	5	8	11
Movement	17	1	7	11	21	27
Christian Democrat	38	28	26	32	22	20
Social Democrat	20	42	29	24	22	11
Socialist	10	19	19	12	16	22
Regionalist	1	3	1	2	2	3
Others	3	2	9	14	7	8

Source: Amando de Miguel et al., Vida Politica y Asociativa, mimeographed (Madrid, 1970), p. 82.

At first glance, we might rejoice that Spaniards have at long last become moderate: the two parties favored by most groups were the Christian Democrats and Social Democrats, the former moderately conservative and the latter welfarist, in favor of a system like that of West Germany. A second glance is more bothersome: blue-collar workers were less interested in these two moderate choices than in either the Falange or the Movement on the right or the militant Socialists on the left. Why should workers favor the extremes? The Socialist showing is not surprising; the Socialist party had great strength among Spanish workers during the Republic. But the workers' interest in the Falange and Movement is something else. There are at least three possible explanations: (1) the workers have been cowed into voicing support for the regime's creations; (2) the quasi-socialist programs of the Falange and Movement have genuinely won them over; or (3) economic growth under the Franco regime has brought relative prosperity to the Spanish working class. The author suspects the workers' responses are a combination of all the above explanations. Either way, responses to the hypothetical question do not show a great commitment to moderate and democratic parties among the working masses of Spaniards. Indeed, Spanish democracy would seem to stand a better chance of survival if elections were limited to the educated classes, but that, of course, would not be democracy.

In sum, the antiquated political institutions of Spain were frozen while Spanish political attitudes evolved along with Spain's economic development. Spanish political attitudes may be more traditional than those of Italy, but not much more. The agonizing problem for post-Franco Spain is how to close this gap by modernizing its political institutions rapidly enough to satisfy an awakened public but slowly enough so that the process does not get out of control and break down. The ghost of the 1930s haunted the Spain of the 1970s.

**PATTERNS
OF
INTERACTION**

TOTALITARIAN SPAIN?

Spain has been described as a totalitarian dictatorship in the mold of Hitler's Germany or Mussolini's Italy. But is this accurate? One widely accepted definition of totalitarian dictatorship characterizes such systems as having an official ideology, an organized mass party, terroristic police, party-controlled mass media and armed forces, and a centrally directed economy.[33]

As such, Spain measures up poorly. In the 1940s Spain may have fitted the model somewhat, but by the 1960s Spain had

1. No official ideology anyone had to bother with
2. The remnants of a single mass party, the Falange, that had not been important for decades
3. Police who were generally unable to crack down on dissidents
4. Mass media run by a variety of groups, not speaking a single viewpoint
5. An army more powerful and important than any party
6. A largely capitalist, market economy

Spain had, to be sure, certain Fascist aspects. The *Guardia Civil*, always patrolling in pairs, brought heavy-handed justice to the Spanish countryside and served as a paramilitary police force in the hunt for terrorists. One never trifled with the Guardia Civil, who were usually equipped with submachine guns.

Economically, Franco in 1941 copied Mussolini's IRI (Istituto per la Recostruzione Industriale) with his own INI (Instituto Nacional de Industria), whose investments include steel, oil, hydroelectric power, shipbuilding, fertilizer plants, automobiles, and the national airline, Iberia. Producing 12 percent of Spain's industrial output in 1973, INI is less important than the nationalized industries of Britain, France, or Austria, especially since private capitalism surged ahead in Spain in the 1960s.[34]

---

[33] See Carl J. Friedrich and Zbigniew K. Brzezinski, *Totalitarian Dictatorship and Autocracy* (New York: Praeger, 1956), pp. 9–10.

[34] See Anderson, *Political Economy of Modern Spain*, pp. 39–40; and *New York Times*, January 26, 1975, sec. 3, p. 41.

If Spain is not a totalitarian dictatorship, then what is it? Juan Linz classifies Spain as "authoritarian" but not totalitarian because under Franco the regime deliberately held down political mobilization, even pro-regime, preferring instead passive acceptance.[35]

A SORT OF PLURALISM

Even under Franco Spain's government was not a totalitarian monolith, dictating all phases of Spanish social, economic, and political life. Instead, there was a sort of pluralism in Spain. It by no means included all Spaniards, but was limited to the established pillars of support of the regime. But these pillars shifted; a key support in one decade languished in the background the next. These pillars also displayed a great deal of autonomous life of their own; they were far from merely the creatures of Franco. On the contrary, it was Franco who had to take their demands into account, carefully balancing them and not letting any one get too powerful for too long. Beneath the appearance of one-man rule, the various elite groups of Spain conducted a half-submerged struggle for predominance. Which are these groups? The original three pillars of the Franco regime were widely believed to be the Catholic Church, the armed forces, and the National Movement. Let us review them first.

The Roman Catholic Church   The Church suffered under the Republic, which was strongly anticlerical. Churches were burned and priests were killed by far-leftists. The Catholic Church had little choice but to side with the Nationalists in 1936; many devout Catholics, including some priests, fought for Franco. The Church was favored under the Franco regime: its power was restored in education, it received state subsidies, and attendance at mass grew under regime encouragement. But things were changing in the Catholic Church. The old churchmen were dour ultraconservatives, the younger ones not. Triggered by Vatican concern over social problems, young priests increasingly identified with Spanish workers, sponsoring a Catholic worker movement, the *Hermandades Obreras* (Workers' Brotherhoods), which sometimes engaged in illegal strike activity but was sheltered from the regime's wrath by its association with the Church. Basque priests supported Basque cultural autonomy; several Basque priests were imprisoned for their efforts. In 1974 the government threatened to end its Concordat with the Vatican, a treaty, in effect since 1953, that granted the Spanish Church special privileges and the regime a say in the naming of bishops. The Catholic Church had thus moved from pillar of the regime in the 1940s and 1950s to semiopposition in the 1970s.

---

[35] Juan J. Linz, "An Authoritarian Regime: Spain," in *Cleavages, Ideologies and Party Systems*, ed. by Erik Allardt and Yujo Littunen (Helsinki: Academic Bookstore, 1964).

The Armed Forces   The armed forces were a shaky pillar of the regime in the 1970s; they were not the same armed forces that had brought Franco to power. The top generals who fought in the Civil War were mostly as old as Franco and dying off and retiring, the younger officers not so conservative. Drawn now from all ranks of society and holding down after-hours civilian jobs to make ends meet, junior officers are no longer a separate tradition-bound caste apart from society.[36] In the mid-1970s a group of several hundred officers, mostly captains and majors, formed a secret Democratic Military Union to make sure the Spanish military would not be used to *oppose* liberalization. The regime tried to stamp out the group by arresting and trying dozens of its leaders. Thus the military was something of a split pillar, the old guard conservative and the younger men liberal.

The National Movement   The Movement cannot be counted on as a major support for the post-Franco regime. Never ideologically cohesive, membership in it became purely a formality for government people. Ironically, some Movement members, pursuing the radical orientation of the original Falange, pressed for "major and radical changes in the structure of the economy and society."[37] Some of the old Falangists even dropped out of the Movement to join the opposition. In the first post-Franco cabinets, some of the younger and more liberal members were Movement people.

In sum, of the three pillars of the Franco regime, none could be counted on by the post-Franco regime. This means that the regime is open to influence from other forces. Let us now turn to the most interesting of these.

THE OPUS DEI

Founded in 1928, Opus Dei started as a Catholic lay organization dedicated to making Spain (and other Catholic countries) into societies that really lived by Church teaching. Opus Dei (Latin for "God's work") proposed to do this not on a mass basis, but by taking over the elite of society; it aimed at enrolling upper- and upper-middle-class Spaniards into a disciplined, hierarchical, and secretive movement to infiltrate the leading positions. Since the 1940s Opus thinking has moved from utterly reactionary (e.g., Russia and America are equally degenerate because both partake of rationalist heresy), to qualified acceptance of democracy, economic growth, and rationality.[38] During the 1950s it occurred to Opus Dei

---

[36] See Enrique Tierno Galván, "Students' Opposition in Spain," *Government and Opposition*, I (August 1966), 470–71. Its author, fired from his university professorship in 1965 for supporting a student protest, became a Socialist leader and attorney.

[37] Anderson, *Political Economy of Modern Spain*, p. 102.

[38] For an excellent discussion of the changes in Opus Dei ideology see Leslie Mackenzie, "The Political Ideas of the Opus Dei in Spain," *Government and Opposition*, 8 (Winter 1973), 72–92.

intellectuals that the best way to take over society's reins was by means of modern, American-style business management techniques. These fanatic Catholics became spokesmen for capitalist free enterprise and rationalization of the creaky Spanish economy. It was as if the Catholic Church had converted the Harvard Business School—or vice versa.

Opus Dei was partially successful and has become an element in the Spanish elite that has to be reckoned with. Using the traditional Spanish technique of hiring their brothers when job openings occurred, Opus members penetrated the Spanish professoriate, particularly in economics and business administration. Admitted into the cabinet in the late 1950s, Opus technocrats opened up Spain's economy to major innovation and growth during the 1960s. But not all Spaniards appreciate Opus Dei; many resent its secretiveness—membership figures have never been announced, and individual members try to keep their affiliation concealed. Opus's conspiratorial infiltration of top positions made Madrid wags call them "Octopus Dei." The quasi-monastic life of Opus leaders—many of whom are celibate ascetics who live in special Opus houses—deepened suspicion. One Madrid sociologist fumed, "Military dictatorships are a disease of the twentieth century, but Opus Dei is a disease of the thirteenth!"

THE BUREAUCRACY

In Spain the bureaucracy is a political interest group in its own right. Almost unchanged organizationally since 1852, each department recruits and trains its own officials and over the decades "a strong sense of corporate self-interest developed with loyalty to the corps taking priority over all other administrative obligations."[39] Old usages have persisted, particularly that of the right of each department to collect *tasas*, or fees for the services it performs, as well as shares of taxes. The financial inspectors, for example, get a percentage of the taxes they collect. In most modern governments such practices have long been ended, and all income must go to the central treasury. In the absence of effective controls, the Spanish bureaucracy has retained its flavor of autonomous fiefdoms.

The bureaucracy is also represented in the Cortes and even formed a majority of the last Franco cabinet. Bureaucrats were thus in a position to protect their interests. Kenneth Medhurst points out that Cortes amendments to cabinet proposals "are frequently a means for moderating attacks upon special interests" of the departments. Medhurst finds that "much of the conflict within the Cortes is between spokesmen for competing bureaucratic interests."[40] It is

---

[39] Kenneth Medhurst, "The Political Presence of the Spanish Bureaucracy," *Government and Opposition*, 4 (Spring 1969), 239.

[40] Ibid., p. 243.

interesting to note that a 1974 reform proposal to bar bureaucrats from holding Cortes seats was squelched in that body by those affected.

CATHOLIC ACTION

Catholic Action was not an important political force under Franco, but with his passing the movement seemed ready to come into its own as the chief building block of a Christian Democratic party. In Mussolini's Italy, Catholic Action was granted autonomy to spread Church doctrine among the people. But it also served as a seedbed for Italy's postwar Christian Democrats, both in terms of organizational strength and leading personalities. The same is happening in Spain—a Catholic lay movement is spawning a center-right party.

In Spain's first post-Franco cabinet, named in December 1975, three ministers associated with a Catholic Action affiliate known as the *Unión Democrática Española* were included. In the second post-Franco cabinet, named in July 1976, three UDE men were again named, plus five others associated with another Catholic study group more conservative than the UDE. As in Italy, the Spanish Christian Democrats who emerged from Catholic Action had no clear-cut program but could offer themselves as a catchall party, moderately conservative but in favor of democracy, proregime but tied to the Church.

THE CABINET AS ARENA

The fortunes of the various political groups of Spain can be examined by their position in the cabinets that were named on the average of every five years. As we see in Table 3–3, cabinet members identified with the Falange (or Movement)

Table 3–3   Spain's Cabinets: Members' known political affiliations

	1938	1939	1945	1951	1957	1962	1965	1969	1974	1975	1976
Falange	23%	27%	21%	22%	25%	18%	18%	11%	16%	24%	16%
Military	32	42	37	28	33	34	32	22	16	21	21
Monarchist	18	—	—	6	3	—	—	—	—	11	—
Technician*	23	19	25	25	17	13	5	19	63	18	16
Carlist	4	8	—	6	6	8	5	—	—	—	—
Catholic Action	—	4	17	13	6	5	11	6	5	16	42
Opus Dei	—	—	—	—	11	21	29	42	—	11	5

*Unaffiliated technicians with no known political background.

Sources: 1938–39, compiled from Ramon Tamames, La Republica, La Era de Franco (Madrid: Alianza Editorial, 1973), chap. 13. Cabinet named in 1974 from Amando de Miguel, Sociologia del Franquismo (Barcelona: Euros, 1974), chart 3, before p. 93. First post-Franco cabinets named in 1975 and 1976 from information supplied by the U.S. State Department's Bureau of Intelligence and Research, with the author's special thanks to Ray Caldwell.

held about steady at a quarter of the ministers except for the 1960s. A Falangist political background does not necessarily mean one is conservative or fascist; some of the more liberal and innovative ministers have risen through Falange ranks. Further, since just about everyone is a nominal member of the Movement, it is hard to tell an unaffiliated technician from a believing Falangist.

Military officers reached a peak of 42 percent in 1939, as the Civil War was ending, but since then have seldom exceeded a third, and in the 1970s were largely confined to their traditional ministries of army, navy, and air force. This underscores the point made earlier that the military is not quite the regime's pillar it used to be.

Unaffiliated technicians have generally occupied less than a quarter of the cabinet positions. In Franco's short-lived last cabinet of 1974, however, they were an actual majority. Neither monarchists favoring a restoration of the Bourbon line (which Franco ultimately did) nor Carlists have assumed much numerical prominence.

One really interesting shift is the rise and abrupt fall of Opus Dei in the cabinet. Getting a foothold in the 1957 cabinet, Opus increased its influence during the 1960s until it was the dominant voice in the 1969 cabinet. A major reshuffle in 1974, however, ousted all ministers of known Opus affiliation and brought in more people with Falange background. Opus got its foot back in the door again in the first post-Franco cabinet, named in December 1975.

As noted above, people affiliated with Catholic Action emerged as the major force in the 1976 cabinet; eight of nineteen ministers were from Catholic "study groups," which served as a vanguard for the establishment of a Christian Democratic party, a political force that would probably play a major role in post-Franco Spain.

A BALANCING ACT

The more we study the so-called dictatorships, the more we realize that far from being simple one-man rule, they are actually complex and ever-shifting balancing acts between various groups that the regime relies on. In later chapters we will see how Tito of Yugoslavia and Ulbricht of East Germany played such balancing acts with great skill. Never entirely committing themselves to one group or one point of view, the successful dictators first let power and policy flow in one direction, then change officials and lay down new lines so that power and policy flow another way. The "dictator" is actually a flexible compromiser between diverse viewpoints. If he cannot shift, his rule tends to be short lived.

Franco proved himself adept at such shifts. At the outbreak of the Civil War, his power base was exclusively in the military. Franco then broadened his base by merging the Falange with the Carlists and naming himself leader of the new movement. Seeing the need to spur the economy in the late 1950s, Franco then brought in technocrats who happened to be affiliated with Opus Dei. As

Opus Dei gained strength in the cabinet, Falange influence shrank. Although Opus Dei members were ousted from the cabinet in 1974, they remained a potent force, one that had the ear of Spain's powerful bankers and industrialists.

The one big problem with such a balancing act is that it is a tough act to follow. Does Juan Carlos have the ability to play the game that Franco had? The possibility that Juan Carlos and his advisors would become inflexible returns us to the basic flaw of Franco's Spain: one-man rule. If Franco's successor is unable to shift and balance as shrewdly as the old man, it is probable that one or more important groups will become alienated from the regime. Franco, therefore, did not leave behind a legacy of stability, because it was doubtful whether the system could operate without him.

WHAT THE
SPANISH SYSTEM
PRODUCES

THE ECONOMY

The first part of the Franco period was marked by economic autarky; that is, an effort at total self-reliance with few or no exports or imports. Considered foolish by most modern economists, the policy of autarky grew out of both the regime's isolationist predilections and the simple fact that shortly after the Nationalist victory World War II broke out and there were few countries in Europe with whom Spain could trade. The 1940s were grim years for Spain, not only because of the thousands of political executions that took place but economically as well. Even after World War II ended in 1945, most nations boycotted Franco's Spain because it had been associated with Hitler (although Spain was officially neutral through the war). Only Argentina, ruled by dictator Juan Peron, shipped wheat to drought-striken Spain. Barred from receiving Marshall Plan aid, many sectors of the Spanish economy did not recover to pre–Civil War levels until the early 1950s.

Things began to improve in the 1950s. With the deepening of the Cold War, the Western powers rethought their relationship with Spain and soon forgot that Franco had been a quasi-enemy. In 1950 the United Nations voted to lift its trade boycott on Spain, and that same year President Truman delivered a modest $62.5 million in foreign aid to Spain. The Spanish economy leaped upward; industrial production more than doubled during the 1950s (but, alas, so did the cost of living) as Spain came out of its isolated shell and started bringing in foreign capital and modern economic ideas.

The 1960s were excellent years for the Spanish economy; many sectors tripled or quadrupled their production. A program drawn up by Opus Dei technocrats, called the 1959 Stabilization Plan, devalued the peseta (Spain's currency) to a more realistic level and trimmed back some unnecessary government controls. The net effect of the Stabilization Plan was to bring Spain definitively into the capitalist (sometimes called "neocapitalist") era by abandoning the old autarkic goals and corporatist concepts of the Falange. While capitalism is viewed as a conservative doctrine in more advanced countries, in Spain capitalism was a new approach and brought with it some political liberalization and melioration of drastic class differences. From 1962 to 1972 Spain's economy grew at the admirable average rate of 6.8 percent a year, the highest in Western Europe.

THE FOREIGN CONNECTION

Spain did not do all this by herself; much of the growth depended on foreign help. First, as mentioned earlier, a million Spaniards went north of the Pyrenees to work, sending back home badly needed foreign currency and holding down the unemployment rate in Spain. Second, during the 1960s Spain grew into the world's most popular tourist country. West Europeans and Americans poured into Spain for bargain vacations and spent an average of $1 billion a year. Sections of the Spanish Mediterranean coast began to resemble Miami Beach as Germans, French, Dutch, Swedish, and other foreigners purchased summer and retirement residences. And third, foreign, particularly American, firms invested heavily in new industries that ranged from automobiles to detergents. The foreign enterprises brought in not only capital but managerial expertise as well.

There is at least one major catch to this foreign connection, and it could become Spain's Achilles' heel. Some Spanish economists argue that Spain is too dependent on these foreign capital sources and has not sufficiently developed her own sources. Critical economists even doubt that the "tourist industry" represents real industrialization. Tourism, because it depends on foreigners' preferences, is inherently unstable. Political unrest, for example, could keep tourists away, and Spain had plenty of potential for political unrest. Further, the secondary or spinoff effects of tourism in Spain are quite limited. Concentrated on the coastal margins, tourism does little to help the impoverished center of Spain. Tourism, to be sure, stimulates construction and infrastructure improvements (highways, sewage, etc.), but only in certain areas. Underscoring the unreliability of tourism as a basis for long-term growth, in 1976 Spain suffered a falloff in foreign visitors, and a shudder went through the Spanish economy.

Some Spanish observers hold that the Spanish elite has not really changed its archaic, precapitalist viewpoint but merely lends its family names and prestige to foreign money and brains, never picking up the vigorous entrepreneurial attitudes necessary to sustain modern industry. Still, as the years passed, Spanish managers and engineers have picked up the skills to form a new, modern elite.

A further problem of Spain—one linking the economic and political worlds—was its labor movement, or rather two labor movements, one legal but ineffectual and the other illegal but with clout. The former is that of the sindicatos, the original Falange idea (borrowed from Mussolini's fascism) of uniting labor and management in nonantagonistic corporations, each representing a whole branch of industry. Workers were prohibited from striking and employers from lockouts and arbitrary dismissal. Wages were to be determined centrally. Twenty-eight sindicatos were in operation, ranging from food production to banking. Every working Spaniard, in principal, belonged to a sindicato and was represented by it in the Cortes.

In actual practice, Spain's sindicatos functioned no better than Mussolini's corporations; both served largely as devices for holding down labor demands. Many Spanish workers came to recognize that their interests were not adequately represented by their sindicatos and so turned to illegal or extralegal labor action. Strikes, although illegal, started appearing in the 1950s. In the 1960s shadowy *comisiones obreras* (workers' committees) grew up in the larger factories to bargain with management and to strike when satisfactory agreements were not forthcoming. Management attitude was generally tolerant; in order to preserve labor peace, management dealt with the comisiones and soon most factory wages exceeded the official rates, which in effect turned into wage minimums. Some years wage increases reached 15 percent and were clearly inflationary, but the regime found it expedient to give in so as to appease potential worker opposition. Even the official sindicatos began to take a more aggressive stand in favor of the workers.

In 1967 Spanish workers gained a limited right to strike. Strikes were no longer automatically illegal so long as they were peaceful and without political intent. In this the regime was giving in to reality; there had been plenty of strikes, and the government's reluctance to suppress them forcefully had made the antistrike law a dead letter. In 1974 there were nearly twenty-two hundred strikes.

A variety of political viewpoints were represented in the comisiones obreras: Socialist, Communist, and even Catholic. The Catholic Action workers' movement, the Hermandades Obreras (Workers' Brotherhoods), sometimes cooperated with underground Communists in labor actions.

By the 1970s the workers' commissions had heavily infiltrated the official sindicatos. Shop stewards backed by the comisiones were elected to sindicato office, thus giving some underground Communists and Socialists an official cover for their activities. "We occupied the fortress," said one Communist active in the workers' commissions. The illegal comisiones clearly were gaining over (and within) the official sindicatos.

Franco hated parties, but he was unable to prevent their gradual reemergence. At first in private but increasingly in public, Spaniards began identifying themselves as Christian Democrats, Social Democrats, Socialists, and regional autonomists. One could even meet Spanish Communists.

With Franco's death in late 1975 this process of parties coming out of the closet accelerated. "Discussion groups," "unions," or "alliances"—labels used to avoid the word "parties"—began to coalesce into parties. Underneath the authoritarian surface of Franco Spain had lurked a party system as fragmented and complex as Italy's, and now it was coming into the open.

In 1976 parties were made legal. Upon the initiative of Juan Carlos and his prime ministers, laws were pushed through a somewhat reluctant Cortes—still a holdover from the Franco era—dropping the ban on parties, political propaganda, and public meetings. The Communists stayed banned.

Keeping the Communists illegal posed some problems. In the first place, many Spaniards pointed out, it wasn't really democratic to ban one party. Second, and perhaps more pragmatically, it might be better to have the Communists out in the open rather than underground. Spain's Communists, under their Paris-based leader Santiago Carillo, took a strongly Italian line: cooperative, conciliatory, moderate, and swearing independence from Moscow.

Elections for the new lower house of the Cortes were set for 1977. How would Spaniards vote? In the mid-1960s Juan Linz speculated that if Spaniards were to vote like Italians, then according to occupational distributions the two countries' votes would compare as shown in Table 3–4.

Table 3–4   If Spaniards Voted Like Italians

	Communists— Left Socialists	Democratic Socialists	Christian Democrats	Conservatives, Monarchists, Neo-Fascists
% of Vote in Spain	40.9	4.7	40.5	13.9
% of Vote in Italy	36.9	4.5	42.4	16.2

Source: Juan J. Linz, "The Party System of Spain: Past and Future," in Party Systems and Voter Alignments: Cross-National Perspectives, ed. by Seymour M. Lipset and Stein Rokkan (New York: Free Press, 1967), p. 269.

Since the first post-Franco governments suppressed Communists and Left Socialists, it is likely that early Spanish elections will show two large, moderate parties, the Social Democrats and the Christian Democrats. A large Social

Democrat vote, however, probably will not reflect actual voter sympathies, for many voters would undoubtedly go further left if permitted to.

Political activity quickened as Franco neared the grave; previously docile groups began to speak their minds. While Franco still lived the regime's response was to crack down where it could. With the advent of King Juan Carlos, however, the regime's tactics became more complicated—or perhaps confused is a better word. While Premier Arias vowed to move toward democracy "without hurry and without pause," his dilemma was how to go fast enough to satisfy the Left and slow enough to satisfy the Right.

On the labor front, for example, the regime first allowed numerous strikes. Spanish workers, at long last tasting freedom, seemed bent on having as many strikes as French or Italian workers. Railroad workers, postmen, truckers, and even policemen threatened to shut the country down. So the regime responded toughly, conscripting tens of thousands of strikers into the army so they would have to return to work under military orders.

Initially the new regime allowed some political protest meetings, but soon these meetings grew bigger and louder, and riot police waded in with tear gas and truncheons. Arrests started anew: critical lawyers, labor leaders, Catalan autonomists, militant priests. Franco's death did not bring instant happiness and democracy to Spain.

The problem was how to depressurize without exploding. The Communist regimes of Poland, Hungary, and Czechoslovakia faced the same problem when they began to de-Stalinize. Closer to home, Portugal went through instability and violence after the overthrow of the Salazar-Caetano regime in 1974. There is no easy way to go from a more authoritarian regime to a more democratic one. Demands and frustrations built up during decades of harsh rule come rushing to the surface, demanding speedy gratification. But the older, more conservative elements fight back, fearing collapse of the entire system and loss of their positions.

Accordingly, Spain at the start of the post-Franco era held the potential for much violence and upheaval. Here are some possible scenarios for Spain:

Constitutional Monarchy This is seen by many as the most desirable and feasible route for the gradual democratization of Spain, requiring the least upheaval. It is the route King Juan Carlos chose. But would he be able to implement this gradual approach, given the social and political forces now unleashed? So many things could go wrong, for example:

Breakaway Provinces Separatist agitation in Catalonia and the Basque country grew during the 1970s. The Catalans generally sought cultural autonomy by nonviolent means. Some Basques, on the other hand, sought full independence and did not hesitate to use violence. The ETA (for *Euzkadi ta Azkatasuna,* Basque Nation and Freedom) robbed banks, shot police, and in 1973 even blew up Franco's friend and premier, Admiral Luis Carrero Blanco, on a Madrid street. But if the breakup of Spain was ever a serious threat, it would trigger the next possibility:

Military Takeover   The Spanish military has long considered itself the ultimate guardian of Spanish unity. Any threat to that unity—breakaway provinces, a general strike, far-leftist terrorism—could persuade the army to take over. Many observers prayed that any post-Franco upheaval would not come for some years, after the last of the ultraconservative generals and admirals of Franco's generation retired or died off. They reason that by the 1980s there will be a much more moderate and professional generation of generals at the top of the Spanish military who would either not intervene directly into governmental affairs or would do so on a leftist basis, which brings us to yet another scenario:

The Portuguese Model   Liberal and leftist Spaniards were thrilled and delighted by the military coup that ousted Portugal's authoritarian regime in April 1974. Some hoped the Spanish army could play a similar role. With the dying out of the old, reactionary generals and the rise of younger officers, a "Nasserist" type of military involvement could not be excluded. In 1975 and 1976, dozens of younger officers were detained on unprecedented "sedition" charges. They were members of the Democratic Military Union. One major factor, however, that politicized the Portuguese military was missing in Spain: overseas wars. While the Portuguese fought three wars at once for more than a decade in Africa, Spain in 1975 simply pulled out of the Spanish Sahara. Furthermore, within two years of the Lisbon coup, political and economic chaos in Portugal had turned off Spaniards from going that route.

Renewed Authoritarianism   Not all Spaniards approved of the liberalization of Spain during the 1970s. Important conservative and fascistic groups demanded a return to the old ways. Rightist demonstrators howled for more death sentences against leftist revolutionaries and killers of policemen. Spanish police were naturally partial to "law and order" demonstrators and did not interfere with rallies demanding a *mano dura,* a "strong hand." A far-right group, *Guerrilleros del Cristo Rey* (Combatants of Christ the King), bashed leftists with impunity. If the extreme right entered the government it would possibly trigger:

Another Civil War   While this scenario is the least likely, it cannot totally be ruled out. Spain has probably changed too much;

economic conditions have greatly improved, a large middle class has arisen, and hardly anybody wants new bloodshed. But at the same time, expectations of progress have been awakened while exasperation with the regime's cautious reforms mounts. With few and weak structures to channel political participation, no one could tell which way popular unrest might surge. For actual fighting to break out, however, there would have to be a split in the Spanish military, or between the military and the Guardia Civil, for they monopolize weapons.

Spain at the beginning of the post-Franco era was a gigantic question mark, which is precisely what makes it so fascinating to study. It could go any way. Along with most Spaniards of good will, we can only hope that the divisions of the Civil War have finally healed.

ITALY
4

A report from the U.S. Embassy in Rome to Washington is alleged to have read: "Italy passes from disaster to disaster, none of them serious." In this manner have observers of Italy over the postwar decades shrugged off the possibility of systemic upheaval; they cautioned against taking Italy's seeming chaos and near-permanent crisis too seriously. Italy had always muddled through before and would again.

By the mid-1970s, however, much of the complacency vanished. A sour economy, growing violence, and an increase in the Communist vote made people wonder whether Italy would muddle through again. The possibility of a political explosion loomed.

Whether Italy explodes or not, long-buried problems show Italians and foreigners alike how fragile and unstable the Italian system really is. Of the Western European democracies the reader may be studying, Italy clearly must rank as the weak sister. Italy's history gives little ground for encouragement, but we might remember that the stronger systems of Western Europe had to overcome similar problems and did so successfully.

THE
IMPACT
OF THE
PAST

LATE UNIFICATION

Metternich is alleged to have remarked that Italy was not a country but "merely a geographical expression." At the time he said it (about 1815), he was right: there had never been a political unit known as "Italy," even in Roman times. Through the Middle Ages and Renaissance, Italy was divided into duchies, republics, city-states, and papal dominions. From the sixteenth through early nineteenth centuries large areas of the peninsula were ruled by Spain, Austria, and France. The domination by Spain of the southern part of Italy, many historians believe, had particularly bad effects on administration, taxation, and popular attitudes toward government.

One is tempted to compare divided Italy with divided Germany—both were unified only in the middle of the nineteenth century. There were some important differences, though. The many German principalities were seldom dominated by foreign powers for long; portions of Italy were under foreign rule for centuries. The unification of the two countries offers some comparison. In both Germany and Italy it was vigorous northern areas—Prussia and Piedmont respectively—that aggregated the more southerly territories to form the new nation-states. The monarchs of Prussia and of Piedmont became, respectively, the monarchs of Germany and of Italy. In both cases, nationalism was triggered by French ideas and occupation under Napoleon, but again there were important differences. By the time Bismarck finished consolidating the Second Reich in 1871, many Germans were enthusiastically nationalistic. German unification was genuinely popular at the mass level. In Italy, on the other hand, the masses were largely indifferent to the unification, which was completed in 1871, and in the South there was considerable hostility to rule by the northerners.[1] At no time did the Italian *Risorgimento* (resurgence) rally the population against foreign and native despots; it relied instead on a few thousand armed Italians—mostly northern middle- and upper-class romantics—plus help from the French in expelling Austria. The patriotic rhetoric of Garibaldi, Cavour, and Mazzini was not widely shared by the still locally oriented peasant majority. Italy seemed to be as unified as Germany, but its unification was superficial.

To this day, observers speak of the South of Italy, starting at Rome, as a different country, much poorer, still traditional, and inhabited by Mediterranean people. Since most Italian emigrants to the United States (one American in ten is of Italian descent) were from the South, Americans have only a partial picture of Italians and of Italy. The Center and North of Italy are quite different, the former characterized by productive farms (many of them worked cooperatively), the latter by large industry. People, manners, work habits, and even language are different in all three regions, but the big dividing line is between the South and the rest of Italy.

The forced amalgamation of the various regions into a united Italy, with the best of intentions, made things even worse for the South, called in Italian the *Mezzogiorno* (midday, like the French *Midi*). The end of internal tariffs allowed Northern products to flood into the South, wiping out its infant industries. Centralized administration in Rome was unable to cure the problems of the

---

[1] For a fictionalized portrayal of the arrival and effects of unification on Sicily, see the fine novel by Giuseppe di Lampedusa, *The Leopard* (New York: New American Library, 1961).

South. Economic growth was concentrated in the North's Industrial Triangle of Genoa, Milan, and Turin. A hundred years after unification, the Mezzogiorno had grown relatively *poorer* in comparison to the booming North. In sum, the South of Italy is a distinctly Mediterranean land, comparable to parts of Spain, Greece, and North Africa; the North is a European land, comparable to parts of France, Switzerland, and Austria. North Italians tend to look down on their southern compatriots. The alliance between the two has never been firmly cemented.

THE CHURCH AS SORE LOSER

Another divisive factor from Italy's past has been the attitude of the Roman Catholic Church. Until Italian unification, the Vatican was not only a spiritual center but a temporal power as well, controlling a large area of central Italy known as the Papal States. With these lands incorporated into the new Italian state, which was heavily anticlerical in spirit, the Church became bitterly antistate. The Vatican had never welcomed Italian unification, seeing it as a threat to its own power, and for the first half-century of the new state's existence the Church instructed faithful Catholics not to participate in national politics, not even to vote. Thus a large section of the Italian people, especially in the tradition-bound South, were brought up to disdain the civil institutions of their country. During the first decades of this century, however, the Church quietly sanctioned Catholic political participation and a Popular party (forerunner of the present Christian Democrats) sprang up as a moderate force. If the Church had brought its basically moderate forces into Italian politics earlier it might have helped stabilize the system and prevent Mussolini's rise.

The anticlerical–Catholic split still runs deep in modern Italy and is capable of generating fiery controversy. Catholicism is still the official religion (about half of Italians are practicing Catholics), and many Catholic schools and charitable organizations receive state funds. The right to grant divorces was a monopoly of the Church until 1970. The Vatican has been extremely jealous of its prerogatives in Italy, and the last hundred years can be read as a rearguard action by the Church to keep its vestiges of temporal power. The Catholic Churches of France and Germany have long since made their peace with the state, but not the Italian Church.

THE RISE OF FASCISM

As the student might judge from the above, the first half-century of unified Italian government was not a great success. Large sections of the Italian population either did not want to participate or were barred (by a restrictive voting franchise) from doing so. Politics fell into the hands of a relatively few men in the dominant Liberal party, which was actually quite conservative by our standards. Behind-the-scenes manipulation and payoffs (called *trasformismo*, the "transformation" of political adversaries into allies by various forms of compensation) were used by crafty prime ministers to circumvent the factious and quarrelsome parliament.

Social and economic progress was made in the late nineteenth and early twentieth centuries, but many Italians became fed up with and alienated from the political chicanery in Rome. On the Left, the Socialist party pursued a "maximalist" course and talked about revolutionizing Italy. The Socialists' bark was worse than their bite; many of their demands were pure rhetoric that they never seriously considered implementing. But the Socialists did succeed in alarming the propertied classes, both middle and upper, many of whom sought a means to block the rise of the Left.

Italian intellectuals increasingly despaired of parliamentary democracy. Brilliant social thinkers like Gaetano Mosca and Vilfredo Pareto argued that democracy was a sham and rule by elites inevitable. Romantic nationalists dreamed of Italy in an imperial role with expanded frontiers and overseas colonies. The Liberal governments around the turn of the century responded to these demands, seizing Somaliland in 1889 and Eritrea in 1890, but losing a battle to Ethiopia in 1896, one of the few times Africans beat Europeans. In 1912 Italy wrested Libya from Turkey. Italy, with her pieces of desert, pretended she was in the same imperial league as Britain and France, and this was her undoing.

When World War I broke out in 1914 the majority of the Italian people favored neutrality; it was not their war and they had no reason to be involved. But by 1915 nationalists were in power and, with an assist from the king, brought Italy into the war on the side of Britain and France in return for secret promises of territory in Austria and Turkey. The war was a near-disaster for Italy. While the romantic poet Gabriele d'Annunzio extolled the patriotic struggle, the masses of conscripts loathed the war. On October 24, 1917, the Italians broke at Caporetto in the Alps in a dreadful rout depicted by Ernest Hemingway in *A Farewell to Arms*. Italy was saved by the Austro-German collapse the following year and received for her pains in the war the Austrian province of South Tyrol, bringing under Italian control a quarter of a million German-speaking people, the only sizable minority group in Italy, and a reluctant one.

But Italy was drained and bitter. Nationalists, dissatisfied with Italy's meager rewards, marched on the port of Fiume on the Adriatic, which was to go to the new country of Yugoslavia, and seized it under the leadership of d'Annunzio. The 1919–20 Fiume episode is often treated as comic opera —d'Annunzio abdicated his "regency" at the first cannon shot—but to an extent it was a dress rehearsal for the Fascist takeover of all Italy in 1922. Mussolini incorporated d'Annunzio's flare for spectacle, including the arm-outstretched Roman salute, into the Fascist movement.

Benito Mussolini, who before the war had been a militant Socialist leader and journalist, became a superpatriot and in 1919 grouped a grab-bag of malcontents (Futurists, syndicalists, nationalists, unemployed veterans, and decaying aristocrats) around him. The movement was called fascism, after the bundle of sticks around an ax (*fasces*) that symbolized authority in ancient Rome, but no one could define precisely what fascism stood for. H. Stuart Hughes points out that fascism had particular appeal to the Italian middle classes, which felt their property and/or status threatened by the noisy Socialists. Fascism was, in this sense, a class movement.[2] But at the time it was so thoroughly cloaked with themes of law and order, patriotism, antileftism, corporatism, national rejuvenation, and such that it seemed to many Italians to be a plausible alternative to corrupt parliamentarism or revolutionary socialism. The Church, which had never accepted the old regime, thought fascism might be some improvement. The elected leaders of Italy, used to behind-the-scenes manipulation, underestimated the threat of the rising Fascists. The Italian police, who had little love for Socialists, generally winked as the Fascists beat and sometimes murdered their opposition. Finally, as the Black Shirts (their uniform) marched on Rome in October 1922, King Victor Emmanuel, an indecisive weakling, refused to sign an order to the army to crush them. Instead, the king bade Mussolini (who did not himself march on Rome but arrived by sleeping car from Milan) to form a new government.

THE FACADE

The Fascist regime that Mussolini consolidated during the 1920s impressed many outsiders. There was order, stable currency, no strikes, much monumental construction, and, as they used to say, "the trains ran on time." Beneath the surface, however, the Fascist period was characterized by improvisation, inefficiency, economic stagnation, waste, and corruption. Promising a breakthrough in political organization, Mussolini set up twenty-two "corporations" in various sectors of the economy in which workers and owners would cooperate and be represented in a National Council of Corporations, to replace the parliament. In reality, the corporate state gave owners pretty much of a free hand but kept workers closely in check.

There was considerable unemployment, but much of it was concealed by the military draft and by a Fascist law requiring peasants to stay in their villages unless they had police permits to move. In attempting to make Italy self-sufficient, Mussolini excluded many imports, and the price of food and other commodities soared. The Fascist regime papered over but did not solve most of Italy's long-standing problems.

Although Italy was the first Fascist state, it did not equal its imitator, Nazi

---

[2] H. Stuart Hughes, *The United States and Italy*, rev. ed. (New York: W. W. Norton, 1965), p. 66.

Germany, in thoroughness, brutality, or racism. The Fascists murdered some opponents, but most survived either in exile, in prison, or banished to remote provinces. Under German pressure, laws against Jews were adopted only in 1938 and were widely evaded, like most laws in Italy.

Remnants of the Fascist period remain in modern Italy, including some laws and many civil servants. Mussolini's 1929 Concordat with the Church, defining the Vatican as a sovereign state and giving the Church extensive control over education and divorce, was incorporated into the postwar Italian constitution. A Fascist scheme to save faltering firms by buying control of them, the IRI (*Istituto per la Ricostruzione Industriale*), remains to this day a giant semistate holding company that runs a good deal of Italian industry.

Ramshackle as the Fascist structure was, it might have lasted if Mussolini had steered clear of overseas adventures. But, still trying to make Italy a major power, Mussolini ordered the conquest of Ethiopia in 1935 and then sent units to support Franco in the Spanish Civil War. Mussolini was drawn into cooperation with Hitler; the Rome-Berlin "Axis" was set up in 1936. While Italy did not enter the war along with Germany in 1939, when Hitler crushed France in the summer of 1940, Mussolini could not resist an easy victory and invaded the South of France. Next Mussolini tried to conquer Greece, but the Greeks pushed the Italians out until Hitler came to Mussolini's rescue in 1941.

Italy was ill-prepared both materially and psychologically to fight a war. Italian armaments were few and light, mostly for show. Defeatism was widespread among soldiers who wanted no part of the war. As the British and Americans overran Sicily in July 1943, King Victor Emmanuel—still the legal head of state—finally dumped Mussolini and took Italy out of the war. Mussolini was spirited out of detention by Nazi commandos and ordered by Hitler to set up a Fascist republic in Central and Northern Italy. In the twenty months this puppet rump state existed some quarter of a million anti-Fascist Italian Partisans fought Germans and Italians alike, liberating whole cities before the Allies arrived. The bedraggled *Duce* (leader) tried to reach Switzerland, but Partisans caught and executed him and displayed his body in Milan.

With strong American backing, a democratic Italy was set up. Let us now consider what Italy has done with her postwar freedom.

THE
KEY
INSTITUTIONS

THE STABILITY OF INSTABILITY

In her first three decades of postwar development Italy had more than three dozen governments. An Italian government "fell," on the average, every ten months. Although this seems to be constant turmoil and absence of leadership, things are not quite that bad. As we pointed out in the chapter on Sweden, the European term "government" is often used to mean simply "the cabinet." When a government "falls" it just means that the cabinet has resigned, either because the parliament has voted no confidence in it, or because the various parties in the governing coalition cannot agree.

The typical Italian "government crisis" is the latter. In France of the Third and Fourth Republics, many cabinets were ousted in votes of no confidence. In Italy, such votes are rare. Instead, Italy's Center-Left coalition, trying to hold together Christian Democrats, Socialists, and smaller parties, frequently comes apart when one or more of the coalition partners finds the government's (i.e., the cabinet's) stance unacceptable.[3] When a cabinet resigns, a caretaker cabinet runs things for a few days or weeks (the "crisis" period) until a new coalition cabinet can be negotiated, usually with the objectionable policy modified. The new cabinet usually includes the same parties as before, and often the same personalities return to the same jobs! Some Italian cabinet ministers have more years of service than their American counterparts. As the French say of their system: The more it changes, the more it stays the same.

The problem with Italian government is not rapid change but the opposite: very little change, sometimes called "immobilism." An Italian cabinet can institute few new departures in policy because one or more of the coalition partners will object. Italy lacks a single party popular enough to govern alone. Whereas Sweden has a large Social Democratic party that can rule alone with tacit Communist support, Italy's largest party, the Christian Democrats, is not big enough to rule without partners. The Christian Democrats are, furthermore, composed of a number of factions that prevent the drawing up of a reasonably clear political program. Thus Italy, which is often described as unstable, turns out to be in many respects too stable, unable to handle the tremendous changes and pressures of postwar Italy. Why is this so?

THE CONSTITUTION

The 1948 constitution established Italy as a republic. The monarchy, tainted by its acquiescence to fascism, had been abolished by a 1946 plebiscite in which 54 percent voted for a republic. Thus from the very beginning, the Republic of Italy was on shaky ground, endorsed by a bare majority. It is interesting to note that a majority in the traditional South favored retaining the monarchy.

The first third of the 1948 constitution includes a number of socialist-sounding clauses that opened the way to the nationalization of industry and land reform. Most of the first fifty-four articles are so vague and idealistic that they

---

[3] See Raphael Zariski, *Italy; The Politics of Uneven Development* (Hinsdale, Ill.: Dryden Press, 1972), p. 153.

merely serve the Left as ammunition to attack centrist governments for failing to fulfill the grandiose aims.

One of these articles, however, is not vague and has caused trouble. Article 7 incorporates the 1929 Lateran Pacts negotiated by Mussolini and the Vatican. The Concordat recognizes the Vatican as a sovereign state and gives it control over divorces; the Italian state in effect handed over one of the civil powers of modern states to an outside agency. Until recently there was no civil divorce in Italy, a point of considerable irritation. Curiously, the Communists cooperated with the Catholics in 1948 to include the Concordat; even then the Communists were trying to demonstrate their moderation.

A CLASSIC SYSTEM

Italy has most of the classic institutions of parliamentary democracy on the model of the French Third and Fourth Republics. But while de Gaulle's Fifth Republic curtailed the power of the French parliament in favor of a very strong presidency, Italy continues with a comparatively weak president elected by parliament and a cabinet formed by and dependent upon a majority of votes in parliament.

Italy is a unitary state, unlike the federal systems of West Germany and Yugoslavia, but she has moved in the federal direction by setting up twenty regions with limited local powers. To represent these regions Italy's parliament has an upper house, the Senate, composed of 315 members. Each region gets one senator for every 200,000 inhabitants but is entitled to a minimum of 6. Italy's most populous region, Lombardy, sends 45 senators to Rome. The regions in turn are divided into districts. If a candidate for the Senate gets at least 65 percent of the vote in his or her district he is elected; if not (as is overwhelmingly the case), senators are elected by proportional representation from party lists in each region.

The lower house, the 630-member Chamber of Deputies, is elected by proportional representation from thirty-two electoral districts. This system produces two chambers that are almost carbon copies of each other with nearly identical percentages of the various parties. Both chambers have coinciding five-year terms. The only slight difference is that voters for the Senate must be twenty-five years old while voters for the Chamber need be only eighteen. Critics hold that the Italian Senate serves no useful purpose, representing citizens in almost the same way as the Chamber of Deputies. In the Yugoslav system, as we shall consider, the two houses of parliament are like two U.S. Senates. In the Italian system, the two chambers are analogous to two U.S. Houses of Representatives.

Both chambers of the Italian parliament must pass a bill before it can be signed into law by the president, who has a weak veto power. He can send the bill back with his comments, but a simple majority overrides. The Italian legislature does have one unique power that speeds up the handling of some matters. When meeting *in sede deliberante,* one of the fourteen standing committees in the Chamber (eleven in the Senate), can actually pass a bill without bringing it before the full house. If one-tenth of the committee's members demand, however, the bill must be reported back to the chamber. Since all the parties are represented proportionally on the committees, a bill passed *in sede deliberante* actually goes through a miniature of the parent chamber.

The formal institutions of Italian government are not all that different from those of many other European countries. Why has Sweden's system worked smoothly and with stability while Italy's has not? Why does the present Italian system resemble France of the Third and Fourth Republics? To answer these questions we must turn to the political parties.

PARTY SYSTEM

The Italian party system is one of the last classic political spectrums left in Europe. The many parties of Weimar Germany have coalesced into two big parties and one small party. The French Fifth Republic is actually a presidential system, and there too the many parties have tended toward two large groupings. Sweden has also evolved into two large groupings with no confessional or far-right parties, and its Social Democrats nearly monopolize the working-class vote, which in Italy is divided among several left-wing parties. The Italian party system has everything. It is a sort of living museum of the way European politics used to be before World War II, and, as such, it is particularly interesting to students of comparative politics. Now let us turn to, in order of electoral strength, Italy's main parties.[4]

Christian Democrats   Democrazia Christiana, or DC, is Italy's largest party, getting around 40 percent of the vote, although this has been declining in recent years. Aside from its ties to and support of the Roman Catholic Church, the DC has no program except to stick to the center. It is a "catchall" party whose several factions span from as far left as the Socialists to as far right as the Liberals. Founded after the war with U.S. blessings and CIA subsidies, the DC is a lineal descendant of the old Popular party. Christian Democratic voters tend to be middle class, rural, serious Catholics and disproportionately female. Its geographic strongholds are in the Northeast (around Venice) and South, traditional Catholic areas.

---

[4] For details on the parties and their support, see Giorgio Galli and Alfonso Prandi, *Patterns of Political Participation in Italy* (New Haven: Yale University Press, 1970), chap. 2; and Dante Germino and Stefano Passigli, *The Government and Politics of Contemporary Italy* (New York: Harper & Row, 1968), chap. 4.

Communist Party   Partito Comunista Italiano, or PCI, is the second largest growing from a fifth to over a third of the Italian vote. A 1921 offshoot of the Socialist party, the Communists went underground during the Fascist period to emerge as one of the main forces in the Resistance in Northern and Central Italy in 1943–45. Strongly rooted among blue-collar workers in Central Italy and the Northern industrial cities and growing more recently among Southern peasants, the Communists have been gaining strength. Although subsidized secretly by the Soviet Union, the PCI is often critical of Moscow and denounced the 1968 invasion of Czechoslovakia. The PCI has been at great pains to demonstrate how moderate and independent it is, but has not been in any cabinet since 1947.

Socialist Party   Partito Socialista Italiano, or PSI, is the third largest Italian party but lags far behind the DC and PCI, getting only about one-tenth of the electorate, chiefly skilled and white-collar workers. Plagued by factions since its 1892 founding, the PSI has historically been Marxist and "maximalist" in revolutionary rhetoric, working closely with the Communists after World War II. By 1963, however, the PSI had become sufficiently moderate to enter into a coalition with the Christian Democrats, called the "opening to the left," which governed Italy into the 1970s.

Social Democrats   Partito Socialista Democratico Italiano, or PSDI, split rightward from the Socialists in 1947. Declining to less than 5 percent of the vote, the Social Democrats are very moderate, advocating welfare rather than nationalization. They have been in coalition with the DC.

Liberal Party   Partito Liberale Italiano, or PLI, was the dominant force in Italian politics from unification to after World War I. The Liberals lost much of their constituency to Christian Democracy after World War II and now win only a small percent of the vote. Economically conservative but anticlerical, the Liberals draw their strength from better-off voters.

Neo-Fascists   Movimento Sociale Italiano, or MSI, sprang up in 1946, although a revival of Fascism is technically prohibited in Italy. The MSI draws from assorted misfits who remember the Mussolini era with nostalgia, along with young toughs who crave violence against the Left. In combination with the shrinking Monarchist party, the MSI rose to 9 percent of the vote in 1972 but dropped to 8 percent in 1976.

Monarchists   Partito Democratico Italiano di Unita Monarchica, or PDIUM, is nearly extinct. There is no chance of reviving the Italian monarchy. In 1972 it ran on a combined ticket with the Neo-Fascists. Its orientation is similar to the Liberals', but pro-Church.

Socialist Proletarian Unity   Partito Socialista Italiano di Unita Proletaria, or PSIUP, split off leftward from the Socialists in 1963 when the PSI entered the DC coalition. In some respects this small party is further left than the PCI, as the PSIUP is unwilling to compromise with moderate parties.

Republican Party   Partito Repubblicano Italiano, or PRI, is Italy's oldest party; Republicans are the party of the unification. Never a mass party, the PRI attracts intellectuals who favor nonrevolutionary reform and economic planning. Although often in coalition with the DC, the Republicans are the strongest anticlericals of all.

Most party systems can be expressed by a simple left-to-right spectrum, but things are not so simple in Italy, for we must also indicate where a party stands on the clerical issue. For example, the Liberals are very close to the right wing of the Christian Democrats but part company with them on the question of support for the Church. Likewise the left wing of the DC is quite similar to the Socialists, except that the DC Left has a Catholic slant. A schematization of the Italian party system would thus have not only the usual left-right axis but also an anticlerical-Church axis:

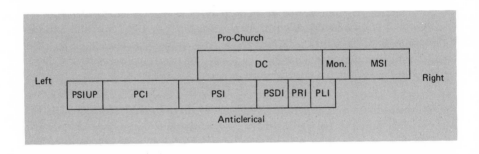

The Center-Left coalition that came to power in the 1963 "opening to the left" consisted of the Christian Democrats, Socialists (PSI), Social Democrats (PSDI), and Republicans (PRI). The previous coalition had been similar, except that it included the Liberals (PLI) on the Right instead of the Socialists on the Left. Few or no other coalitions have been possible, and that is the crux of Italian immobilism.

The Christian Democrats, with the largest share of the Italian vote, cannot stray far from the Center. A Center-Right coalition of DC, Monarchists, Liberals, and Neo-Fascists is absolutely unacceptable to the left wing of Christian Democrats.

The Communists, on the other hand, in 1973 proposed a *compromesso storico* (historic compromise) in which Catholics and Communists would over-look their differences and form a coalition, the two being Italy's largest parties. Initially this idea was unacceptable to all but the leftmost Christian Democrats. For years the Communists have been on their best behavior, stressing modera-tion and flexibility—they would even keep Italy in NATO!—to show the Chris-tian Democrats that they would make good coalition partners. The long-term trend of Italian voting may force the DC to take up the Communists' proposal, for the Christian Democratic vote has been faltering while the Communists' has been growing. During the 1970s the PCI lost some of its frightening image and many non-Communist Italians began to perceive it as a plausible member of the government.[5]

ITALIAN
POLITICAL
ATTITUDES

THE UNCIVIC CULTURE

An old saw goes: "People get the government they deserve." Thus calm, rational Swedes get a calm, rational political system. Mistrustful, fractious Italians get an untrustworthy, fragmented system. But which comes first? Do popular attitudes create the government, or does the government create the popular attitudes? In Italy—indeed, in most places—we cannot be sure.

The Italian political culture is something to behold; it is often cited as an example of how bad things can get. Italians, says Joseph LaPalombara, are "isolated into mutually antagonistic subgroups of the society, basically disin-clined to engage in pragmatic bargaining—the give and take—of a pluralistic democratic polity and at times completely alienated from the political system."[6] Gabriel Almond and Sidney Verba sum up Italians as "particularly low in national pride, in moderate and open partisanship, in the acknowledgement of the obligation to take an active part in local community affairs."[7] Edward Banfield studied a town in the South where people could think of nothing that did not concern their immediate families; he called it "amoral familism."[8]

---

[5] For an excellent discussion of these trends see Giacomo Sani, "Secular Trends and Party Realignments in Italy: The 1975 Election," paper delivered at the 1975 meeting of the American Political Science Association, San Francisco, September 2–5, 1975.

[6] Joseph LaPalombara, "Italy: Fragmentation, Isolation, Alienation," in *Political Culture and Political Development,* ed. by Lucian W. Pye and Sidney Verba (Princeton, N.J.: Princeton University Press, 1965), p. 282.

[7] Gabriel A. Almond and Sidney Verba, *The Civic Culture: Political Attitudes and Democ-racy in Five Nations* (Boston: Little, Brown, 1965), p. 308.

[8] Edward C. Banfield, *The Moral Basis of a Backward Society* (New York: Free Press, 1958), pp. 83–86.

Laws are something to be circumvented. An Italian who attempts to live by the written rules is often considered *fesso*, a fool. If, for example, an Italian declares his or her income honestly, he or she will be taxed even more than the fair share, for the assessor automatically assumes he or she is lying and adds on a percentage to make up for it. The person Italians often admire is *furbo*, foxy or crafty, adept at skirting the law and profiting from it.

Government and politics are widely disdained in Italy. Almond and Verba found that 62 percent of Italians claimed never to follow political affairs, and 66 percent said they never talk politics with others.[9] Only 3 percent were proud of their governmental institutions.[10] Only 10 percent said a man should be active in his community.[11] Italian political culture is poor soil in which to grow a democracy.

There are a number of explanations for how things got to be this way.

History   History has not been kind to Italy. Ruled, usually misruled, by foreigners for centuries, Italy did not have a chance to develop its own institutions and pride in them until relatively recently. Italians learned to knuckle under to their foreign rulers, chiefly Spanish and Austrian, becoming obsequious to the powerful, but shrewd and calculating behind their masters' backs. The survival of one's family was all that mattered; the common good took last place.

The Family   The Italian family thus became a miniature state, and a rather authoritarian one at that. LaPalombara notes that "the Italian family fails to provide its members with a coherent view of the national political system or with a sense of effectual involvement concerning it." Politics is seldom discussed and children learn to disdain the subject. Fathers demand unquestioning obedience; "there is little training in the kind of pragmatic give-and-take that a democratic polity requires." The authoritarianism of the Italian family thus provided a psychological basis for fascism.[12]

Economic Conditions   The material conditions of life in Italy have until quite recently been terrible. Parts of the South are still more North African than European; hunger stalked the area for centuries. Throughout Italy jobs were scarce until the 1960s. Competition for food, jobs, even for survival has been merciless. Difficult economic conditions have left even present-day Italians insecure, jealous, and mistrustful of other Italians, especially those who are better off. This in turn deepens class conflict.

[9] Almond and Verba, *The Civic Culture*, pp. 54 and 79.

[10] Ibid., p. 64.

[11] Ibid., p. 127.

[12] LaPalombara, "Italy: Fragmentation, Isolation, Alienation," pp. 318–19.

Class Conflict   Italian class conflict is one of the sharpest and nastiest in Europe. The gap between rich and poor is large; the rich live extravagantly while the poor scrape by. Until the postwar economic boom, social mobility was low and it is still retarded because university education, the chief avenue of social mobility, is overwhelmingly middle class. Class resentment fuels the Left vote and helps account for the large Communist party. The middle and upper classes in turn react in horror at this threat to their property and status. The result is an extremely hostile Left and Right with little possibility of the kind of rational compromise that goes on in Sweden. The political style turns shrill and demagogic and extremist groups turn to violence. In contrast to calm, orderly Swedish political rallies, Italian rallies are guarded by platoons of riot police.

THE TRIUMPH OF CYNICISM

Factors such as the above produce an extraordinarily cynical kind of politics. Italians tend to assume that politics is self-interest: politicians merely seek their own advantage; votes are cast to win favors; party membership is to help you keep your job. These attitudes are especially deep among older Italians.

While voting turnout is high, over 90 percent, and some four million Italians are members of a political party, a good deal of participation is tinged with skepticism. The Italian takes politics with more than a grain of salt. Italians, holds Luigi Barzini, place little store in ideologies and political institutions "because all of them will always function defectively in Italy," in itself a pretty cynical statement.[13] Things are changing, though. Economic, social and cultural changes are rapidly propelling Italy into the modern era; Italian politics cannot lag behind forever. One case study of this kind of change is worth examining in some detail.

THE DIVORCE REFERENDUM

The 1929 Lateran Pacts, incorporated into the postwar constitution, gave the Church control over divorce in Italy. Since the Church forbids divorce, the only legal way to end a marriage in Italy was by a difficult and expensive papal annulment. Italians with a more modern viewpoint thought this was ridiculous (see the film *Divorce Italian Style*), and finally the anticlerical parties in parliament (a majority) passed a moderate divorce law in 1970, which allows couples to file for divorce after a separation of at least five years. There was no divorce boom in Italy after the enactment of this law, but pro-Church forces, chiefly Christian Democrats, acted as if the heavens were falling. Using a neglected clause in the

[13] Luigi Barzini, *The Italians* (New York: Bantam Books, 1965), p. 236.

constitution that sets up a referendum upon petition by half a million citizens, antidivorce forces gathered 1.5 million signatures to repeal the law in a May 1974 referendum.

On the surface, the referendum was about divorce; underneath, it represented the clash of two subcultures, one secular and leftist, the other religious and conservative. Just as there are Two Spains, so also are there Two Italies. Amintore Fanfani, then the head of the DC, was widely believed to be using the referendum as a de Gaulle-type plebiscite to establish his one-man rule. Anticlerical forces took the referendum as a showdown with Church interference in politics. The propaganda grew extreme, and banners, posters, and leaflets blanketed Italy's cities. *Divorzisti* called their opponents Fascists (some were), while *antidivorzisti* called their opponents Reds (many were). The antidivorce side was especially primitive and emotional, claiming that the divorce law automatically meant the collapse of the family and the rise of drug use, homosexuality, and abortion. Fanfani even exhorted the very *macho* Sicilian males that their wives would leave them for young girls!

The antidivorce forces severely misjudged modern Italy; indeed, their exaggerations may have backfired. When the ballots were counted, 59.1 percent were for keeping the divorce law, 40.9 percent were for repealing it. Only the South, still traditional, voted a majority (52.4 percent) for repeal; the North and Center of Italy went 62.5 and 63.9 percent respectively for keeping the law. The strongest supporters of the divorce law were men, younger people, those with at least a junior high school education, irreligious people, and those voting for parties of the Left.[14]

The defeat was a severe setback for both the Christian Democrats and the Church. Indeed, the left wing of the DC voted against repeal and some priests refused to support the Church's stand. In local and regional elections the following year, the Christian Democratic vote declined sharply while the Communists' rose. For the Christian Democrats the divorce referendum was a foolish tactic to try; it showed how out of touch they were with the modern, secular Italy that is emerging.

PATTERNS

OF

INTERACTION

AN ABUNDANCE OF GROUPS

Some theorists of democracy hold that a multiplicity of interest groups, each struggling to make its impact on governmental decisions, is the foundation of democracy. If this be so, Italy is the most democratic country in the world, for

---

[14] Bulletin of the Milan public opinion survey organization Demoskopea, *Richerche Demoscopiche*, May–June 1974, pp. 5–10. The author expresses his special thanks to Demoskopea director Giampaolo Fabris.

myriad Italian interest groups battle to make their voices heard. Joseph La-Palombara counted almost twenty-four hundred associations in Rome alone, not all of them, of course, political in nature.[15] In Italy, as you may have noticed, nothing works precisely as it is supposed to, and Italian interest groups contribute little to democracy; they may serve to undermine it.

The problem is not a shortage of interest groups. Indeed, there may be too many. There are far fewer interest groups in "organization Sweden," but they are cohesive and strong. The tendency in Sweden is to amalgamate interest groups into bigger and more powerful units. In Italy the tendency is toward fragmentation. In most areas, there is more than one association, usually political, trying to speak for any given group. Thus there are Communist, Social Democratic, Catholic, and even Neo-Fascist labor unions. The same thing is true for sports federations, women's groups, and farmers' organizations. Each sector of Italian society speaks not with one voice but with many. The voice that gets heard the most is the one with the best connections in the bureaucracy and in the ruling Christian Democratic party. Catholic interest groups start with a built-in advantage in Italy, while many of the other groups feel shut out and ignored. This does little to build democratic feelings of participation among those whose voices are not heard. In Italy, then, the strong life of interest groups does not foster democratic "pluralism" as it does in other countries.

Here are some of the more important Italian interest groups:

Economic organizations

Confindustria, representing 100,000 firms with a total of 3 million employees.

IRI, a giant semistate holding company whose interests include Alfa Romeo, Alitalia, all of radio and television broadcasting, and three large banks.

ENI, the National Hydrocarbons Authority, also semistate, which has over 200 companies and monopolizes the petroleum industry.

Labor unions

CGIL, the largest, with 3.5 million members, led by Communists and Socialists.

CISL, led by Christian Democrats, with 2.5 million members.

UIL, led by Social Democrats and Republicans, with 1 million members.

Agricultural organizations

Coltivatori Diretti, organizes 1.75 million small, family-run farms under DC leadership.

Confagricoltura, speaks for large, commercial farms.

Catholic organization

Catholic Action, which groups together several Catholic associations totalling 3.5 million members.

The two giants, almost universally believed to have the greatest influence, are Confindustria and Catholic Action. They operate however, in two rather distinct ways.

---

[15] Joseph LaPalombara, *Interest Groups in Italian Politics* (Princeton, N.J.: Princeton University Press, 1964), p. 128.

Joseph LaPalombara has divided the way Italian interest groups make their voices heard into two general patterns, the *clientela* and *parentela*, or "clients" and "relatives." The clientistic relationship is that of a government agency that works very closely with an interest group, viewing it as a natural constituency, fighting for its interests, and relying on information and ideas it supplies. The government agency, in effect, becomes a spokesman for the special interests, a situation not unique to Italy. The parentela relationship is a broader one between interest group and political party in which the group has close ideological ties with the party, works for the party and has a good deal to say in party policy.[16]

The strongest example of the clientistic relationship is that of Confindustria and the Ministry of Industry and Commerce. Many officials in the ministry view the relationship as good and natural, the only way the ministry could function. Confindustria enjoys what LaPalombara calls "structured access" to the Ministry of Industry and Commerce; that is, the bureaucracy is especially and permanently receptive to suggestions from Confindustria. One key factor in this is the bureaucracy's dependence on industry for expertise and data. The government agencies in Rome do not have research staffs adequate to generate their own data independently. One Industry and Commerce official commented, "Every time we need a single datum, we have to turn to Confindustria or the other professional associations. We are completely dependent on them and literally at their mercy."[17]

On the parentela side, Catholic Action is the giant interest group. Catholic Action sees itself as the connecting link between the Church and Italian society. Although not formally under Church discipline, Catholic Action closely follows the lead of the Vatican and local Church authorities, particularly bishops. Catholic Action also works closely with the Christian Democrats and is a major influence inside the party. Neither controls the other, but it is unlikely that the DC could adopt a policy in opposition to Catholic Action. Indeed, some DC politicians are former Catholic Action leaders; the founder of Christian Democracy, Alcide de Gasperi, guided Catholic Action through the Fascist era, preserving its autonomy and developing it as a power base for the postwar period. Although not as powerful as it once was—the divorce referendum showed the limits of Catholic Action's political power—the organization still plays a considerable role in translating Church teaching into social practice by means of film censorship and influence on the appointment of university professors, staffing of the bureaucracy, and governance of semistate enterprises.

[16] LaPalombara, *Interest Groups*, pp. 262, 306.

[17] Quoted in LaPalombara, *Interest Groups*, p. 283.

SOTTOGOVERNO

Much of governance everywhere does not take place in public or in formal institutions. A good part of politics consists in deals, arrangements, payoffs, special favors, etc., behind the scenes. In the United States, the resignations of Nixon and Agnew and the revelations of Ralph Nader have underscored the unseen aspects of American politics. The Italians have understood this kind of thing for a long time and have given it a name, *il sottogoverno*, the "undergovernment," where much of the real governing of Italy takes place.

The importance of sottogoverno in Italy grows out of the fact that the formal institutions of Italian government manage to get little done. The parliament is frozen into hostile blocs and the ruling coalition is vulnerable to the objections of its member parties—and at least one member party is bound to object to every new policy. Merely to pass a law in Italy—and so many are passed they are impossible to enforce—means little. To get something done in Italy, pressure groups turn from formal institutions to the grey area of sottogoverno. If demands cannot be handled by parties, parliament, and laws, is it then not inevitable that they will be handled in other ways, out of the public eye?

Sottogoverno is analogous to Sweden's "Harpsund democracy," where the big interest groups meet privately to work out deals that in theory should be public. The difference here is that in Sweden the deal thus made soon becomes public knowledge and often must be approved by parliament. Furthermore, the Swedish system takes pains to elicit all viewpoints; no important groups are left out. The Italian system, on the other hand, grossly shortchanges sectors of the population that either are not organized into effective groups or are organized but ignored by the bureaucracy. While Confindustria, IRI, and Catholic Action enjoy "structured access" to friendly bureaucracies, poor rural people and urban slum dwellers are unrepresented. The large, Communist-led labor union and many other mass organizations are likewise not heeded by the bureaucracy. Such treatment heightens the feelings of estrangement that many Italians hold toward their government and especially their bureaucracy.

THE BUREAUCRATIC MAZE

The Italian civil service receives few kind words. It is widely considered to be corrupt, inefficient, lazy, inflexible, officious, and slow. Many Italians believe, perhaps incorrectly, that the only way to get anything done is to slip the right official a *bustarella*, a little envelope full of money. Indeed, Italians' feelings of alienation from their political system stem in large part from their very real mistreatment (or nontreatment) at the hands of the bureaucracy.

How did Italian administration get this way? One cultural factor contributes: a large disproportion of Italian civil servants are recruited in the South and bring with them southern attitudes. Bright lads from the North and Center prefer the higher salaries and greater opportunities of private industry. For a bright southern lad, though, government service appears to be a fine way out of poverty and into respectability. Southern attitudes can be described as precapitalistic. There is an emphasis on deference rather than on work. Instead of dynamic efficiency there is tradition and legalism. Instead of facilitating change there is preserving of the existing order. Instead of promotion based on performance, there is promotion based on staying out of problem areas and going by the rule book.

The rule book is another problem. There are laws for (usually against) everything in Italy, many of them contradictory. The parliament churns out hundreds of *leggine* (little laws) that, if enforced, could bring the country to a standstill. A bureaucrat is often familiar enough with the laws to know that whatever he does may run afoul of one or more of these regulations. So he tends to be ultracautious, preferring to delay or to send something to another office rather than commit himself and risk hurting his career.

Extreme centralization is another problem. As in France, most decisions must come from the capital. Predating the new regions, Italy has ninety-two provinces, each with a prefect (as in France), but each prefect has little power to initiate or change anything without word from Rome. By the 1970s, twenty autonomous regional governments had been set up, but instead of returning some power to the grass-roots level, the regions seemed only to add another layer to the bureaucratic maze.

Stories of the Italian bureaucracy abound. Decades after natural disasters, the victims still wait to receive compensation that has been voted by parliament. Housing and social service programs are on the books but not implemented. A citizen petitioning a governmental agency must fill out myriad forms (most of them requiring a tax stamp), must usually wait hours to see an arrogant official, and then often gets no results. The Italian bureaucracy may be a symptom of the Italian malaise, but it is also an important contributor to it.

**WHAT THE
ITALIAN SYSTEM
PRODUCES**

THE ECONOMY

From the above, one might suppose that Italy has accomplished little as a republic. To put Italy's problems in perspective, we might note that Italy has experienced a healthy rate of economic growth. From 1962 to 1972 Italy's GNP grew at an annual average of 4.6 percent, which was lower than France (5.7 percent) but higher than West Germany (4.5), Britain (2.9), or the United States

(4.1). Italy, being less developed than the others, had an easier time registering larger percentage gains than the already highly developed U.S. and West German economies. Still, Italy has become an important economic power, producing much of Western Europe's automobiles and shoes.

The per capita income and consumption levels of individual Italians have also soared. By the early 1970s, most Italians were living far better than they had in the past. Over ten million passenger cars clogged Italy's streets. The Italian diet shifted from all pasta to more meat. These two items—cars and beef—deepened the severe economic problem that hit Italy in 1974. Italy had been importing massive quantities of petroleum and beef to match the Italians' newly acquired tastes. In 1974 several calamities hit at once: Oil prices quadrupled; world beef demand increased; a general economic slump chopped Italy's exports; and Italian workers were sent home from north of the Alps. Italy's international payments went some $10 billion into deficit, inflation hit 24 percent, and unemployment increased. It was a scary time, and some observers began to doubt whether Italy would muddle through again.

But Italy did. Italians again tightened their belts, as they had so many times in the past, and the following year the economy recovered nicely. Still, Italy's economic problems were not solved; they continued. The giants of Italian industry have shown little social responsibility; when things get rough they send their funds abroad, chiefly through the Italian-Swiss banking town of Lugano. The labor unions threaten to shut down the entire economy; they do not show the kind of wage restraint that Swedish and West German unions have been capable of. Since 1969, Communist and non-Communist unions have been acting in concert to win 15 to 20 percent annual wage increases. Governmental power in Rome, fragmented among the several parties, manipulated by big interest groups, and poorly executed by the bureaucracy is too weak to control the situation.

One economic problem, for example, seemed incurable: the sick South. Since unification, governments have tried to raise up the *Mezzogiorno*. Mussolini carried out numerous public works projects in the South, but they were mostly governmental buildings rather than productive facilities. The republic instituted the *Cassa per il Mezzogiorno* (Fund for the South) in 1950, but the sums at its disposal were unable to make much of a dent in the Southern problem, in large part because the subculture of the South is not yet oriented to modern, entrepreneurial attitudes.

The main relief from wretched conditions in the South has been emigration. Since the war over two million southerners have moved to northern cities in search of jobs; another million or so went north of the Alps for work. This pattern of migration northward is identical to the trend in Spain and Yugoslavia. Italians encountered discrimination in Northern Europe, and southern Italians even found discrimination in northern Italy. Many north Italians want the southerners to go back home. The Visconti film *Rocco and His Brothers* portrays the ordeal of a southern family attempting to survive in a hostile Milan.

Instead of bringing southerners to the jobs in the North, the government has tried to bring jobs to the southerners at home. Tax breaks are given to set up new plants in the South, and IRI and ENI by law must put the bulk of their annual investment into the South. But in Italy, as in Yugoslavia, investment in a backward area is less productive than in an area that already has a good infrastructure and trained labor force. The expectation that new industries would create "pockets of growth" in the South failed to materialize. Said one ENI technocrat of the forced investment in the South, "We have been building cathedrals in the desert."

THE LONGING FOR A BREAKTHROUGH

Italy has been called a "stalemate society."[18] Serious problems have remained untouched. Reform measures have taken decades to pass parliament and then are often not executed. First and foremost the bureaucracy needs to be overhauled, but new laws have just made it more complicated instead of simpler. The university situation is bad: the number of students has increased exponentially but facilities and instructors are slow in coming. This has led to monumental overcrowding and student radicalization.

Other problems piled up. Luxury apartment construction has boomed, but underfunded housing programs for the poor leave a class of hovel-dwellers on the outskirts of Italian cities. Around Rome alone, an estimated 60,000 immigrants from the South lived in shacks, caves, or other substandard dwellings. Riots occurred when some of these people moved illegally into newly finished apartments and were expelled by heavily armed police. Cholera, thought to have been wiped out in Europe, reappeared in Naples in 1973, leaving at least sixteen dead. The Naples sewer system, it seems, had not been repaired in a century.

Italians use the word *slittare* (to slide) to describe their government's inability to deal with these problems. Badly needed reforms are let slide; the solutions proffered are superficial and makeshift, and the makeshift then becomes the permanent. This sort of stalemate produces a longing for really sweeping change, for a breakthrough, to end the immobilism. But in which direction might this breakthrough go? Here are some of the possibilities for Italian politics:

More of the Same   Jolted by growing Communist strength, Italy's feuding moderate parties—the Christian Democrats, Socialists, Social Democrats, and Republicans—may huddle together again in their old Center-Left coalition. One key split would have to be overcome: the DC is against abortion and the Socialists for it, and abortion is hard to compromise on.

---

[18] The author is grateful to sociologist Guido Martinotti of the University of Milan for much of this discussion of Italy's current problems.

Furthermore, many Italians are fed up with DC ineffectualness, temporizing, and outright corruption. The Christian Democrats held power for three decades and catch a lot of the blame for everything that goes wrong in Italy. In the 1970s DC voter appeal declined; the party had probably passed its high point. Very much against its will, Italy's Christian Democratic leadership may be driven to:

Historic Compromise   When the Communists first proposed forming a coalition with the Christian Democrats in 1973 it was considered out of the question. Within a few years it became highly plausible. The PCI has bent over backwards to demonstrate pragmatic moderation and has enjoyed great success at the municipal level, emerging as the largest party in Italy's six biggest cities. Bologna has elected Communist municipal governments ever since the war, and they have made Bologna Italy's best-run city, free of the corruption that plagues most other towns. In some cities, Communists and Christian Democrats have long worked together in municipal government. The upsurge in the Communist vote in the 1976 elections showed that an increasing number of Italians respected the Communists' abilities in local administration.

The leader of the PCI, Enrico Berlinguer, appeared to be the right man for a *compromesso storico*, being something of a historic compromise himself. This leader of the workers' party is the scion of a noble Sardinian family of Catalan origin. The well-tailored Berlinguer is an atheist, but his wife and children regularly attend mass. Moderate as Berlinguer was, many Christian Democrats made it clear they would not stand for a coalition with the Communists. This then leads to another possibility:

Popular Front   If Italy's Left parties—PCI, PSI, PSIUP—together win a majority of the vote, they might try to form a sort of coalition known as a "popular front" of all the Left parties. Curiously, the Communists opposed a popular front, fearing that it would push Italy leftward too far and too fast, possibly triggering a military coup or rightist takeover. Berlinguer often warned against going the way of Allende's Chile; he preferred a coalition with the Christian Democrats. One variation on a popular front might be possible. The DC is so faction-ridden that one or more of its leftwing factions could break off to join with the parties of the Left.

A Labor-Management End Run   With despair growing over governmental weakness during the difficulties of the mid-1970s, there was increased talk of the giants of Italian industry and labor reaching an understanding on wages, prices, investments, social policy, and the like, without bothering to work through the ineffectual governmental apparatus. Neither labor nor management could benefit from anarchy, observers reasoned, so they might set up their own shadow government to run things. We might remember here how important the Saltsjöbaden Agreement between Swedish labor and management has been in promoting stability and growth in that country. Although unlikely, a labor-management end run would be in keeping with the Italian pattern of sottogoverno.

The Growth of Violence Starting in 1969 and continuing through the 1970s, extremist groups planted bombs in public places that killed dozens. These were largely neofascist splinter groups of the MSI such as the "Black Order" (after Mussolini's Blackshirts). On the extreme left, groups like the "Red Brigade" turned to kidnapping of prominent persons to raise money and win the release of their imprisoned comrades. On balance, it appeared that neofascists caused more bloodshed than the far-Left. Police described neofascist groups as well supplied with arms and money and operating training camps in remote areas. If violence continued to grow, the following could not entirely be ruled out:

The End of Italian Democracy? Observers pointed out certain similarities between the mid-1970s and the early 1920s when Mussolini rose to power: economic difficulties, labor unrest, the growth of the Left, governmental paralysis, and the longing for a political breakthrough to end the Italian malaise. History seldom repeats itself exactly, however, and any such comparisons ignore the differences between the two periods: Italy's economic progress, a far more sophisticated population, a strong labor movement, and Italy's ties to the Common Market and NATO. This analysis does not preclude other brands of authoritarianism, though, particularly from the armed forces and police.

In 1974, for example, several top army officers were implicated in a rightist plot to set up a secret "anti-Communist defense," reportedly backed by wealthy industrialists. The example of the 1967 military takeover in Greece was on many Italians' minds. In general, though, the Italian armed forces were believed to be largely apolitical and supportive of democracy.

Difficulties might come from another source: Italy has three national police agencies totalling 200,000 persons. The most famous of these are the *Carabinieri*, a paramilitary force of 80,000, which like Spain's Guardia Civil mostly patrols the rural areas. Additionally, 80,000 Public Security Police concentrate on the cities and 40,000 Finance Guards look for tax dodgers and smugglers. Together they would form a formidable force, but usually they view each other as rivals and sometimes work at cross purposes. Fragmentation touches everything in Italy.

In 1968 a former carabinieri commander, General Giovanni Di Lorenzo, was accused of preparing a coup d'état, illegally keeping tabs on thousands of key Italians, and drawing up a list of 700 persons to be arrested. Nothing like the Di Lorenzo affair has come to light since, and the carabinieri have stayed aloof from politics. Still, many Italians worry that if a political breakthrough does not come on the civilian side, it might come on the side of the military and the police.

YUGOSLAVIA
5

Tourists visiting Yugoslavia are often surprised when they learn it is a "Communist" country, for in outward appearances Yugoslavia resembles very little the disciplined orderliness of East Germany or the shabby giantism of the Soviet Union. The newer buildings and shops are right up to Western European standards, modern and generally well stocked. Urban Yugoslavs are well clothed in the latest Continental fashions. Swarms of automobiles clog the streets. There are many private shops. A Yugoslav magazine rack seems to hold a year's issues of *Playboy*. Customs formalities are minimal; most visitors can get visas on the border without delay. And even more surprising, Yugoslavs are free to leave and reenter their country. Can this be communism?

Looking deeper, though, the visitor learns that Yugoslavia is indeed governed by a Communist party and that there are hundreds of political prisoners. Although the economy is organized in a market system like Western economies, there are no big capitalists because the enterprises are controlled by and ostensibly for their workers. The private shops are limited to five employees. Although Yugoslav "revisionism" has been savagely denounced at various times by both the Russians and the Chinese, Yugoslav thinkers are convinced that they are on the path to building real socialism. In fact they think that other East European countries can (and do) learn a lot from Yugoslavia. Some Yugoslavs even go so far as to proclaim their system the only authentic Marxist system in existence.

If the visitor is perplexed by this seeming gap between rhetoric and reality, he has a right to be, for Yugoslavia is undoubtedly the most oddball, chimerical country in Europe. It resembles nothing, and nothing resembles it. But the possibility that the Yugoslavs have found a better form of Marxism and a better way to build socialism stands as a rebuke to the Soviet contention that theirs is the only way, that they alone understand what Marx had in mind. The idea of a "third way" between Western capitalism and rigid, Soviet-style communism has been and will continue to be infectious in Eastern Europe, and this is

Yugoslavia's real importance. Ideas can be dynamite, and Yugoslavia has developed new ideas on socialism that eventually could be a threat to the "state socialism" of the Soviet Union. Let us consider how this unique system came into being.

THE
IMPACT
OF THE
PAST

THE FATAL SPLIT

Yugoslavia is not an old country; it was founded only in 1918. Its component parts have long histories of their own, though, and these have given Yugoslavia its number-one headache, the nationality problem. There is historically no such thing as a nationality called "Yugoslav" (which simply means South Slav). Instead there were several Slavic tribes that slowly pushed their way south, down the Balkan (Turkish for mountain) Peninsula between the first and seventh centuries A.D. In the area of present-day Yugoslavia, the two most important groups were the Serbs and the Croats, the Serbs settling in the central portion of Yugoslavia and the Croats in the northwest and along the coast.

This has been Yugoslavia's fatal split, a problem that plagues the country to this day. Although Serbs and Croats spoke more or less the same language (or several dialects of the same language), now called Serbo-Croatian, they diverged culturally over the centuries. The first divergence was religion: Serbs received Christianity from Constantinople, becoming Eastern Orthodox; Croats received Christianity from Rome, becoming Catholics. Thus Serbia had an eastern orientation and Croatia a western orientation. Further, the Serbian alphabet grew out of Greek; it is called Cyrillic and is like the Russian alphabet with some additional characters. The Croatian alphabet was taken from Latin, with extra marks added for the special Slavic sounds.

Foreign conquest deepened Serb-Croat divergence. While both Serbia and Croatia enjoyed brief independent kingdoms, the Croats were absorbed by Hungary in 1102, and the Serbs were conquered by the Ottoman Turks in 1389. Thus Serbia was ruled for five centuries by the Turks while Croatia was an Austro-Hungarian province for eight centuries. The cultural differences implanted by the two empires on their subject peoples persist to this day in their food, architecture, economic development, and political attitudes. To travel from Zagreb, capital of Croatia, to Belgrade, capital both of Serbia and of Yugoslavia as a whole, is still a journey from the edge of Austria to the edge of Turkey.

Two smaller nationalities in Yugoslavia show this difference even more markedly. Slovenia, in the extreme northwest corner of Yugoslavia, was thoroughly Austrianized; only the Slovene language (also a Slavic tongue but quite different from Serbo-Croatian) kept the culture alive. Today Slovenia is the most prosperous and industrialized republic of Yugoslavia, virtually a Slavic Austria. The southern part of Yugoslavia is Macedonia, whose people speak a Slavic language close to Bulgarian. Macedonia is one of the poorest areas of the country, almost a Slavic Turkey. Slovenia is traditionally Catholic; Macedonia traditionally Orthodox.

The mountainous spine of Yugoslavia has a large Moslem minority. In Bosnia the Turks were able to convert a part of the population to Islam. Today one can still see there mosques and minarets with an Alpine backdrop and blond, blue-eyed Moslems. The other inhabitants of Bosnia are Catholic or Orthodox, and identify themselves as Croats or Serbs accordingly. Bosnia too is a backward area.

One small area of Yugoslavia was never conquered by Turks or Austrians. Tiny Montenegro (meaning Black Mountain), nestled in the coastal mountains just north of Albania, fended off the Turks for over four centuries. Montenegrins, who are basically Serbs, are the tallest nationality in Europe. The men became renowned both as fierce anti-Turk warriors and as terribly lazy. The area is a backward one.

Other cultural influences washed up on Yugoslavia from neighboring countries. Venice dominated most of the Adriatic coast for centuries, and the Italian influence in architecture and music is still evident. Hungarians and Romanians have long inhabited the northeast corner of Yugoslavia. Albanians spilled over into the south of Serbia, now the poorest part of Yugoslavia with by far the highest birth and infant-mortality rates. The fantastic heterogeneity of the peoples of Yugoslavia make it a fascinating country to travel through.

This heterogeneity has also made nation building an extremely difficult task, one that has still not been completed. At least as much as Spain and Italy, Yugoslavia suffers from monumental North-South differences. The North is central European, the South Balkan. As one travels from South to North, incomes, productivity, standards of living, and modern attitudes increase while infant mortality and illiteracy decrease. Yugoslavia is not one country but many.

THE YUGOSLAV IDEA

It was Serbia that started the drive for national independence. Revolting against the Turks in 1804, the Serbs gradually expanded a small kingdom and nurtured the idea of expelling all the foreign occupiers and establishing a South Slav state, under Serbian leadership, naturally. Fired by the example of Italian unification led by little Piedmont, Serbs thought of themselves as the founders and freedom fighters of a Greater Serbia, a monarchy that would gather in and protect the neighboring South Slavic peoples. The flaw in this conception was that it did not accord equality to the other peoples.

The spark that ignited World War I was struck by Serbian nationalism.

Austria, partly out of fear of growing Russian strength in the Balkans, expanded her empire by annexing Bosnia in 1908. Serbians living in Bosnia, infected by Serbian nationalism and linked to Belgrade by secret societies, bitterly resented the Austrian move. When Austrian Archduke Franz Ferdinand visited Sarayevo, Bosnia's mountain capital, on June 28, 1914, young Serb Bosnians assassinated him with weapons loaned by Serbian officers. The action was in no sense an official Serbian move, but Austria took it that way and, demanding impossible concessions from Serbia, began the war. Russia, bound to Serbia by treaty, came to its aid. Germany, bound to Austria by treaty (and fearful of the gigantic Russian mobilization), came to Austria's aid.

The Serbs at first repelled the Austrians, but next year a German army pushed the Serbian forces across Albania to Corfu. Under a French general, the Serbs later participated in the successful northward thrust from Salonika. The Croats and Slovenes fought—sometimes not too enthusiastically—on the Austrian side. Indeed, the young Tito, born Josip Broz in 1892, chose to serve in an Austrian rather than a Croatian regiment. Sent to the Russian front, Sergeant Broz was wounded, captured, and later converted by the 1917 revolution.

Obtaining the sometimes reluctant agreement of the country's various nationalities during the war, King Alexander of Serbia proclaimed a new state in December 1918, the Kingdom of Serbs, Croats, and Slovenes. The name Yugoslavia came only in 1929. The union was precarious from the start. Governments changed every few months. The Croats especially resented the unitary, centralized monarchy, which treated the new country as a big Serbia; they would have preferred a federal republic. Many Croats found the transfer of control from Budapest to Belgrade no improvement at all. Bitterness grew when some of the top Croatian politicians were gunned down on the floor of parliament in 1928. By 1929 King Alexander was so exasperated with the turmoil that he proclaimed a royal dictatorship, trying to erase the traditional national areas by setting up artificial districts named after rivers. Alexander was assassinated in Marseilles in 1934 by a gunman employed by both Croatian and Macedonian separatists and backed by Hungary and Italy.

Yugoslavia as a country simply did not jell in the interwar period. It took more foreign occupation to forge a sense of Yugoslav nationality. Drawn under Axis influence as World War II began, Serbian officers, with British encouragement, overthrew the regime in 1941 and shifted sympathy to the Allies. Hitler, in a rage, attacked a few days after the coup and in just eleven days forced the Yugoslav surrender. The old Yugoslavia, riven by national resentments and chronic instability, hardly put up a fight.

THE RISE OF THE COMMUNISTS

In sharp contrast to the establishment of Communist party regimes in East Germany and elsewhere in East Europe, the rise of the Yugoslav Communists to power was largely their own doing. Ulbricht and his group spent the war in

Moscow and were installed in East Germany by Soviet bayonets. Tito and his men fought their way to power against Germans, Italians, and even fellow Yugoslavs; they owed little to the Soviets.

How was it possible for a small political party in interwar Yugoslavia to take over the country in four years, from 1941 to 1945? The Communists were few but well organized. Following Soviet orders, they waited until the Germans attacked Russia before rising against the invaders in their own land. They were neither the only nor the largest armed group of Yugoslavs. Remnants of the army formed a Serbian guerrilla force called the Chetniks; its goal was a restoration of the old Serbian-dominated monarchy. As such, the Chetniks were not a viable rallying point for other Yugoslav nationalities. In the 1930s a native Fascist movement grew up in Croatia, the Ustasha, which set up a Nazi puppet state, doubling the size of Croatia and slaughtering Serbs; obviously the Ustashas could not form a movement to rally all of Yugoslavia. Only the Communists, who formed fighting units known as Partisans, were above the old national quarrels; they alone held out the hope of new system with justice for all national groups. The Chetniks fought for Serbia; the Ustashas for Croatia; the Communists for all Yugoslavia.[1]

The Partisans tied down several German divisions in fierce guerrilla fighting, much of it in the rugged mountains of Bosnia. In reprisal, the Nazis massacred whole villages, but this just convinced more Yugoslavs to join the Partisans, who numbered some 800,000 by late 1944. In this way, Nazi brutality helped the Partisans grow powerful enough to liberate about half of the country. In 1945, the Soviet army pushed the remaining Germans out of the other half.

To an extent, then, it was circumstances that brought the Communists to power in Yugoslavia. First, Hitler destroyed the old regime. Then there was no other group that could speak for all of Yugoslavia and was willing to fight the invader. The Partisans suffered some 350,000 fatalities and 400,000 wounded, achieving considerable moral authority in the eyes of their countrymen. By 1945 the Communists were the most powerful force in a country horribly disfigured by war. Over 10 percent of the population had been killed; three and a half million were homeless. The Royal Yugoslav government, operating in distant London, no longer had any political base in the country; the Communists took over.

THE TITO-STALIN SPLIT

Tito was an ultraloyal Stalinist and had been ever since he rose through party ranks in the 1920s and 1930s. The regime he installed in 1945 was thoroughly pro-Soviet. Yet only three years later Yugoslavia and the Soviet Union were locked in bitter confrontation. What happened? The problem was not ideologi-

---

[1] For an excellent discussion of ethnic composition of the Partisans, see R. V. Burks, *The Dynamics of Communism in Eastern Europe* (Princeton, N.J.: Princeton University Press, 1961), pp. 118–26.

cal. The system that the Communists built after World War II aped the Soviet model in detail. If anything, the Yugoslav Communists were 200-percenters, destroying the bourgeoisie and building socialism faster than the Soviets recommended. The Yugoslav constitution of 1946 was a copy of Stalin's 1936 constitution. Agricultural collectivization was quickly begun. Non-Communist political groups were soon liquidated and thousands arrested in the best Stalinist style. It looked as though Yugoslavia were the perfect Soviet satellite.

If the Tito-Stalin split can be attributed to one thing, it must surely be Stalin's personality. Tito may have been completely loyal, but he had his own power base, and that was something paranoid Stalin could not tolerate. All the other Communist leaders of Eastern Europe were personally and militarily dependent on Stalin; none had come to power on their own. Stalin found Tito's independent power base increasingly annoying and by 1948 decided to dump him. Stalin assumed that when he signalled his displeasure with Tito by expelling Yugoslavia from the Moscow-controlled Cominform, the "healthy elements" in the Yugoslav party would dispose of Tito and then place the Yugoslav party at his feet. The expulsion was announced on June 28, 1948.[2]

To Stalin's chagrin, the Yugoslav Communists ignored Stalin almost to a man and rallied around Tito. Soviet propaganda blasts depicted Tito as an American agent, but they did not shake his position. At first the Yugoslav Communists could not believe their ears; they had been trained to worship Stalin. For some months Belgrade expected Moscow to cease its obviously insane charges and patch things up with Tito. The invective did not cease, and gradually the Yugoslavs came to realize they were on their own, that the Soviet Union was as great a threat as the capitalist West, and that Stalin had constructed a monstrous system. By 1950 the Yugoslavs had resolved to build their own system, a non-Soviet socialist system, which we will now explore.

**THE
KEY
INSTITUTIONS**

YUGOSLAV FEDERALISM

Soviet federalism permits little local autonomy. Such is not the case with Yugoslavia whose six "republics" really do have great autonomy and are staffed by local talent. The problem with the Yugoslav system is not whether it gives the republics enough autonomy but whether it gives them so much that Yugoslavia could fall apart.

The nationality question was the biggest problem of the interwar kingdom,

---

[2] The best analysis of the split is Adam Ulam's *Titoism and the Cominform* (Cambridge, Mass.: Harvard University Press, 1952).

which was much too centralized and dominated by Serbs. The Communists resolved to settle the problem by federalism, and they drew the boundaries of the six republics to end territorial squabbles between the nationalities. To account for two large minorities, Hungarians and Albanians, two autonomous provinces (Voyvodina and Kosovo, respectively) were designated as part of Serbia. Here are the 1973 populations of Yugoslavia's components:[3]

Serbia	5.3 million
Croatia	4.5
Bosnia	3.9
Slovenia	1.8
Macedonia	1.7
Montenegro	.5
Voyvodina	2.0
Kosovo	1.3

Each republic has a mixed population with, for example, many Serbs in Croatia, some Croats in Serbia, and both Serbs and Croats in Bosnia. The mixing of ethnic groups has accelerated with Yugoslavia's postwar industrialization. As in Italy, the poor people in the South come up North for jobs.[4]

In any case, Serbia is the largest republic and Serbs are the largest nationality. Shorn of verbiage, the function of Yugoslav federalism is to prevent Serbia and Serbians from again dominating the whole country as they did before the war. (We will explore this more fully in the section "Patterns of Interaction.") Part of Tito's success in holding Yugoslavia together can be attributed to his non-Serbian origin: his father was Croatian and his mother Slovene. Tito's closest colleagues, Edvard Kardelj and Stane Dolanc, are both Slovenes. Although there are many Serbs in the federal government, Serbs do not play the leading role, for that would reawaken old resentment at Serbian domination.[5]

EXPERIMENTAL CONSTITUTIONS

We tend to think of a constitution as relatively fixed, a document that should be changed only cautiously. The U.S. Constitution for example, has scarcely been touched in its basics. The Yugoslavs have a totally different approach to constitutions. They write them and discard them without sentimentality. A constitution, Yugoslav theorists claim, merely describes relationships that have already

---

[3] Yugoslav Federal Office for Statistics, *Indeks*, April 1974, p. 12.

[4] See George W. Hoffman, "Migration and Social Change," *Problems of Communism*, November–December 1973.

[5] For an excellent discussion of this problem see R. V. Burks, *The National Problem and the Future of Yugoslavia* (Santa Monica, Calif.: Rand Corporation, 1971).

evolved into being; as things change so do constitutions. As a result there have been four Yugoslav constitutions since World War II, adopted in 1946, 1953, 1963, and 1974. We can conclude that the Yugoslavs are experimenting and that the 1974 constitution is not necessarily the last.

The 1963 constitution illustrates this kind of experimentalism. It provided for a legislature of *five* chambers, each with 120 members: Federal (the most powerful), Economic, Education and Culture, Social Welfare and Health, and Organizational-Political. The Yugoslav legislature of the 1960s looked more like a cabinet. Laws were passed concurrently by the Federal Chamber and the other chamber in whose area the subject of the law fell.

The 1974 constitution, a mammoth document the size of a book, scrapped the five chambers in favor of two, but it was equally experimental, adopting corporatist concepts. Delegates to the new Federal Chamber were to be elected from "self-managing organizations" that included business enterprises, state institutions, farmer groups, and the army. These various organizations propose candidates to the Socialist Alliance, a mass front much larger than but guided by the Communist party, which in turn draws up lists of candidates at the republic level. Although the party has a major and often decisive influence in selecting candidates, many positions are contested and the voters are sometimes able to reject candidates. Each republic then holds elections to send 30 delegates each to the Federal Chamber; the two autonomous provinces send 20 each. Thus each republic is represented equally in the 220-member Federal Chamber, regardless of population.

The other house of the Yugoslav parliament, the Chamber of Republics and Provinces, is composed of delegates from the republic assemblies, twelve from each republic and eight from each autonomous province. The obvious flaw in this arrangement, at least by American standards, is that neither house of parliament takes population into account. Tiny Montenegro has the same representation as Croatia or Serbia, which have several times the inhabitants. The present Yugoslav bicameral arrangement would be like the United States' having not a Senate and a House, but two Senates, one large and one small.

The two Yugoslav chambers are assigned somewhat different tasks. The Federal Chamber is aimed at passing statutes, while the Chamber of Republics and Provinces is aimed at economic matters. Included in the latter's powers are the determination of which republics should get which share of investment funds, an extremely sore point that we shall consider later. The division of labor between the two houses is none too clear—clarity has never been a strong point of Yugoslav constitutions—but the eighty-eight member Chamber of Republics and Provinces seems to be the more powerful, controlling (in agreement with republic assemblies) the money supply, foreign exchange, tariffs, development funds, taxation, wages, and the federal budget. The power of the purse belongs to the Chamber of Republics and Provinces.

The presidency of Yugoslavia is no longer (supposed to be) held by one man. It is now a council of nine, one from each republic and autonomous province (elected for five-year terms by their respective assemblies) plus the head of the country's Communist party. The Yugoslav presidency seems to be a partial copy of the Swiss Federal Council (which has seven members). In both, the actual president is elected by his peers for just one year; he is to be merely a *primus inter pares*, a first among equals, not a figure who towers over the group. An exception is made for Tito, who may be reelected without limit.

How the Yugoslav presidency will function after Tito—who, although amazingly healthy and young-looking in his eighties, must leave the scene sometime—is problematic. On paper, the constitution would prevent one man from ever holding as much power as Tito. But in practice power may tend to accrue to the head of the party, the pattern in virtually all Communist systems. Whether or not the party chief formally occupies the president's chair, he will automatically be in the presidency and will likely be the most powerful of the nine. The Swiss system, based in an ultrastable country may prove inapplicable to Yugoslavia.

The strict equality of republics in both houses of the legislature and in the collegial executive demonstrates how federal the Yugoslav system is. Under the new constitution, Belgrade serves as merely the meeting ground for the republics. On paper, Belgrade seems to be less powerful than Washington in the American federal system. There may be a danger here in granting too much power to republics, which have a history of separatism. But this centrifugal force in Yugoslavia is now offset by a centripetal force, the Communist party.

THE LEAGUE OF COMMUNISTS

The League of Communists of Yugoslavia, or LCY, has been the party's official name since 1952, a change made as part of a reform effort to differentiate the Yugoslav from the Soviet system. These reforms were indeed major: Party meetings were opened to the public, organization was reformed, power in the party was decentralized, considerable autonomy was granted to lower organs, and candidate membership was abolished.[6] As with the rest of the Yugoslav system, no change is the last, and the LCY has oscillated between looser and tighter discipline. It cannot be allowed to get too loose—and Yugoslav leaders recognize this—because the LCY is the cement that holds the system together.

The student is entitled to wonder how Yugoslavia's constantly changing, experimental federal structure can hold the country on an even keel. It may be argued that the latest reorganization in Belgrade does not matter all that much because the party still runs things quietly behind the scenes. Particularly important have been the 100,000 or so party members who survived the war as

---

[6] For a fuller description see George W. Hoffman and Fred Warner Neal, *Yugoslavia and the New Communism* (New York: Twentieth Century Fund, 1962), pp. 176–79.

Partisans. (The Communists formed the leadership stratum of the Partisans, only a minority of whom were party members.) These are the people who cast their lot with the party in its most difficult period; they tend to see themselves as the saviors of Yugoslavia and to form an "old boy" network. For three decades few persons who were not Partisan fighters reached leadership positions.[7] The intellectual level of most of these *Partizani* was not always high—many were illiterate peasants—and positions after the war were staffed with well-connected incompetents, a situation that has gradually been remedied over the years. The strapping Montenegrins were overrepresented in Partisan ranks and in elite positions after the war. There were snide remarks about how Montenegrins went "from Cetinye to Dedinye," that is, from the village-capital of Montenegro to Belgrade's best residential district.

The growth and occasional shrinking of LCY membership illustrates the periods of loosening and tightening. From a mere 140,000 party members in 1945, the party swelled to over half a million just four years later, in 1949, then to three-quarters of a million in 1952. In June 1953, Tito, in an effort to curb liberalization and enforce discipline, initiated a purge. In the next two and a half years over a third of a million members were expelled from the LCY. Some new faces were accepted so that by the end of 1955 there were 643,000 members.[8] That episode of tightening up was caused in part by the sliding of one of Tito's closest protegés, Milovan Djilas, from Marxism to liberal democracy. Djilas bitterly attacked the formation of a "new class" of privileged party members.[9] Djilas, who at one point might have been Tito's successor, was expelled from the party and subsequently imprisoned (from 1957 to 1967) for publishing his criticisms abroad.

After the mid-1950s shakeout, the LCY grew for more than a decade until membership reached 1.15 million at the end of 1968. The next few years were again a period of tightening party discipline and ousting "anarcho-liberals" and republic separatists: 144,000 members were dropped. With some newcomers added, LCY membership stood at 1,076,711 in December 1973, an even 5 percent of Yugoslavia's population.[10]

As in most Communist countries, Yugoslavia has had difficulty in keeping the LCY a party of workers and peasants. According to official statistics, the percentage social composition of the LCY, shown in Table 5–1, has undergone some striking changes.

[7] See Bogdan Denitch, "Mobility and Recruitment of Yugoslav Leadership: The Role of the League of Communists," in *Opinion-Making Elites in Yugoslavia*, ed. by A. Barton, B. Denitch, and C. Kadushin (New York: Praeger, 1973), pp. 104–7.

[8] Hoffman and Neal, *Yugoslavia and the New Communism*, pp. 196–97.

[9] See Milovan Djilas, *The New Class: An Analysis of the Communist System* (New York: Praeger, 1957).

[10] Figures from League of Communists of Yugoslavia, *Draft Report on the Activities of the League of Communists* (Belgrade: League of Communists of Yugoslavia, 1974), p. 138.

Table 5–1   Yugoslav Party Membership

	Workers	White-Collar	Peasants	Other
1946	27.6%	10.3%	50.4%	11.7%
1948	30.1	13.6	47.8	8.5
1950	31.2	19.0	43.4	6.5
1952	32.2	18.9	42.8	6.1
1954	28.3	29.8	22.6	19.2
1958	32.7	34.8	14.7	17.8
1962	36.7	36.4	9.6	17.3
1966	33.9	39.0	7.4	19.6
1968	31.2	43.8	7.4	18.7
1971	28.8	—	—	—
1973	29.1	—	5.6	—

Source: Bogdan Denitch, "Mobility and Recruitment of Yugoslav Leadership: The Role of the League of Communists," in Opinion-Making Elites in Yugoslavia, ed. by A. Barton, B. Denitch, and C. Kadushin (New York: Praeger, 1973), pp. 104–7; and League of Communists of Yugoslavia, Draft Report on the Activities of the League of Communists, (Belgrade: League of Communists of Yugoslavia, 1974), p. 137.

The workers' party has seldom reached one-third worker membership. Peasants, the main element of the Partisans, have dwindled almost to extinction in party ranks. There are two reasons for this. In the first place, the portion of peasants in Yugoslavia's population declined by almost one-half since World War II, from over 70 percent to under 40 percent. Second, since most of Yugoslav agriculture is private, the party has little to do in the countryside and there is no career advantage for a peasant to join the party. The LCY has become a heavily white-collar institution, composed of administrators, managers, intellectuals, and security and army personnel.

The problem facing the League of Communists of Yugoslavia is this: Tito expects a disciplined, ideological, Soviet-type party in the context of a relatively free, consumer-oriented, market society, a context Tito himself largely created. The Yugoslav reforms of the 1950s ushered in a totally different system, one in which the LCY is not supposed to and does not play the same role the CPSU does in Soviet society or the SED in East Germany. Yugoslav thinkers propose a new brand of Marxism, based on worker management of economic enterprises, in which the party is supposed to lead only indirectly, by discussion and example. The vigor of a market economy is to propel Yugoslavia into socialism. But a market economy brings considerable income differentials and an emphasis on living the good life as practiced in Western Europe. Since party membership helps to get the best jobs, the LCY is invaded by opportunists. Tito thus finds it necessary, in order to keep the party ideologically socialist, to purge it periodically of "careerists" and to restore "worker control." No purge of the LCY, however, can be the last, for within a few years the same kinds of opportunists, careerists, and self-seekers again emerge in party ranks. One can't kill weeds by mowing them.

The dilemma of the League of Communists of Yugoslavia is the dilemma of the country as a whole: how to stay ideologically socialist while in practice abandoning most of the traditional Soviet-type controls over the economy. Can the Yugoslav party, or the society as a whole, stand poised forever with its head in Marxism and its body in consumerism? Let us now consider this Yugoslav schizophrenia.

YUGOSLAV POLITICAL ATTITUDES

THE SOCIALIST IDEAL

Yugoslavia loudly proclaims itself a socialist country; its official name since 1963 has been the Socialist Federal Republic of Yugoslavia. Previously it was the Federal People's Republic of Yugoslavia. Thus Yugoslavia has promoted itself to the same level as the Soviet Union, which also bills itself as socialist in its full name. Of the other East European countries, only Romania has also promoted itself from People's to Socialist Republic. Even East Germany, probably the most advanced Soviet-type system, still modestly calls itself the German Democratic Republic.

The official Yugoslav rhetoric is Marxist. Students study Marxism in school—although not nearly so much as in the Soviet Union—and newspapers and magazines engage in considerable Marxist analysis, but again, not as much as in the Soviet Union. The Yugoslavs are particularly proud of their "self-managing socialism," which they contrast elaborately with the Soviets' "statist socialism."[11] By turning over power at the enterprise level to workers, they claim, they have gone much farther than the Soviets toward eliminating exploitation and de-alienating the proletariat. Yugoslav thinkers grant that there are income differences, as well as differences in the relative wealth of the republics, but they argue that such differences are inevitable and temporary in an economy that still has a long way to grow. The task of the party, they hold, is to promote both overall growth and gradually to eliminate income differences, but this takes time.

The more candid Yugoslav thinkers admit that some opportunists have gotten into the party but that in general LCY members are idealistic and committed to building socialism. A talk with a Yugoslav party intellectual is an exciting experience, for he paints a picture of a unique, experimental effort at

---

[11] See Rudi Supek, "The Statist and Self-Managing Models of Socialism," in *Opinion-Making Elites in Yugoslavia*, pp. 295–315.

building a working utopia. The party intellectual is idealistic and pragmatic at the same time: building socialism is a difficult, tentative, trial-and-error thing, but we are gradually perfecting our system, which in some respects is the most advanced in the world.

THE REALITIES

Yugoslav realities are at considerable variance with the ideals. Numerous young Yugoslavs have accepted the official rhetoric and joined the party only to become appalled at the self-serving careerism among party members. Many of these young people drop out; a few even leave the country. The ones who stay in the LCY often become cynical themselves and join in the careerism. Cynicism lives cheek by jowl with idealism in Yugoslavia.

This is not to say there is much actual disloyalty to the system. Most Yugoslavs support the system, and support for Tito personally and for Yugoslavia's neutral foreign policy are quite high. The *idea* of self-management is also widely accepted, and this may be part of the problem. In practice, self-management has a spotty record. Communist party members are usually the leading figures in a self-managed enterprise—many Yugoslavs believe that enterprise directors *must* be Communists, which is mostly true.[12] To some Yugoslavs, it is like saying, "We want you to manage your own factory, but under our watchful eye." The not-infrequent bumbling and inefficiency in self-managed enterprises also provokes cynicism.

Yugoslav-American sociologist Bogdan Denitch points out that the rotation of representatives on self-managing boards "means that a major part of the working population at one point or another participates in running its own institutions."[13] This, believes Denitch, is rooting self-management deeper and deeper into the Yugoslav system, but we cannot be sure until we have reliable data on what the participants candidly think of their experiences in self-management. From this author's conversations with Yugoslavs, it appears that many are vexed with the interminable meetings that eat into both their work and leisure hours. This brings us to another aspect of Yugoslav political life.

THE FUNCTION OF WORDINESS

Not only self-management meetings, but scholarly presentations and constitutions in Yugoslavia are inordinately wordy, yet they often convey little informa-

---

[12] Many advertisements for enterprise directors in Yugoslavia's leading newspaper, *Politika*, specify "proper moral and political attitude," which are understood to mean "party member."

[13] Bogdan Denitch, "Notes on the Relevance of Yugoslav Self-Management," *Politics and Society*, 3, no. 4 (Summer 1973), p. 479.

tion. In ordinary usage Serbo-Croatian is not a verbose language, but as soon as a Yugoslav enters the public arena, either spoken or written, he or she seems to follow this dictum: "Speak endlessly and say nothing." A Yugoslav anthropologist has suggested that long-windedness in Yugoslav public expression is an oriental characteristic acquired from the Turks. There may be some truth to this theory, but the author has a different explanation.

To speak endlessly and say nothing is a highly functional device for individual survival in a constantly changing system where the norms are unfixed and often contradictory. In such a system, someone who makes a brief, clear, penetrating statement might be penalized for it. Some are. A young university teacher, Mihailo Mihailov, was imprisoned for trying to establish a critical opposition journal. Eight Belgrade professors were fired for their views. At various times, Croat autonomists, Serbian nationalists, democratic socialists, and even pro-Soviets have been arrested and imprisoned for merely expressing their divergent views. From 1965 to 1975, an estimated 8,000 Yugoslavs were jailed for alleged political offenses. Accordingly, it is much safer to ramble on about vague abstractions than actually to say something pointed that might catch the attention of the authorities. This quality of empty wordiness has not helped the growth of a viable socialist political culture in Yugoslavia.

NATIONAL FEELINGS

The Communists claimed to have solved the national problem once and for all by granting nationalities their own republics in a truly federal system. For some time the problem did seem to be solved. A 1964 survey of 2,700 Yugoslavs found that 81 percent responded that relations between the country's nationalities were good or satisfactory. A 1966 survey found an almost identical percentage (80.4) indicated very slight or negligible attitudes of "ethnic distance," (e.g., unwillingness to enter into friendship or marriage with another Yugoslav nationality). A 1967 study found that the more modern and "mobilized" the respondent was, the more he or she tended to "cultural universalism," away from national orientations.[14]

Without doubting the honesty or ability of the Yugoslav social scientists who carried out these surveys, we can be skeptical about the respondents' candor. The years of Stalin-type terror in the late 1940s are still remembered in Yugoslavia; many people had friends and relatives unfairly imprisoned during that time. This author found to his surprise that a dinner host, a successful writer, had spent three years in solitary (starting at age nineteen) as an alleged "American spy." The presence of such individuals in the society serves as a constant reminder that one must be careful about public utterances. In private Yugoslavs

[14] For a summation of these surveys see Gary K. Bertsch, "The Revival of Nationalisms," *Problems of Communism*, November–December 1973, pp. 5–7.

say whatever they want. In responding to a survey on the national question, a strongly political matter, it is doubtful that interviewees completely speak their true feelings. Accordingly, the author believes that survey data on the national question in Yugoslavia is inaccurate, understating the amount of hostility that still exists.

Some of this hostility came out in the late 1960s and early 1970s in Croatia, where not only the people but many party members turned strongly nationalistic; some even suggested that Croatia leave the Yugoslav federation and become an independent country. Many Croats objected to calling their language Serbo-Croatian. Some of their grievances were economic; they claimed the profits of their industries were unjustly siphoned off and sent to other republics. As in the 1920s and 1930s, domination by the Serbs was alleged. In 1971, a wholesale purge of the Croatian party was carried out and a new leadership was promoted to crack down on the growing nationalism. This purge spread nation-wide, and alleged "nationalist elements" were expelled from the party in all the republics.

PEASANTS IN THE CITIES

One of the striking features of postwar Yugoslavia is its rapid urbanization. From 1921 to 1953, the urban population of Yugoslavia increased by only 5 percent, to 21.9 percent of total. By 1961, however, it had become 28.3 percent urban, and 35 percent by 1971.[15] A once peasant country has become heavily citified.

More than half of Yugoslav city dwellers were born in the countryside, and this has had various effects. It has probably benefited the regime, since people off the farm were less politically sophisticated than the old urbanites and more appreciative of an urban standard of living. It is among the old urban bourgeoisie, in fact, that foreign visitors hear the most criticism of the regime. In part, this author believes, the old urbanites react against the influx of peasants into the city, particularly into the housing and jobs of the old urban class. Resentment at being displaced by perceived social inferiors bothers them at least as much as the new socialist order. Peasants were the backbone of the Partisans, and after the war they claimed their rewards in jobs, housing, and university education, elbowing aside the old urbanites.[16]

A SYNTHETIC POLITICAL CULTURE

It's hard to generalize about a "Yugoslav" political culture because Yugoslavia is such a strange and rapidly changing mixture. The regime recognizes this and

---

[15] Hoffman, "Migration and Social Change," p. 21.

[16] See Lenard Cohen, "The Social Background and Recruitment of Yugoslav Political Elites, 1918–48," in *Opinion-Making Elites in Yugoslavia*, p. 54.

tries to foster feelings of national solidarity. We might say that they are trying to synthesize a political culture where previously none existed.

An old device is used for this: "Attack from outside." The Yugoslav media (like the Soviet) emphasize the German invasion and Partisan resistance, portraying the war as a great national epic that all Yugoslavs can identify with. That is an exaggeration: most Yugoslavs were not Partisans and some even fought against them. The Partisans "won" in the classic guerrilla manner by running away from and outlasting the enemy. But to see Yugoslav movies, one would think the entire country rose up and trounced the Germans. This kind of mythology is necessary national cement in Yugoslavia, and the media chiefs lay it on with a trowel.

Another epic is Yugoslavia's 1948 ouster from the Soviet camp and subsequent go-it-alone course. It is emphasized as a source of intense pride in the media: we've built our system by ourselves, threatened by the capitalists on one side and the Stalinists on the other.[17] These two themes feed into a third: the uniqueness and trail-blazing quality of the curious brand of communism that the Yugoslavs have evolved, which we shall now consider.

**PATTERNS
OF
INTERACTION**

SOCIALIST PLURALISM

In sharp contrast to the Soviet and East German systems, which are at most only latently pluralistic, Yugoslavia has made groups and their interaction the cornerstone of its system. Marx foresaw the withering away of the state, and Yugoslav thinkers have taken this idea to heart. The Yugoslav state since the reforms of the 1950s is officially supposed to be withering, or at any rate confining itself to the minimum tasks of modern statehood (national defense, currency, nationwide legal standards, etc.). The Soviet path of constantly increasing state power is, Yugoslavs note gleefully, profoundly anti-Marxian. Yugoslav law professor and constitution writer Jovan Djordjevich emphasizes that "the essence of socialist statehood lies in its *reduction and weakening*, not in expansion and strengthening."[18]

The Yugoslavs are serious about trying to shrink state power. The number of federal bureaucrats, for example, has declined since Yugoslavia's Stalinist period, although there are still plenty at the republic and municipal level.

---

[17] See for example Vladimir Dedijer, *The Battle Stalin Lost: Memoirs of Yugoslavia, 1948–1953* (New York: Viking, 1971).

[18] Jovan Djordjevich, "Interest Groups and the Political System of Yugoslavia," in *Interest Groups on Four Continents*, ed. by Henry W. Ehrmann (Pittsburgh: University of Pittsburgh Press), p. 200. Emphasis in original.

Instead of state supervision, each of Yugoslavia's 500 communes and 15,000 enterprises are supposed to be self-managing, that is, run by and for their members through representative bodies. This self-management process is not unfettered—the Communist party is always in the background, selecting representatives, establishing guidelines, and curbing excesses—but there is still a good deal of autonomous interaction.

WORKERS' CONTROL

Yugoslav theoreticians point out that worker self-management is not a new idea but was discussed by the utopian socialists, syndicalists, the Webbs, and even Lenin, who liked the idea but wanted to postpone it until Russia was industrialized. They further point out that where the old system collapses workers begin to take over their enterprises and run them as they did in 1917 in Petrograd and in 1956 in Budapest. By citing these antecedents, Yugoslav thinkers try to demonstrate that their system is natural and rooted in the socialist tradition and is in fact the culmination of that tradition.[19]

If such is true, one would not have known it in Yugoslavia prior to 1950. In the late 1940s, the Yugoslavs, then Stalinists, entertained no thoughts of decentralization and debureaucratization. Such ideas came only after 1950, as the Yugoslavs groped for ways to distinguish their system from the Soviet one. Decentralization and self-management reforms were introduced and repeatedly modified from the top down. The movement was not a spontaneous one.

For the sake of Yugoslav unity that is probably just as well, for if fully implemented, "self-management" could lead to chaos. For example, once workers found themselves in charge they started voting themselves wage increases out of line with productivity or profits. The result was major inflation, which had to be corrected by government requirements that wages be based on complicated formulas that restrain increases. Even so, in 1973 Belgrade had to freeze wages and prices and in some areas roll back prices. Inflation and self-management seem to go hand in hand in Yugoslavia.

The sheer time consumed by various self-management meetings also eats into productivity. A study of a shipyard found that the average worker spent the equivalent of 26.8 working days a year in meetings; the total loss of man-days could build one small ship. Some Yugoslav critics charge that the endless meetings are merely devices to avoid working.

While self-management opens up opportunities for citizen participation —something like one out of five workers has served on a council at one time or another—power still tends to accrue to the more educated. Using Yugoslav data, American political scientists Sidney Verba and Goldie Shabad concluded that on self-management councils "unskilled workers are greatly underrepresented;

---

[19] See Yugoslav theorist Branko Horvat, *An Essay on Yugoslav Society* (White Plains, N.Y.: International Arts and Sciences Press, 1969), pp. 26–43.

skilled workers are overrepresented; and white-collar workers with high levels of education are the most overrepresented."[20] Thus while worker participation is in theory open to all, in practice some play a larger part than others.

Do the workers' councils actually control their enterprises? The amount of worker control has varied, almost like a pendulum swing from one period to another and geographically as well. In some years observers have found the workers' councils really setting the course and telling the director what to do. But more often the director (invariably a party member) lays down policy to the workers' council. Typically, directors "propose" to their councils that one-third of the enterprise's profits be distributed to the workers and two-thirds go for investment and taxes. Some Yugoslav social scientists believe, however, that as workers gain more education they will erode the directors' monopoly on information and expertise. To this end, the republics have set up "workers universities" to train blue-collar types in management, law, psychology, and economics.

The Yugoslav regime is sincere in trying to build genuine worker self-management, but the task is far from finished. Perhaps the greatest limiting factor in making complete self-management function is apathy. The Yugoslav system, like the East German, presumes tremendous interest on the part of nearly everyone. In East Germany, participation is patently at odds with a still largely centralized system. Yugoslav leaders claim they want worker and citizen participation, but they do not always get the enthusiasm desired. In the first place, everyone knows that the Communist party hovers in the background and intervenes quietly in economic and governmental affairs. Thus many Yugoslavs feel that since the party will get its way in the end anyhow, there is no point in pretending to participate in decision making. But more basically, many persons detest the long meetings, boring speeches, and difficult decisions required by self-management. Many workers just want a fair paycheck and decent job conditions. Yugoslav ideologists strongly deny that workers may be apathetic about self-management, for to admit it would undermine the basic assumption that the proletariat is alienated and can be made whole only by directly controlling the workplace. If this revisionist Marxist view were abandoned, the Yugoslav system would veer either toward a statist Soviet or an oligarchical capitalist conception of the way economies should operate. Thus worker interest in self-management may be the necessary myth of the Yugoslav system.

STRUGGLE BETWEEN REPUBLICS

The levels of development of the republics are still strikingly different. Per capita gross material product (a lower figure than GNP) for the six republics and two autonomous provinces in 1972 shows:[21]

[20] Sidney Verba and Goldie Shabad, "Workers' Councils and Political Stratification: The Yugoslav Experience," paper delivered at 1975 meeting of the American Political Science Association, San Francisco, September 2–5, 1975, p. 68.

[21] Calculated from figures in *Indeks*, April 1974, p. 12.

Slovenia	$1,520
Croatia	970
Voyvodina	880
Serbia	750
Montenegro	570
Macedonia	540
Bosnia	520
Kosovo	250

The mostly Albanian people of Kosovo produced only one-sixth as much as Slovenians. The economic distance between regions in Yugoslavia is greater than in Spain or Italy, although all three are characterized by rich Norths and poor Souths.

If one drew an imaginary line under the northern third of Yugoslavia, including all of Slovenia, most of Croatia, and half of Serbia, he would have divided the country into a rich North and a poor South, with the northerners producing about twice as much as the southerners. Much of the tension in modern Yugoslavia grows out of this sharp difference. The rich republics, Slovenia and Croatia, have wanted to keep their earnings at home and invest them locally, where, they argue, they will have the biggest payoff. The poor republics, usually led by Serbia, have wanted earnings distributed nationwide with a good portion going to industrialize the backward areas.

In this debate the rich republics have economics on their side; funds invested in an already productive region where there is a good infrastructure and skilled labor force pay off much better. The poor republics have equity on their side; funds invested in backward areas lift living standards, reduce unemployment, and help unify the nation. The argument has been over how much of profits from the North should be diverted to the South.[22]

This kind of "economic nationalism" between the republics has led to considerable waste and duplication. Each republic has demanded its own steel mill, even if it is a money loser. Each has achieved its own outlet to the sea, with the exception of Macedonia. Serbia made a huge investment in a railroad line that was not absolutely necessary, but it reached the sea through friendly Montenegro rather than through rival Croatia, which commands most of the Adriatic coastline. Both Slovenia and Bosnia set up expensive port facilities on their few miles of coastline, as if they could not trust Croatia to handle their cargos. Given the relative weakness of the federation in economic planning, little can be done to restrain the republics from their economic foolishness.

To pacify the poorer republics, a Federal Fund for the Accelerated Development of Underdeveloped Regions was set up to extract earnings from the

---

[22] For an excellent study of this problem see Paul Shoup, *Communism and the Yugoslav National Question* (New York: Columbia University Press, 1968), especially chap. 6, "Economics and the National Question."

richer republics and send them southward. Even though the fund was modest, Belgrade had difficulty in securing the needed contributions from the donor republics. No one is satisfied—the North complains that demands are too high and the South complains that the amounts delivered are too low.

LIBERALS AND CONSERVATIVES

Conflict between the Yugoslav republics has become linked to another, more general struggle: one between liberals and conservatives. In the Yugoslav context, a liberal is someone who wants to carry the reforms that started in the 1950s to their logical conclusions: a truly self-managed society relatively free of direct party domination. (Djilas, who suggested many of the early reforms, kept going down that path until he was no longer a Communist.) Yugoslav liberals also want nearly total press freedom. Many are also liberal in the economic sense, wanting each enterprise to prosper or decline according to its abilities so as to increase overall efficiency and productivity. (This is liberalism in the classic, nineteenth-century sense, not in the current American usage.) Liberals favor more contact with the West (trade, cultural exchange, etc.). Liberals also favor more autonomy—approaching independence—for the republics, and a sharp reduction of Belgrade's central power. Thus Yugoslav liberals tend to be Slovenes and Croats.

A Yugoslav conservative is one who thinks decentralization has gone too far already, and that tighter control is needed over the republics, the economy, and the party. The Yugoslav conservative takes self-management with a grain of salt: Self-managed organizations need guidance by reliable party people to keep them from anarchy. The conservative wants to retain a fair degree of central control over the economy, both to prevent the formation of an elite managerial class (which might undermine his power) and to redistribute investment funds southward, into the backward republics. Conservatives are leery of contact with the West; they are a bit pro-Soviet. Not surprisingly, Yugoslav conservatives tend to be Serbs and Montenegrins, the nationalities that always favored centralization of power in Belgrade.

The strength of Yugoslav liberals and conservatives alternates in a pendulum-swing manner. Periods of liberalization tend to lead to economic growth, freer mass media, growth in party membership, new ideological proposals, and a general lessening of anxiety in the country. Unfortunately, these same periods tend also to produce inflation, a class of rich managers, increased income differences between individuals and republics, and a feeling that the system has become unglued. When things seem to be getting dangerously chaotic, Tito passes the word to tighten up. Dubious party members are expelled, new controls are placed on the economy, the mass media drop controversial material, the richer class stops flouting its private villas and Mercedes cars, and people watch their conversations a bit. After a few years, when the divisive threats seem to have been overcome, Tito urges greater economic growth, cautions the party against abusing power, and stresses the gains of self-management. The cycle is then ready to start over again.

One such cycle began in 1966 with a period of liberalization marked by the firing of Aleksander Rankovich, vice-president of Yugoslavia, boss of the Serbian branch of the LCY, and chief of the security (i.e., secret) police, which was largely staffed with Serbs and Montenegrins. Rankovich, at one time considered Tito's possible successor, was stripped of his positions (but allowed to stay in the party) for using his secret police to block economic reforms.[23] He also had some of Tito's residences bugged. Rankovich fitted most of the above characteristics of a conservative, and it is interesting to note the Serbian reaction to the ouster of the Rankovich clique. Many Serbs hated and feared the secret police, but quite a few were sorry to see the country's top Serb get the ax. Their attitude was similar to an American general's alleged comment on Chiang Kai-shek: "Sure he's a bastard, but he's *our* bastard."

Liberalization, though, brought with it the problems mentioned above, particularly in regard to Croatian nationalism. Tito fired the Croatian leadership in 1971 and over the next two years expelled from the party thousands of "anarcho-liberals," a term for those who want more liberalization and democratization. The term may be unfairly pejorative, but it does recognize that if things go too far, Yugoslavia could fall apart as a country. Accordingly, liberalization has very definite limits in Yugoslavia.

WHAT THE YUGOSLAV SYSTEM PRODUCES

ECONOMIC GROWTH

Economic growth in Yugoslavia averaged a very respectable 6.6 percent a year from 1948 to 1972. During the same period, per capita income increased over two and a half times. Particularly helpful to Yugoslavia's per capita growth rates has been its modest rate of population growth, 0.9 percent a year. Sometime in the early 1970s Yugoslavia passed $1,000 a year per capita income, considered by some economists to be the point separating poor from affluent countries.

While still poor by West European standards, Yugoslavia is losing some of its reputation as one of the most backward areas of Europe. In the interwar period, economic growth averaged 2.9 percent a year and about three-quarters of the population was in agriculture. By 1974, only 38.5 percent of the labor force

---

[23] See Shoup, *Communism and the Yugoslav National Question*, pp. 209–10, 247–48, and 257–58.

was in agriculture. Yugoslav agriculture, in contrast to that of the rest of Eastern Europe, is mostly private. About 85 percent of the arable land is private, as is 96 percent of the agricultural labor force. But recently only 71 percent of production has been private. This is because the small "social" sector of agriculture concentrates on cereals and is more mechanized. The private sector concentrates on labor-intensive items like vegetables, cows, and sheep. Peasants can bring their wares to open-air markets in each town and sell directly to housewives at whatever prices they can get. Some peasants have become rich, and stories abound of how grizzled illiterates pay cash for a new tractor or car. Yugoslavia, by not forcing agricultural collectivization (but encouraging it indirectly), produces food not only for itself but for export as well.

It is in industrial growth, though, that Yugoslavia has scored the biggest gains. Tax laws penalize enterprises that pay themselves too much; this encourages heavy reinvestment of profits. Indeed, the ratio of investment to GNP has reached as high as a phenomenal 29 percent, while industrial output has grown at an average of over 10 percent a year. Only 18 percent of Yugoslav output in 1947 was industrial, in 1972 it was 38.1 percent.[24] Yugoslavia has become a middle-industrialized country.

While Yugoslavia can offer itself as a model of socialist development, its economic system has three distinctly nonsocialist features: unemployment, pronounced income differences, and inflation.

Unemployment   Few other East European systems have unemployment (East Germany and the Soviet Union are seriously short of manpower). In the early 1970s, Yugoslav unemployment averaged over 7.5 percent and hit 10 percent in 1975. Self-managed enterprises in a relatively free market are under no obligation to absorb unemployed workers, for that could lower their efficiency and competitiveness. With the advantages of a market system comes the disadvantage of unemployment.

The number of jobless in Yugoslavia would be even higher but for close to one million Yugoslavs working in other countries. About 10 percent of Yugoslavia's labor force go to West Germany, France, Sweden, Austria, and elsewhere in Western Europe to take jobs ranging from construction and shipbuilding to professional soccer playing and architecture. Paris alone is said to harbor a colony of 3,000 graduate Yugoslav architects. Architecture is one of the most popular subjects in Yugoslav universities, which produce many times the number of architects needed. Yugoslavs abroad remit an average of $880 a year back to Yugoslavia, netting the country over half a billion dollars in valuable foreign exchange a year. Thus Yugoslavia helps hold down the number of

---

[24] Yugoslav Federal Office for Statistics, *Materijalni i Društveni Razvoj, SFR Jugoslavije, 1947–1972* (Belgrade: Federal Office for Statistics, 1973), p. 44.

unemployed and earns foreign currency at the same time. There is no constraint on those who wish to leave (except for some political problem cases); passports are easy to get.

Income inequality   According to official figures, income inequality is a good deal lower than in Western Europe. Considering, however, that there is no class of big capitalists, the amount of inequality remaining in Yugoslavia is considerable, nearly that of the United States. In 1963 the Gini Index of inequality of household incomes was 0.32.[25] By 1968, it had increased to 0.34; that is, family incomes had grown less equal. In comparison, the Gini Index for U.S. household incomes grew from 0.35 in 1964 to 0.38 in 1970. Although income inequality is lower in the United States than in virtually all of Western Europe, the United States makes no pretense of being a socialist country.

Yugoslav social scientists claim that the growth of income inequality of the 1960s was stopped or reversed in the early 1970s. The attainment of levels of equality similar to those of other East European lands will take some doing. In 1969, highly qualified Yugoslav workers earned 2.75 times as much as unskilled laborers, a considerable gap to bridge. With some republics and some enterprises much more efficient than others, inequality is the natural consequence. One device being tried to hold down income differentials is a requirement that within a republic (but not nationwide), an individual's wage cannot be more than 5 times the republic's average wage. Five times the average is hardly equality.

Inflation   Another difference between Yugoslavia and other socialist countries that have centrally administered prices is the amount of inflation. There is little inflation, for example, in East Germany. In the early 1970s consumer prices in Yugoslavia climbed at rates of from 15 to 19 percent a year and topped 30 percent in early 1975. To a certain extent, Yugoslavs over the years have gotten used to steady inflation of 12 to 15 percent a year and do not overly mind it, so long as salaries keep pace. In the mid-1970s, however, an inflationary time the world over, real income declined in Yugoslavia. How long Yugoslavs will stand for the erosion of their income is an open question. What can they do about it? Here we have another point of difference between Yugoslavia and most of the rest of Eastern Europe: Yugoslavia tolerates strikes, and there have been a few. Although strikes are awfully embarrassing for a system that claims to be under worker control, they have at times served as needed warnings against high-handed enterprise directors who ignore the demands of their workers' councils. (Poland too experiences occasional strikes.)

Another point of differentiation is Yugoslavia's cultivation of foreign, including American, investment in joint ventures. The Soviet Union likes to buy

---

[25] For a brief explanation of the Gini Index see Karl W. Deutsch, *Politics and Government: How People Decide Their Fate*, 2nd ed. (Boston: Houghton Mifflin, 1974), pp. 135–40.

American technology but refuses to let American firms penetrate its economy. Yugoslavia is delighted to get both American capital and know-how and requires only that the Yugoslav side control 51 percent of the joint venture. American firms setting up production in Yugoslavia recently include Gillette (razor blades), Dow Chemical, and Black and Decker (hand tools).

A MIDDLE WAY?

Yugoslav theorists strongly deny that Yugoslavia is a middle way between the Communist East and capitalist West. They say Yugoslavia is a firmly socialist country. Nonetheless, in terms of how the system actually works, Yugoslavia is indeed a mixture of East and West, a sort of zig-zag middle route, a market economy led by Communists, stumbling uncertainly toward some kind of socialism.

One key support for this middle way is Yugoslavia's foreign policy. Nonalignment has been the basis of Yugoslavia's international position since its expulsion from the Soviet bloc. Yugoslavia does not stay precisely in the middle between East and West, but rather oscillates back and forth, as do other trends in Yugoslavia. In the early 1950s, Yugoslavia turned to the West, accepting American economic and military aid and recognizing West Germany. In line with domestic tightening up in the mid-1950s—and thanks to Khrushchev's 1955 apology for Stalin's abuses—Belgrade sidled a little closer to Moscow and recognized East Germany. But in 1958, after the Soviets' problems with Poland and Hungary, they denounced Tito and the atmosphere chilled again. Trying to hold an even balance in the 1960s, Yugoslavia became alarmed at the Soviet 1968 invasion of Czechoslovakia and loudly warned she would defend her independence. Presidents Nixon and Tito exchanged warm visits in 1971 and 1972. By the early 1970s, however, Tito, fearful that Western influence and Yugoslav liberalization was going too far, warmed up ties with Moscow.

The balancing act may never end, and in the Yugoslav case there would be no purpose to ending it by drifting permanently into one camp or the other. Nonalignment not only opens trade with both East and West (more with the latter) but has allowed Belgrade to assume a leadership role among the world's large group of neutralist countries. Tito knows personally most of the leaders of the Third World, and this has opened new economic possibilities for Yugoslavia. In short, there would simply be no percentage in Yugoslavia's altering its international status as neutral and nonaligned.

CAN IT LAST?

Yugoslavia in the twilight of the Tito era faced problems similar to Spain on the evening of the Franco era. (Both men were born in 1892, but Tito appeared much younger and healthier than Franco, who died in 1975.) As we discussed in connection with Spain, can one man do? Both Franco and Tito performed adroit balancing acts, but can their successors? In this regard, Yugoslavia is in better shape than Spain, for Tito constructed a political backbone for Yugoslavia, the League of Communists, while Franco neglected to do anything similar for Spain. Accordingly, the transition to the post-Tito era in Yugoslavia will probably be easier than Spain's transition in the post-Franco era.

Still, there is plenty that can go wrong in Yugoslavia. As in Spain, any major threat to the unity or continuity of the system could trigger military intervention. If the breakup of Yugoslavia were ever threatened, the armed forces would simply take over and prevent it, as the constitution enjoins them to do.

Could Yugoslavia shift from its relatively open and experimental system back toward the Soviet model? Such fears were raised in the mid-1970s as Tito tightened controls as if in preparation for difficulties that might arise upon his departure from office. Dissidents were sentenced to jail for criticism; lawyers who tried to defend them were also threatened with jail. New laws banned the "spreading of false news" and the "disparaging of state organs." Eight critical professors were fired from Belgrade University. The Zagreb periodical *Praxis*—which often pointed out that real self-management was not being practiced—was shut down. The Yugoslav press turned nasty toward the United States with accusations of pressure and infiltration. Some observers feared the trend could lead Yugoslavia back into the Soviet camp, giving the Russians the direct outlet on the Mediterranean they have longed for and seriously unsettling the balance of power in Europe.

But the crackdown of the mid-1970s was aimed in both directions, against the Soviet Union as well as the West. In 1974 and 1975 some 200 "Cominformists"—Belgrade's parlance for pro-Soviets—were arrested, and alleged Soviet designs on post-Tito Yugoslavia were pointedly directed at Moscow. Tito wished his country to go neither East nor West after his departure.

A permanent shift in either direction seems unlikely. Yugoslavia has evolved so far from the Soviet model, and Yugoslavs have become so used to Western contact, that the re-Sovietization of the country could probably not be accomplished by any means short of war. This author believes, rather, that the tightening up of the mid-1970s was the sort of thing that happened before in Yugoslavia and that it would likely give way again to a new period of liberalization.

EAST
GERMANY
6

In 1974 the United States finally granted diplomatic recognition to a European country that Washington had tried for twenty-five years to ignore: East Germany. Germany to most Americans meant glittering West Germany, the Federal Republic, "our Germany," with its capital in Bonn. American soldiers, tourists, scholars, and business people felt at home in West Germany, but most never set foot in gray, somber East Germany, the Germany beyond the Wall, or even considered doing so.

Americans and West Germans even had trouble settling on a name for the territory to the east. In the 1940s and 1950s it was called the Soviet Occupation Zone, implying that it had no government of its own. In the 1950s and 1960s Americans began calling it East Germany while West Germans called it *Mitteldeutschland* (Middle Germany) to emphasize that there were former German territories still farther east that Poland and the Soviet Union had absorbed. In the 1960s people began grudgingly to call the area "the so-called German Democratic Republic," after its official name, *Deutsche Demokratische Republik*. As Bonn and Washington in the early 1970s began to establish normal relations with East Germany, their statesmen finally dropped the "so-called" and acknowledged that East Germany had the right to call itself what it wanted.

Some contend that the names West and East Germany are Cold War terms and should no longer be used. We will use them because they are a good deal shorter than Federal Republic of Germany (FRG) and German Democratic Republic (GDR). Besides, both West and East German are necessary as adjectives and to describe citizenship. What else could we call these people—German Democratic Republicans, GDRniks, Federal Germans?

THE
IMPACT
OF THE
PAST

East Germany is the youngest of our five countries; it was founded only in 1949. Historically, though, the division of Germany is nothing new. Indeed, for most of history there has not been one Germany but many. At one point over 400 principalities covered Germany like a crazy quilt; they were set up according to their princes' religion, Catholic or Protestant. Gradually German rulers consolidated these tiny units into bigger ones, and in 1870 Bismarck united Germany into the Second Reich (Charlemagne's was the First, Hitler's the short-lived Third). For a millennium before Bismarck, Germany had not been a political entity but a linguistic-cultural area. Out of this area Austria and Switzerland have emerged as states in their own right. Likewise, the East German regime fights to prevent reabsorption into a united Germany.

Although the Germanic peoples have a long history of division, their territory was never before divided the way it is now. That division stems only from World War II, specifically from the 1944 Yalta talks in which the United States, Britain, and the Soviet Union agreed to divide postwar Germany into three (later four, when France was added) zones for temporary administration. The Soviet zone was about one-fourth of the territory of prewar Germany, an area slightly smaller than Tennessee. It appears that the Russians at that point did not plan on setting up a Communist satellite in their zone. Berlin, located in the Soviet zone, was to be jointly administered by the Allies. This "temporary" arrangement was inherently unworkable and became one of the key factors in starting and continuing the Cold War.

While all the Allies were vindictive toward conquered Germany, the Soviets, who had suffered horribly from the Nazis, were adamant about economic reparations from Germany. The Russians immediately began dismantling whole factories in their zone and shipping them home. Industry in the Soviet zone was set back severely, an indication that the Russians had little on their minds at this time but revenge and were not then contemplating an East German state. If they had had that in mind, they would not have been trying to ruin its economy.

The division of Germany grew in large part out of the different attitudes of its Western and Eastern occupiers. With Soviet takeovers in Eastern Europe, the British and Americans decided to build up rather than tear down the economies of their zones. Starting in 1948, the Marshall Plan pumped in millions of dollars to aid recovery. Matters came to a head that year over the issue of currency. The Soviets, still intent on looting, were flooding the country with inflated military currency that they had the right to print along with the other Allies. The British and Americans, trying to stabilize the economy in their zones, introduced a new Deutsche mark. The Soviets, angered by this currency reform, reacted by blocking ground traffic to West Berlin, which was supplied for nearly a year by the amazing British-American airlift.

Meanwhile, in both the Eastern and Western zones there were people working for statehood under, respectively, Soviet and American sponsorship. In the West, Konrad Adenauer urged the founding of the Federal Republic of Germany and achieved it in September 1949. Walter Ulbricht pressed for a German Democratic Republic and got it in October 1949. The founding of the Bonn republic was the point of no return for the Soviets, forcing them to give to Ulbricht what he had been demanding.

The Soviets had not planned on setting up an East German state. It was forced on them by the overall East-West confrontation, to which, of course, they were important contributors. As Jean Edward Smith points out, the Soviets hesitated for years before establishing the GDR and at times seemed willing to sell out their German Communist protegés for Soviet strategic interests.[1] The Soviets suggested repeatedly that Germany could reunite provided it turned neutral and unarmed. The West feared a Soviet trick to take over all of Germany. Tension between purely Soviet national interests and the survival of East Germany continues to this day; the East German regime fears that détente will open them up to West German penetration. GDR leaders know that their foundations are still shaky.

THE RISE OF THE SED

The political backbone of East Germany is its leading party, a variation on the classical Communist parties called the Socialist Unity party of Germany (*Sozialistische Einheitspartei Deutschlands*, or SED for short). The GDR would not exist without the Soviets, but it would not work without the SED.

The SED is in part a continuation of the pre-Hitler German Communist party, which at one point (1932) racked up 13 percent of the German national vote (but was always smaller than the Social Democrats). Communist refusal to cooperate with the Social Democrats, whom they called "Social Fascists," opened the way for Hitler's rise to power. The Communists held that Hitler would merely be a temporary phenomenon, and after his regime collapsed Germany would go Communist. Instead, Hitler crushed Social Democrats and Communists alike. Some German Communists made it to exile in the Soviet Union where they later assisted in the anti-Hitler war effort. Among them was

[1] Jean Edward Smith, *Germany Beyond the Wall: People, Politics . . . and Prosperity* (Boston: Little, Brown, 1969), chap. 10.

Walter Ulbricht (1893–1973), a carpenter from Leipzig who became a founding member of the German Communist party in 1919 and later its expert on party organization. For years Ulbricht was characterized in the West as a colorless, Stalinist bureaucrat. His survival through Stalin's purges and the war and postwar periods, however, bespeaks considerable shrewdness and astute attention to detail. Ulbricht's strong point was like Stalin's: the ability to organize political structures. Ulbricht was able to follow the changes of Moscow's post-Stalin leadership and even disagree with Soviet leaders when it came to East Germany's national interest.

In April 1945, in the wake of Red Army advances into Germany, the "Ulbricht Group" consisting of Ulbricht and some of his exile associates was flown into Soviet-occupied Germany and began setting up a civil administration and reviving remnants of the old German Communist party. In local elections in 1945 the Communists were beaten by the reviving Social Democrats (SPD). Ulbricht then urged the merger of the Communist and Social Democratic parties, which occurred (in the Soviet zone only) in April 1946.

Observers hostile to the Communists call this a "forced merger." Others point out the considerable desire on the part of the SPD to heal the breach with their former antagonists—that antagonism had helped the Nazis—and form a common left front. British political scientist David Childs believes "it is fair to say that [the merger] was due to a mixture of conviction and coercion."[2] The Social Democrats contributed 52 percent of the initial membership of the new SED, the Communists 48 percent. In later years the forceful aspect of the merger came to the fore and many former Social Democrats were expelled from the SED; they had served their purpose. One former Social Democrat, Otto Grotewohl, became the SED's first chairman and later president of the GDR, although real power unquestionably stayed in Ulbricht's hands.

THE SHAKY REGIME

In some respects the East German regime, which made East Berlin its capital, has faced a much more difficult situation than other Soviet-linked countries in Eastern Europe. Millions of refugees poured in from former German territories that Poland and the Soviet Union had taken over (many of the refugees subsequently left for West Germany). Industry suffered from the Soviet reparations policy, which squeezed an estimated $20 billion from the area. The Soviet troops, which had at first been welcomed as liberators in some areas of East Europe, were generally seen as conquerers by Germans. But worst of all for the East German regime, their country had a perfect escape hatch right in its middle: Berlin. The East Germans, like the Czechs, could seal off their border with West

---

[2] David Childs, *East Germany* (New York: Praeger, 1969), p. 19.

Germany, but Berlin, under Allied agreements, remained open to free circulation. An East German who was dissatisfied with his or her political or economic situation did not have to sneak across a mine field to get out; all he or she had to do was visit East Berlin, take the subway to a refugee center in West Berlin, and be flown out to West Germany, complete with West German citizenship. Some three million persons left East Germany, mostly for West Germany, from the end of the war to 1961.

The number of refugees varied from year to year, the peak coming in 1953. In June of that year the East German regime decided to raise work norms in order to boost the lagging economy. East Berlin construction workers, deciding that they already worked hard enough, struck in protest against the new norms. They were soon joined by other protesters, and the demonstrations spread to other cities. As the strikes turned into antiregime riots, the Ulbricht government asked for help from the occupying Soviet forces, and they quickly crushed the uprising, which was without plan or leadership. An estimated twenty-one demonstrators were killed and seven were later executed. Although not nearly as spectacular as the hard-fought 1956 Hungarian revolt, the riots were immortalized by a photograph of unarmed workers throwing stones at Soviet tanks. In 1953 almost one-third of a million East Germans left for West Germany.

Over the course of the 1950s, the GDR was slowly bleeding to death. There were seldom fewer than 200,000 refugees each year, and they were disproportionately young, skilled, and productive. Thanks to this outflow (plus a very low birth rate), East Germany is one of the few countries of the world that has had zero population growth (and even decline) in the postwar period. The shortage of able people was a severe hindrance to the GDR's economic growth and even to the viability of the system as a whole. In 1960 and 1961 many farmers fled a collectivization drive.

In 1961 the Ulbricht regime did what it had to do: dammed the outflow by building the Berlin Wall, thus sealing off the escape hatch.

Although the Wall stands as a chilling reminder of the East German system's inability to match West Germany's freedom and prosperity, Ulbricht had little alternative to its construction. Every country, no matter what its system, places survival at the top of its priorities, and the refugee exodus made East Germany's survival doubtful. East German authorities explain that the Wall was necessary to block "fascist" penetration from West Berlin, but the real motivation was an economic one, to stop the manpower loss.

Despicable as it may be in our eyes, the Wall worked for East Germany. Persons who may have considered leaving for the West (or at least had it as an option) suddenly found they had no choice; they had to stay. There was little to do but make the best of it. The East German economy expanded vigorously, at rates comparable to those of West Germany's "economic miracle" (*Wirtschaftswunder*). Although the GDR's per capita income and standards of living are about two-thirds those of the FRG, the differences are no longer day and night. Perhaps more important, on the psychopolitical level, East Germans have begun to take pride in their accomplishments and in their system. Our country may not be as opulent as West Germany, many East Germans say, but we started with several disadvantages and all by ourselves have built an economically equitable, socialist system in which everyone has a chance, regardless of class origins.

Thus the real foundation of the GDR as a system dates not from its formal founding in 1949, but from the time it stabilized itself in 1961. This makes the history of the East German system even shorter than at first one would think. It also indicates that the Wall will not come down in the foreseeable future, for few governments voluntarily put themselves out of business.

THE
KEY
INSTITUTIONS

NO MORE FEDERALISM

West Germany, in rejecting the unitary government of the Nazi period, went back to the old German tradition of particularism by adopting a federal structure. The Federal Republic is composed of ten *Länder* (states), which enjoy some autonomy in running local affairs. East Germany opted for a unitary system in 1952 and turned its five *Länder*—Mecklenburg, Brandenburg, Saxony-Anhalt, Thuringia, and Saxony—into fourteen districts named after the leading city of each. These districts (*Bezirke*) are merely administrative subdivisions governed centrally from Berlin; they have practically no autonomy.

One of the more important geographical changes that have occurred since World War II is the disappearance of Prussia, the Baltic foundation stone of the nineteenth-century unification of Germany. Long the home of German expansionism, militarism, and social reaction, Prussia was divided after World War II among the Soviet Union, Poland, and the GDR. Most Prussians fled from the parts taken by the Russians and Poles. The great landed estates were dissolved and parceled out to small landholders in East Germany, thus depriving the Prussian elite of its economic base. The East German farms were later collectivized.

THE FORMAL ORGANIZATION

The 1968 GDR constitution provides for the usual legislature and executive, plus an interesting body in between these two.

People's Chamber Volkskammer, or People's Chamber, is the name given East Germany's unicameral legislature of 500 deputies elected for five-year terms. The Volkskammer has at least two curious aspects. In the first place, it has 66 nonvoting deputies from East Berlin, the very capital of the GDR. Why? The answer goes back to the legal status of both parts of Berlin, which is still theoretically under four-power administration. West Berlin, for example, sends 22 nonvoting deputies to the Bundestag in Bonn. Because the GDR constantly emphasizes that West Berlin is not part of the Federal Republic, they have to go along with the game by pretending that East Berlin too is still a bit special and awaiting final disposition of the Berlin question. If East Germany made East Berlin a full part of its political system, they reason, then West Germany could claim the same right for West Berlin. Germans are great ones for legalisms.

The second curious aspect of the Volkskammer is that it is nominally composed of several parties, an unusual arrangement for Eastern European countries. These parties do not, however, enjoy an independent existence; none serves as an opposition in the parliament. Instead, they are junior partners of the leading SED, designed to mobilize sectors of the East German population who have a traditional antipathy toward the Communist party. These parties, although fake by our standards, show a realistic appreciation on the part of the regime of East German public opinion. For serious Christians (East Germany is 80 percent Lutheran) who are not inclined to give up their religion in favor of the materialism of the SED, there is a Christian Democratic Union (CDU, just as in West Germany) to "represent" their views in the Volkskammer and to transmit the regime's decisions back to them. For businesspersons, shopkeepers, and other traditionally bourgeois elements, there is a Liberal Democratic party (LDPD). For ex-Nazis and military officers there is even a National Democratic party (NDPD). Farmers have a Democratic Farmers party (DBD). Other groups are represented directly in the Volkskammer: the trade union organization (FDGB), the women's league (DFD), the Free German Youth (FDJ), and the German Culture League (DK). One observer sees the East German parliament as an example of "corporatism."[3]

The distribution of seats in the Volkskammer follows a set, unvarying pattern. No party or group can win or lose strength in an election because they all run together as a common National Front. The Volkskammer is composed of "parties" and groups in the following numbers.[4]

---

[3] See James H. Wolfe, "Corporatism in German Political Life: Functional Representation in the GDR and Bavaria," in *Politics in Europe: Structures and Processes in Some Postindustrial Democracies*, ed. Martin O. Heisler (New York: David McKay, 1974).

[4] Federal Republic of Germany, *Bericht der Bundesregierung und Materialien zur Lage der Nation 1972* (Bonn: Bundesministerium fuer innerdeutsche Beziehungen, 1972), p. 57.

SED	127 deputies
CDU	52
LDPD	52
NDPD	52
DBD	52
FDGB	68
DFD	35
FDJ	40
DK	22
Total	500

Occasionally the non-SED parties put in their two-cents' worth on non-critical legislation. The CDU, for example, suggested the GDR's conscription law be amended to allow conscientious objectors to do alternate service, and the SED agreed. The CDU also opposed liberalizing the abortion law. Nonetheless, it is clear that the leaders of the various small parties are chosen and guided by the SED, whose viewpoint they echo.

Another interesting point is the relative youth of Volkskammer members. In 1971, 33 percent were only forty years old or younger. In comparison the West German Bundestag of 1969 had only half that percentage of deputies in this age bracket.[5] The two systems are, of course, completely different. In the Federal Republic, young persons must work their way up through party ranks before they can win a seat in Bonn. In the GDR, bright young talent can quickly be promoted without regard to democratic procedures. The direct representation of the Free German Youth in the Volkskammer also insures at least thirty-five seats for young people. In some respects, as we shall consider more fully later, the GDR affords special opportunities for ambitious youngsters.

The East German Volkskammer, then, has some interesting differences from Soviet and other East European legislatures. It cannot, however, be considered an important decision-making body, for it simply approves legislation placed before it. In the decade from 1961 through 1970, for example, of the 107 laws passed, 62 were initiated by the Council of Ministers, 45 by the Council of State, and none by the Volkskammer.[6]

Council of Ministers   The *Ministerrat* (Council of Ministers) is nominally, like Western cabinets, answerable to and chosen by the legislature to carry out "the political, economic, cultural, social and military tasks of the socialist state" (according to Article 78 of the 1968 constitution). In practice, the Council of Ministers is more like the administrative arm of the SED. Of the thirty-nine ministers holding office in 1970, thirty-three were SED

[5] *Bericht 1972*, pp. 33 and 41.

[6] *Bericht 1972*, p. 63.

members, including sixteen members of the SED's Central Committee and four members of the powerful Politburo.[7] The four token non-SED parties were also represented.

Like the Soviet Council of Ministers on which it is modeled, the East German Ministerrat is heavily occupied with administering the nationalized economy. This leads to ministries that are extremely specialized by our standards. For example, among the twenty-nine ministries existing in 1971 there were separate ministries for the glass and ceramic industry, for processing machinery and motor vehicles, for light industry, and for electronic technology. Old ministries have been dropped and new ones added to foster better economic growth and control.

Council of State   The *Staatsrat* (Council of State) was, until the retirement of Ulbricht, the chief executive agency of the GDR. Although still in operation, the Staatsrat is not nearly so important as it was when Ulbricht used it as his main control device.[8] Like the Ministerrat, the Staatsrat is nominally a branch of the Volkskammer, designed to give continuity of leadership between parliamentary sessions. Since the Volkskammer meets only about five days a year (typical of Communist systems), the twenty-five-member Staatsrat speaks for the larger body year round. Staatsrat decisions have the force of law whether or not they have been approved by the Volkskammer. The Council of State prepares bills for legislative approval and can convene the People's Chamber when it wishes. Under Ulbricht the Staatsrat had oversight of internal security and national defense. The chairman of the body still names GDR ambassadors and receives the credentials of foreign ambassadors, which means that, according to international law, the chairman of the Staatsrat, Willi Stoph, is the functional equivalent of a president. Ulbricht combined this office with that of party chief; its splitting into two offices, one state and one party, in the post-Ulbricht era resembles the post-Stalin shakedowns of the Soviet Union.

As is the case with Yugoslavia, it is clear that ultimate decision-making authority does not reside in the formal mechanisms of government, but in the leading party.

THE SED

At first glance one may be tempted to dismiss the East German Socialist Unity party as just another Communist party, a carbon copy of the CPSU. That would be an oversimplification. In the first place, as we noted, the SED was formed

[7] U.S. Army, *Area Handbook for East Germany* (Washington: Government Printing Office, 1972), p. 123.

[8] John M. Starrels and Anita M. Mallinckrodt, *Politics in the German Democratic Republic* (New York: Praeger, 1975), pp. 190–91.

from a merger of the Communists and Social Democrats in 1946. Subsequently the SED was transformed into a "party of the new type" to more closely resemble the Soviet Communist party model. Membership rolls were cut, particularly to get rid of those still committed to social (rather than socialist) democracy. Instead of open admissions into the party, the SED demands "candidate membership" before final acceptance and carefully scrutinizes applicants' social origins (working-class applicants are preferred) and ideological depth.

Another point to consider is the relatively large size of the SED. With 1,845,280 full and 64,579 candidate members in 1971, the SED enrolled 11 percent of East Germany's population, more than double the approximately 5 percent in the Soviet and Yugoslav Communist parties. The large size of the SED tends to indicate that it does not play precisely the same role as does the CPSU. It is designed to bring in far more members and thus serves as somewhat more of a mass mobilizing device than an elite leadership stratum. We may further suspect that membership in the party by itself is not quite so important as in the Soviet Union: the bigger an elite, the less elite it is. We must then modify our statement on the importance of the SED as East Germany's leadership. The SED as a whole is not the leading elite—it's too big. The leadership is rather a small, elite *part* of the SED.

The organization of the SED strongly resembles that of the CPSU. At the bottom are cells consisting of as few as 3 and as many as 100 members. Copying a Soviet reform, in 1963 the SED reorganized on the "production principle," with divisions based on economic activities (factories, farms, etc.) instead of on the previous "territory principle," based on neighborhoods. Each level of the party nominally elects members to the next highest level, but actually the higher level controls the membership and activities of the lower level. The district organizations in East Germany send delegates to a party congress held every four years to approve (usually by acclamation) the policies of the party leaders and the pre-selected 135 members (plus 54 candidates, in case of death or resignation) of the Central Committee (see Figure 6–1).[9] The Central Committee approves both a 10-member Secretariat, which controls party activities nationwide, and the real peak of power, a 16-member (plus 7 candidates) Politburo. Walter Ulbricht was SED General Secretary, chief of the Politburo and the GDR's head of state. He was powerful.

One of the criteria for admission to the SED is social origin. The party of workers and peasants has tended to attract a disproportionate number of bureaucrats and intellectuals, a tendency common to all East European systems. Thus a candidate who started as a blue-collar worker, a true proletarian, is often more welcome than a professional type of middle-class origin. This is not to say that all those listed by the SED as "workers" currently get their hands dirty; many have

[9] Adapted from *Area Handbook for East Germany*, p. 145.

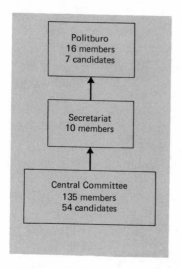

Figure 6–1   Structure of the SED
Leadership

long since been promoted to managerial positions and some have completed
university study. It's the origin that counts, and over the years that has varied
among SED members, as Table 6–1 shows.

Table 6–1   SED Membership Origins

	1947	1957	1961	1966
Wage workers	48.1%	33.8%	33.8%	45.6%
Salaried workers and intellectuals	22.0	42.3	41.3	28.4
Farmers	9.4	5.0	6.2	6.4
Others	20.5	18.9	18.7	19.6

Source: Heinz Rausch and Theo Stammen, eds., DDR—Das politische, wirtschaftliche und
soziale System (Munich: Verlag C. H. Beck, 1974), p. 219.

From 1961 to 1966. Blue-collar workers jumped from 33.8 to 45.6 percent,
a difference of 11.8 percentage points, while white-collar workers and intellectuals fell from 41.3 to 28.4 percent, a difference of 12.9 percentage points. This
major swing raises the suspicion that some members were simply redesignated
as "wage workers" based on their former or their fathers' professions, thus
making the party more "proletarian."

The dilemma for the SED, like that of most Communist parties, is how to
stay a workers' party while awarding and coopting the brainier professions.

Bringing a metal worker into the party is better ideologically, but bringing in his boss, a graduate engineer, makes more sense economically. There is a built-in tension here between a party that tries simultaneously to represent the masses but function as an elite. The ideal solution, and a common one in East Germany, is to find a bright person from a working-class family and send him or her through engineering school, making sure he or she joins the party. In this manner the party hopes to get the best of both worlds, a proletarian elite.

EAST
GERMAN
POLITICAL
ATTITUDES

A TOUCH OF THE PAST

East Germany remains a very German country; indeed, perhaps more German than West Germany. The Federal Republic is chrome-plated modern. American influences have crept into the lifestyles of West Germans, particularly the younger generation. Along with West German affluence has come conspicuous consumption; along with freedom has come pleasure seeking. Much of traditional Germany has disappeared in the Federal Republic, including old political attitudes.

Such is not the case in the GDR. In some respects an old-fashioned German feels more at home there. The stress is on the traditional virtues of order, discipline, and obedience to the state. Crime rates are low, and many East Germans, familiar with skyrocketing crime rates in the West (as reported on West German television) mention this as one of the strong points of their system. In some ways the Prussian discipline and obedience of the GDR represent a continuation of values extolled during the Hitler period.

To take an example the author has personally experienced, one need only ride the subway from East to West Berlin (passing through the proper checkpoint with the right passport, of course) on a Saturday night. East Berlin is still; few persons are on the streets. The streets themselves are rather dark due to the absence of illuminated advertisements. There are some theaters and the opera but practically no "pop" entertainment. To step from this atmosphere out onto West Berlin's famous Kurfuerstendamm is almost unreal. West Berlin on a Saturday night is jumping. Gorgeously dressed young people stroll along the K'damm in the latest continental fashions. Movies, bars, night clubs, most of them stressing sex, do a booming business. The contrast between the two halves of Berlin is admittedly an extreme one; a comparison of small towns would not show as sharp a difference between East German austerity and West German indulgence.

This contrast between lifestyles is precisely what the GDR leadership harps on and is trying to instill as a fundamental part of the East German political culture: the West is sybaritic and decadent; we are serious and dedicated. In a phrase, what East Germany says is, "We are different!" Indeed, this policy of differentiation even has an official name, *Abgrenzung*, or demarcation. Much of the SED's effort since East Germany's establishment is to differentiate it as a system from West Germany, to make reunification impossible. To a certain extent this effort has worked; both East and West Germans who might favor eventual merger have to admit that their social systems are now too different to easily form a single country again.

USES OF THE PAST

The differences that have evolved are instructive. Both Germanies are the remains of Hitler's Reich, but they have handled the Nazi past differently. The Soviet zone was rough on Nazis; those who could be found lost their property and sometimes their lives. Ex-Nazi bureaucrats and teachers were soon displaced from their jobs by hastily trained younger persons who demonstrated the proper "anti-Fascist" (i.e., pro-Communist) orientation. A few repentant Nazis and Wehrmacht officers were enlisted to perform security and military duties, but always under party supervision. Some people who had been nominal Nazis were permitted to join the SED, but the general tenor of political life in East Germany has been militantly anti-Fascist.

The Federal Republic has not been so militant. Although the Western occupiers at first attempted to "denazify" their zones, later many bureaucrats, teachers, and even judges got their jobs back. The properties of Nazis were not confiscated, and many ex-Nazis became prosperous businessmen. Some ex-Nazis got back into politics and attained high office, chiefly in the CDU. One even became chancellor: Kurt Georg Kiesinger. Scandals rocked the Bonn regime when the wartime records of several officials were revealed; they were, to say the least, unsavory. Neo-Nazi newspapers and political parties have been tolerated in the Federal Republic. The political culture of West Germany does not stress the horrors of the Hitler period—schoolbooks tend to play it down —and the average West German would rather just forget the whole thing.

It may be argued that the attitude in the Federal Republic is more "natural" than that in the GDR, where memories of the Third Reich are kept alive as government policy. By stressing Nazi remnants in West Germany, the GDR authorities gain a certain plausibility in arguing that Bonn is "revanchist." SED leaders can point with pride to their long struggle with the Hitler regime—many were imprisoned and killed—while most West German leaders cannot. Willy Brandt was an obvious exception here. The East Germans built a Monument to the Victims of Fascism and Militarism on East Berlin's Unter den Linden. They do not, however, notice the irony in the changing of the guard at this monument—by goose-stepping East German soldiers.

Another element of the German past that the GDR strives to keep alive is the revolutionary tradition. Marx and Engels were, after all, Germans and wrote in the German language. The German socialist movement was the "mother" of such movements the world over in the nineteenth century. In stressing the German origins of Marxian socialism, the SED tries to demonstrate that its power is rooted in German soil (and to obscure its arrival via Soviet bayonets). The SED further claims to be the true heir to the long stream of German socialism; the SPD, they argue, forsook this mantle in 1914 in voting to support the Kaiser's war. Since then, they hold, the SPD has been just another nationalist party little different from bourgeois parties.

NATIONAL PRIDE

These uses of the past, however, have not been notably effective in winning over the support of the bulk of the East German population. More effective has been the slowly growing national pride East Germans feel at having built themselves into an important economic power. This pride is enhanced when East Germans visit the Soviet Union and compare conditions there with the GDR; they feel, rightfully, that they have done a better job of building socialism than their putative teachers.

Most East Germans are well aware of the higher living standards prevailing in West Germany. The element of national pride comes in, though, when they consider that their socialist system has eliminated most of the class biases and differences that still exist in West Germany. They point out that East German education is open to all and free whereas West German education still heavily favors the children of middle-class families. The GDR goes out of its way to get working-class youth into universities; few such youths get into West German universities because most have been "tracked" into nonacademic high schools and apprenticeship programs. All children in the GDR go to the same ten-year polytechnical schools; West German children are segregated early into academic or vocational schools, and most workers' children get the latter. East German workers who decide later to go to a university or technical college are welcome.

These educational opportunities along with the fact that there have been many vacant managerial positions in the GDR have produced great social mobility. Nazi officials, teachers, and managers were fired after the war, and new, reliable people were needed quickly to fill these jobs. Later, before the Wall went up in 1961, many highly trained people departed for the West. Again there were more job openings, especially for young people.[10] This has produced two attitudes among the new, young elite: (1) gratitude toward and appreciation of

[10] West German sociologist (and later Common Market official) Ralf Dahrendorf holds that the replacement of the old elite in the GDR was so thorough that the country has become "the first modern society on German soil." *Society and Democracy in Germany* (Garden City, N.Y.: Anchor Books), p. 401.

the regime that made promotions possible; and (2) opportunism. These two attitudes are not necessarily antithetical; they can exist side by side in the same person, the first fostering loyalty to the regime, the second making that loyalty shallow and superficial.

As in Yugoslavia, there is a great deal of opportunism among party members in the GDR. This is to be expected: When a single party has a near-monopoly on the society's better positions, many people will mouth the party line without real dedication in order to serve themselves. Jean Edward Smith asked two young East German engineers why they had joined the party. They replied, "To get ahead, naturally, like most other people our age. There are a few 'two-hundred percenters,' but not many."[11]

In East Germany, as in Yugoslavia, the regime operates under the fiction that all citizens are politically aware and interested in participating in political activities. Elections, which secure over 99.7 percent of the vote for the single National Front slate, are practically compulsory; if a citizen fails to get his or her name checked off at the polling station, a mobile poll calls on him or her to vote that evening at home, on the assumption that the citizen "forgot" to vote earlier. In a similar fashion, East Germans are deluged with messages via the mass media, billboards, and meetings to "plan with us, work with us, govern with us."

THE TELEVISION PROBLEM

East Germany has a unique problem among the countries of East Europe in establishing a distinctive political culture and sense of legitimacy among its citizens. West German television, in part thanks to the location of West Berlin 110 miles inside the GDR, can be picked up by some 80 percent of East Germans. We cannot be certain how many East Germans actually do watch West German television, but the SED authorities gave up trying to prevent people from watching it. New party chief Erich Honecker decreed that East Germans can tune in to whatever they want, provided they do not spread the news and views to others. The message from West German television, however, is mixed. It shows that West Germans enjoy a higher standard of living, more and better products, and political democracy, but it also reveals the prevalence of crime, violence, crass commercialism, and economic ups and downs.

Television in the FRG is good, drawing from the best of West European networks through Eurovision. It thus affords East Germans a welcome respite from the bleak cultural life of their own country, which one GDR playwright called "the dullest society on earth." Western pop music, blue jeans, and a rebellious lifestyle can easily infect East German youth, and the regime has had some problems in this regard. East German political socialization has not been

---

[11] Smith, *Germany Beyond the Wall*, p. 44.

uniformly successful. Although practically all youngsters belong to the Young Pioneers from ages six to fourteen and the Free German Youth (FDJ) from fourteen to twenty-six, the youthful enthusiasm thus inculcated does not always stay with them into adulthood. Perhaps their most widespread desire is to travel in Western Europe, but permission is rarely granted. If the regime has an escape valve for youthful restlessness, it is sports. The GDR is sports-mad, and with official encouragement and financial support. This paid off in the 1976 Olympics where little East Germany came in second in gold medals won, beaten only by the Soviet Union.

The East Germans' muted enthusiasm toward their political system does not mean they are disloyal. On the contrary, a West German researcher found in several hundred personal interviews over the 1960s that they were growing increasingly loyal to the regime. We have to take surveys in authoritarian countries with a grain of salt—their citizens often say what they think the regime wants to hear—but nonetheless the changes in East German attitudes found by Hans Apel and shown in Table 6–2 are interesting.

Table 6–2   East Germans' Loyalty

	1962	1964	1966
Loyal	37%	51%	71%
Opponent	28	23	14
Ambivalent/"Goes Along"	35	26	15

Source: Hans Apel, "Bericht ueber das 'Staatsgefuehl' der DDR-Bevoelkerung," Frankfurter Hefte, 22, no. 3 (March 1967) as cited in Arthur M. Hanhardt, Jr., The German Democratic Republic (Baltimore: Johns Hopkins Press, 1968), p. 124.

We cannot be certain what East German attitudes would be like if the Wall came down, but the system seems to have at least the general support of a majority of its citizens.

PATTERNS
OF
INTERACTION

THE MONOLITHIC IMAGE

The image of Communist states as monolithic has proven to be a serious oversimplification, more related to now-outmoded theories of "totalitarianism" than to complex realities. In part, the image of a regime in total agreement and without factions or internal conflicts comes from the East European states themselves: They seldom publicize inner-party disagreements.

East Germany is a semiclosed society. Its officials do not openly discuss their problems in front of Westerners. Some sophisticated outside observers, chiefly West German, however, have discerned patterns of interaction that we may group into three main categories: interactions between (1) the party and the populace; (2) technocrats and dogmatists within the party; and (3) nationalists and integrationists with regard to the GDR's position in the Soviet bloc.

THE PARTY AND THE PEOPLE

The relationship of the SED to the population of East Germany can be described as an exercise in confidence building. The party tries to win the confidence of the masses, with greater and lesser success over the years. The ideology of Marxism-Leninism has not contributed a great deal; most East Germans ignore it. The Berlin Wall contributed in a purely negative fashion; that is, it removed the possibility of leaving. The SED has won a certain amount of respect, however, by planning and implementing programs that promoted economic growth and higher standards of living. Political scientist Thomas Baylis calls this respect for results "performance-based legitimacy."[12] A system that delivers the goods is respected, and people work harder for it.

The SED was not in a position to deliver a respect-winning performance during the 1950s, though. Too many able people were leaving for West Germany before the Wall went up in 1961. In 1963 the party introduced a New Economic System (NES), partly on cue from the Soviet debate on economic reforms triggered by the 1962 Pravda article by economist E. G. Liberman. The interesting point here is that "Libermanism" was never fully adopted in the Soviet Union; only some half-hearted measures were introduced, and those in 1965, long after the East Germans had installed their NES.

The East German pupils outdid their Soviet teachers in speed, thoroughness, and success in implementing economic reforms. Basically the NES, as Liberman suggested, brought in certain aspects of the Western market economy such as profitability, cost accounting, bank control of investment loans, product marketability, and even a certain amount of decentralized decision making. It was not a wholesale importation of capitalism but merely sought to borrow some of capitalism's more effective mechanisms while holding the economy under overall "social" control.

The chief innovation of the 1963 reforms was the Association of State-Owned Enterprises (*Vereinigung Volkseigener Betriebe,* or VVB). These are some 110 legally and economically independent trusts, rather like large American corporations, which group together all the enterprises of the same sector of the economy. Each VVB is assigned its role in the national plan but basically has

---

[12] Thomas A. Baylis, "In Quest of Legitimacy," *Problems of Communism,* March-April 1972, p. 49.

to produce the quantity and quality of goods the market wants. Profits rather than sheer numerical output are the indicators of success. The VVB must generate much of its own capital for expansion from the profits of its member enterprises. Individual firms (*Volkseigene Betriebe*, or VEB) reward their workers and management with bonuses based on profits.[13] The reforms did not go nearly so far as Yugoslavia's radical decentralization and return to a market economy, which East German ideologists continue to view with suspicion. The economic results of the East German reforms, though, were rather good (see next section). But in winning the population's respect through a more productive and efficient economy, the SED created new political problems for itself within party ranks.

TECHNOCRATS VERSUS DOGMATISTS

The kinds of people needed to run East Germany's New Economic System were a breed apart from the Stalinist hacks who had previously commanded the GDR's economy. The new people were young, bright, university-educated (mostly in engineering and economics), and dedicated to economic progress rather than doctrinal purity. They have been called "technocrats," connoting their emphasis on technology rather than ideology. Their opponents, generally older, trained during the party's Stalinist period to emphasize political obedience, have been called "dogmatists." This division, of course, is somewhat artificial; there are young dogmatists, old technocrats, and various mixtures in between. But in general terms, the disagreements of these two types characterize virtually all systems dominated by Communist parties.

Peter Ludz, a West German political scientist specializing in the GDR, cautions that the opposition of these two groups is not a clash of liberalism or "humanistic socialism" (such as that propounded in 1968 by Czechoslovak party chief Alexander Dubcek) against Stalinist conservatism but rather "between pragmatic neoconservatism and the dogmatic conservatism of the SED veterans."[14] Both groups want the same thing, the building of socialism under party control, but differ with regard to style.

The technocrats have made some interesting additions to Marxist-Leninist thinking. Pushing traditional concepts like "class consciousness" and "proletarianism" to the rear, some younger East German writers emphasize such modern ideas as economic rationality, operations research, and cybernetics. In their view, anything that builds the material basis of socialism faster must be the correct Marxist thing to do. Marx never specified exactly how society would be

[13] For a complete description of the NES, see Martin Schnitzer, *East and West Germany: A Comparative Economic Analysis* (New York: Praeger, 1972), pp. 221–32.

[14] Peter C. Ludz, *The Changing Party Elite in East Germany* (Cambridge, Mass.: MIT Press, 1972), p. 149.

run after the revolution, but both Marx and Lenin placed great emphasis on technology to lift man into a golden age. The dogmatists fear that this stress on technology and expertise will both erode their personal power and bring in Western economic ideas. The technocrats do not want to overturn the GDR's system but merely to rationalize it.

During the 1960s, Ulbricht seemed to be promoting more of the technocrats to higher positions, particularly to the SED's Central Committee. With Ulbricht's semiretirement in 1971—he gave up his party chieftainship but retained his chairmanship of the Staatsrat—and Erich Honecker's takeover of the top party job, this tendency was reduced. According to Ludz, Honecker preferred to appoint "younger party functionaries (generally in their forties) whose careers have reflected a combination of political pragmatism, ideological activism and organizational capabilities, as opposed to the equally pragmatic but nonideologically oriented technocrats whom Ulbricht tended to lean on in the last years of his leadership."[15]

This covert contest between technocrats and dogmatists—never openly acknowledged, for factions are not allowed in any Communist party—will probably never be settled definitively. The demands of economic growth call for increased reliance on experts and technocrats, but the continued existence of the GDR as a socialist state on the Soviet pattern requires dogmatic ideologues to keep a careful check on political deviation. The two types, technocrats and dogmatists, are not antithetical but complementary to a certain degree; they need each other. Chances are they will coexist in the SED with the top leadership roles going to those who do not belong fully to either camp but can use the skills of both.

NATIONALISM VS. INTEGRATION

The GDR would not exist without the Soviet Union, but that did not prevent the tail from trying to wag the dog. Paradoxically Ulbricht, the devout worshiper of Stalin and faithful Soviet agent, gradually was turning into something of an East German nationalist. The process, to be sure, never was completed; the Soviets nipped it in the bud. The GDR is again firmly committed to full integration into the Eastern bloc, under Moscow's leadership. But the fact that it happened once indicates the behind-the-scenes tension and incipient nationalism that infect all of the East European countries.

There is a built-in contradiction between the existence of East European countries as separate states and their tight integration into the Soviet bloc. National interests, economic efficiency, the personal power of party leaders, and just plain tradition tug in the direction of nationalism. The training of many top

[15] Peter C. Ludz, "Continuity and Change Since Ulbricht," *Problems of Communism*, March–April 1972, p. 65.

party leaders in Moscow, their fear of a popular uprising against communism, the economic ties of COMECON, and the presence of several divisions of the Soviet army tug in the direction of integration. There have been only two clear triumphs of nationalism out of this process in Eastern Europe: that of Yugoslavia in 1948 and Albania in 1961. The other satellite states have stayed within the bounds of the balancing act just described, some years a little more nationalistic, other years a little more integrationist.

East Germany's flirtation with nationalism grew out of its 1963 economic reforms and their subsequent successes. During the late 1960s Ulbricht was so proud of the GDR's progress that he went around touting it to other Communist leaders as a model they should imitate, especially after the crushing of Dubcek's revisionism. Ulbricht's national pride surely irritated Moscow, for, as Peter Ludz put it, "he was projecting himself as a potential rival of Moscow."[16] Memories of arrogant Germans are still vivid in East Europe, and few party leaders welcomed Ulbricht's unsolicited advice.

The most dramatic example of East German economic nationalism was the 1965 suicide of Erich Apel, one of the GDR's top economic planners and drafter of the New Economic System. Apel had also pressed for trade policies that would make East Germany less dependent on the Soviet Union. Faced with a new Soviet-GDR trade pact that was unfavorable to the GDR, Apel committed suicide just a few hours before it was signed. Officially the death was attributed to "overwork," but it is widely believed that Apel was despondent over the pact's terms. The incident illustrates that economic growth can be a highly nationalistic thing in Eastern Europe (as it has been in Romania), tending to pull the country away from integration with the Soviet economy.

More serious disagreement arose in late 1969 over a very touchy question, East Germany's international status. In 1969 Willy Brandt became chancellor in Bonn and began a policy of improving and normalizing relations with East Europe, his famous *Ostpolitik*. Brandt offered Moscow something it had long demanded: West German recognition of the present boundaries of European countries and admission that former German territories taken over by the Soviet Union and Poland were gone for good. This recognition was formalized in the Moscow Treaty of August 12, 1970, which some observers peg as the beginning of the end of the Cold War. Ulbricht was not completely happy to have Bonn and Moscow holding discussions over his head, and the next topic they took up really bothered him: Berlin. Ulbricht had long demanded an end to West Berlin's ties to the Federal Republic. He would have preferred, naturally, absorbing West Berlin and its 2.2 million inhabitants right into the GDR, but he was willing to settle for a "free and demilitarized" independent city. A reaffirmation of West Berlin's ties with the Federal Republic was a nonnegotiable minimum for the Western powers and the Soviets wanted a Berlin agreement to promote détente.

---

[16] Ludz, "Continuity and Change Since Ulbricht," p. 57.

Something had to give, and it was Ulbricht. The loyal Stalinist who had inadvertently grown into a nationalist "resigned" in May 1971 and the four-power Berlin agreement was signed in September. Ulbricht had become too inflexible, too trapped in the past for the Soviets, who undoubtedly played a major role in his ouster.

Once Berlin was more or less settled—and the Berlin problem will never finally be settled so long as it is an island inside another country—the two Germanies, with Soviet blessing, proceeded with negotiations that led to their mutual recognition of each other and their admission as separate countries to the United Nations in 1973. Ulbricht had insisted that negotiations between the two Germanies not start until Bonn granted the GDR full diplomatic recognition. He was ignored. Ulbricht's successors returned to strict adherence to Moscow's guidance, and the GDR stopped touting itself as a model other socialist states should copy. But the fact remains, as we shall consider next, that East Germany *is* more successful than the Soviet system. That, plus the long-time Soviet propensity to put its international interests ahead of those of junior partners, suggests that differences between Moscow and East Berlin may again arise.

**WHAT THE
EAST GERMAN
SYSTEM
PRODUCES**

OSTWUNDER

There are two German economic miracles, one Eastern and one Western. The GDR's economic growth in the 1960s slightly edged that of the FRG. From 1963 to 1970, East Germany's economy expanded by an average of 5.2 percent a year, West Germany's by 5 percent. The GDR, to be sure, started from a lower level and had further to go, factors that make impressive percentage gains easier to show. Nonetheless, East Germany's growth has been impressive, and it now ranks as the world's ninth industrial power.

The interesting thing about comparing East and West German growth rates are the rises and falls of the latter in contrast to the almost unchanging rate of the former. The East German economy, tied by barter deals into the East European COMECON and centrally planned, does not experience the wild swings of most Western countries. It has not soared as high, but neither has it fallen so low. Many GDR citizens appreciate this stable growth.

The GDR's economy is, furthermore, relatively immune from the twin plagues of Western economies: oscillating commodity prices and inflation. The GDR has a rather secure petroleum source in the Soviet Union that delivers oil by direct pipeline. Although the Soviets doubled the price of their oil in 1975, from about $3 to $6 a barrel, this was still only half the world market price. Set by long-term agreements rather than by fluctuating market prices, East Germany can count on many of its raw materials at relatively fixed prices.

Since domestic prices are set in Berlin and change only under official scrutiny, prices in the GDR have inflated little or not at all since the early 1960s, a fact the regime is extremely proud of. On balance, East Germans do not live as well as West Germans. They earn only about two-thirds what West Germans do and pay considerably more for most consumer items. There is a severe housing shortage in the GDR. But citizens of the GDR are relatively insulated from economic ups and downs. The GDR suffers neither from inflation nor unemployment (indeed, there is a severe labor shortage). This economic security fosters considerable support for the system. Many East Germans say they prefer the security of the GDR's economy to the more hectic, competitive pace of West Germany.

East Germans, like all Germans, work hard, but in a socialist economy the element of cutthroat competition is missing. This may deprive East German products and services of the meticulous quality associated with West Germany. But compared to its East European neighbors, the GDR economy produces both more and better. In agriculture, for example, since collectivization was completed in 1960 (by harangue, not terror), the East German *Landwirtschaftlichen Produktionsgenossenschaften* (Agricultural Production Associations, or LPGs) have consistently outperformed their Soviet counterparts, the *kolkhoze*, as well as those of any other East European country. The LPGs produce five times as much wheat per acre as Soviet farms, three times as much barley, and four times as much oats. Indeed, East German per acre yields have matched those of France, Italy and West Germany.[17]

The long-standing East German goal, however, has been to make itself into the technical workshop of the Eastern bloc, a goal it has in considerable measure already achieved. The GDR is the Soviet Union's most important trading partner. East Germany supplies the Soviet Union with chemicals, machinery, and precision instruments and gets raw materials in return. Short on raw materials but with a skilled work force, the GDR has no reasonable alternative. Accordingly, East Germany has made technology into a religion. The country's flag does not show the Soviet hammer and sickle but rather a hammer and machinist's calipers. This strong technological orientation shows up clearly in the GDR's educational system.

EDUCATION WITH AN AIM

Learning is not an abstract thing in the GDR. The great philosophical debate is officially closed there; Marxism-Leninism answers most of man's age-old questions. Further study in history, philosophy, political science, and so on is

[17] Jean Edward Smith, *Germany Beyond the Wall*, pp. 120–21.

therefore not much needed. Instead, secondary and college students are steered toward technical careers. As mentioned earlier, all students in the GDR get the same ten-year polytechnical training, leading either to the production line or to a university.

Some comparisions with West Germany are instructive. Both East and West Germany have highly developed apprenticeship programs, a German tradition. But the East Germans put the largest portion of their apprentices into industry, while the West Germans send more of their apprentices into commerce. Thirty-eight percent more East Germans than West go to vocational schools. East Germany also sends proportionally more of its people to college. Twelve percent of the GDR's population were college graduates in 1970, compared to about 9 percent in the FRG. What they study, shown in Table 6–3, is interesting.

Table 6–3   German Students, East and West

	West Germany	East Germany
Mathematics, Science	11.4%	8.3%
Engineering, Architecture	9.8	26.1
Medicine, Agronomy	14.1	16.6
Economics	10.4	12.7
Philosophy, History, Law	11.6	4.2
Music, Religion, Physical Education	3.6	2.2
Languages	4.3	0.9
Art	2.4	1.6
Education	32.4	27.5

Source: Federal Republic of Germany, Bericht der Bundesregierung und Materialien zur Lage der Nation 1971 (Bonn: Bundesministerium fuer innerdeutsche Beziehugen, 1971), pp. 404–5.

East Germany, with just 28 percent of West Germany's population, turns out almost as many engineers each year.

One serious West German problem is missing in the GDR: student unrest. There are two reasons for this. In the first place, East Germany as a whole is more tightly controlled; open opposition is penalized. Most students must be members of the FDJ, which although it encourages opportunism, insures control. In the second place, the East German university structure is much more modern than the medieval West German one. Curiously, East German universities are organized more on the American pattern, with several professors to a department, rather than in the traditional German style, with one lord-like professor dominating completely "his" institute. As noted previously, universities in the GDR draw from all social classes; West German universities tend to exclude children of the working class. Higher education in the FRG, class-biased, archaic, and reluctant to change, remains the Achilles' heel of the West German system. The GDR does not have such a problem.

If the GDR has a problem in higher education it is in its extreme emphasis on practicality. Universities are designed to have an immediate rather than just a long-term payoff. Some university departments are contractually tied in with VVBs to do research. Curricula and research, Peter Ludz points out, are therefore increasingly applied rather than basic, aimed at today's needs rather than tomorrow's. In time, Ludz believes, this approach could limit East Germany's technological and economic growth.[18]

CONTROL WITHOUT TERROR

Estimates of the victims of Stalin's terror in the Soviet Union vary, but all agree that they run into the millions. An appreciable fraction of the Soviet population was either killed or imprisoned by the regime. Terror has been called the linchpin of the Soviet system. This cannot be said of the GDR. There are several reasons why.

Most obvious is that the Soviet occupiers and later the SED regime took over a system that was already tightly controlled (by the Nazis) and kept it that way. The new authorities did not have to impose control on a population unused to it. Traditionally, police and strict courts are accepted by Germans without hostility. Further, until 1961, potentially antiregime elements could leave the GDR via the Berlin escape hatch. For the same reason, too-tough "administrative measures" could have stampeded skilled people to the West; the regime was thus constrained from a major terror campaign. By the time West Berlin was sealed off, the regime had long imposed a structure of opportunities that was able to involve most of the remaining population. Germans are hard-working and ambitious; presented with an opportunity to advance themselves they seldom decline. Opportunism, not terror, is the cement of the East German system; the former is ever so much more efficient and cheaper than the latter.

As a result, there have been practically no Stalin-style roundups and purges in the GDR. In 1953, in the wake of the June riots, seven persons were executed and about one thousand imprisoned for an average of four years each. Considering that the uprising had been a serious threat to the regime, government reaction was mild compared to what has gone on in other East European countries. On the more intellectual level, those who disagree with the party line are usually just kicked out of the SED. In 1957 Dr. Wolfgang Harich, a brilliant university professor and SED member, was sentenced to ten years in prison for

---

[18] Peter Christian Ludz, *The German Democratic Republic from the Sixties to the Seventies* (Cambridge, Mass.: Harvard University Center for International Affairs, 1970), pp. 15–17.

allegedly plotting the overthrow of the regime. Actually Harich had simply been a Marxist revisionist, urging party democratization, ideological loosening, and Yugoslav-style workers' councils to run factories. In 1964, Professor Robert Havemann, a well-known scientist and SED member who had been imprisoned by the Nazis, was expelled from the party and his teaching job for advocating greater intellectual freedom in the GDR.

The arts are controlled, not by putting offending artists and writers behind bars but by denying them audiences. For example, balladeer Wolf Biermann, a committed Marxist, left West Germany for the GDR only to become a sharp critic of the regime in his songs. Biermann was expelled from the SED and is not allowed to sing in public or publish his songs. Still, he lives in East Berlin on income from his old records sold in the FRG; the police don't bother him and he has a lively circle of friends. No Siberia, no psychiatric hospital, and no exile.

As in the Soviet Union, writers are prohibited from publishing their works abroad without approval. Still, novelist Stefan Heym, who spent the war years in the United States, had three novels published "illegally" in West Germany without punishment. Then later, in 1973, he was notified that the three books would be published in East Germany; they had previously been rejected. In sum, cultural life of the GDR is more restrictive than in Yugoslavia, but not nearly so much as in the Soviet Union.

The GDR is emphatically not a free society in our sense of the word. People, their movements, their jobs, and their leisure activities are all carefully controlled. When relations between the two Germanies were normalized in 1973 and visits by West Germans greatly increased, party and government officials were forbidden to have contact with them—a security concern. Foreign visitors to the GDR report that East Germans invited to hotel rooms are quite nervous about possible listening devices. Foreigners cannot casually tour the GDR but must sign up and pay for a set itinerary in advance.

The most authoritarian aspects of the GDR, however, fall on those East Germans who want to leave. Travel to the West is rare; usually only trusted party people can go on business, leaving their families behind. Those who find the system intolerable can do practically nothing. The border with West Germany is heavily mined and patrolled; the Berlin Wall has been perfected until it is virtually unbreachable with anything less than a tank. The latest "improvement"—ungrabable twenty-inch pipes fixed along the top of the Wall—is much more effective than the old barbed wire. East Germans must stay and build socialism, whether they want to or not.

CAN THE GDR STAND?

Since the Wall in 1961 and the economic reforms of 1963, East Germany has been rather successful for a socialist or Communist system. The question is, can it endure more or less permanently or is it merely the result of a temporary constellation of forces that, when dissipated, will lead to the dissolution of the GDR and its absorption by the larger, more populous, and richer Federal Republic of Germany? The latter was for many years the West German view, shared by the United States. The East German official view once was that the GDR would not only survive and thrive but eventually serve as the nucleus for a reunified socialist Germany. Both Germanies, in other words, had a "magnet theory": our system will be so successful that it will eventually attract the other into it.

Until the Wall went up in 1961, it seemed that the West German version of the magnet theory was more accurate. Gradually both Germanies gave up their respective magnet theories; East Germany especially adopted the much more defensive view that it can survive quite nicely if only the Bonn revanchists would leave "our republic" alone. From the point of view of the GDR's leaders, the greatest threat to East Germany's independent survival is posed by détente. If fully successful, a relaxation of tensions between the great powers could undermine the very basis of the GDR's existence: the division of Germany and the Cold War that keeps 533,000 Soviet troops in East Germany. Thus it is not surprising that East Berlin has been far more reluctant than Moscow about easing tensions in Europe. As we saw, Ulbricht's foot dragging on improving relations with the West annoyed Moscow. Although Ulbricht was dumped, we can assume that his successors face the same dilemma: if Soviet relations with the West get too good, it could mean less Soviet support for East Germany. For example, if Mutual and Balanced Force Reduction (MBFR) really took place in Europe, the departure of American troops would not trouble the internal stability of West Germany, but the same thing might not be true if Soviet divisions decamped from East Germany. What the SED regime wants is time. If the situation can be held about as it is for another couple of decades, they reason, then the GDR's socialist system may be sufficiently rooted to withstand the West German "magnet."

A further illustration of the GDR's defensive attitude is the way it has treated contacts between its SED and West Germany's SPD. In the late 1960s such contacts were encouraged; the SED leadership assumed that they would win converts from a dialogue. When that failed to happen—indeed, when the SPD discussants were making more headway—the SED dropped its interest in a dialogue with the SPD and went back to denouncing the Social Democrats as nonsocialist betrayers of the working class. The SED entertains no hope for further contact with the SPD until it sees the light and becomes a truly socialist party, for example, by nationalizing West German industry.

This pulling away is part of East Germany's *Abgrenzungpolitik*, and it is the logical response to West German Ostpolitik. While Ostpolitik aimed at drawing the GDR out of its shell, Abgrenzung aimed at keeping it in. Ostpolitik was an attempt at seduction; Abgrenzung is a defense of chastity.

Why are the East German authorities so worried? The GDR is the leading system of East Europe. Growth rates are impressive, and the standard of living is slowly creeping up toward West European levels. Citizens of the GDR are not wildly enthusiastic about their system, but neither are they conspicuously disloyal. What then has the SED leadership to fear?

What they have to fear is this: no one knows how deep East German loyalty to the system really goes. A major opening up of East Germany could undo all that the Wall has done. Since 1961 East Germans have felt resigned and have tried to make a go of their situation. But given a different situation, how might they react? GDR authorities are intent on keeping the Wall up.

Public opinion surveys are carried out by a party agency in East Germany, but they are kept secret. Still, in 1970 an indication of East German popular orientation emerged dramatically. West German Chancellor Willy Brandt visited Erfurt in the GDR as part of an exchange to discuss improving relations. His reception in Erfurt was not merely cordial, it was tumultuous, delirious. East German police struggled to hold back a wildly cheering crowd. One had the feeling that if Brandt had given the order, he could have instigated an uprising on the spot. The lesson was not lost on East German authorities; Brandt was not invited back. The image of the Erfurt crowds must haunt the nightmares of the GDR leadership: They have reason to be defensive.

TO COMPARE AND TO CONTRAST

7

| | When faced with a mass of complex data, one hoary |

THE
THREE
EUROPES

When faced with a mass of complex data, one hoary trick of social scientists is to divide the material into three. Just as writers have found three kinds of political parties, three kinds of conservatism, three kinds of inflation, three kinds of anything, so we can discern three patterns of European politics. Although such a simplification will have to be hedged with exceptions and overlaps, it does make the complex manageable and is thus a useful teaching device. As we mentioned in the Introduction, contemporary Europe can be grouped into three patterns: the Northern, the Latin, and the Eastern. Let us now consider these patterns.

NORTHERN EUROPE

This pattern includes Britain, Sweden, and West Germany, and not only because they are all situated in Northern Europe. The three countries have more in common than geography and linguistics. In them the difficult task of the establishment of legitimacy is passed—long ago in Britain and Sweden, recently in West Germany. Government is firmly established, laws are generally obeyed (one exception: the gunmen of Northern Ireland), and the system is widely accepted, although we might wish to put a little question mark by West Germany on this item.

The key question for these three countries, the one that with various nuances dominates their political life, is, How much welfare? All three countries have highly developed welfare programs. Germany's is the oldest, going back to the last century; Sweden's is the most thorough; and Britain's is the newest, having blossomed only after World War II. All three have had Social Democratic regimes for varying lengths of time, and these regimes and their programs present the electorate with a fairly clear choice between more welfare programs and higher taxes to fund them or a leveling off or even rollback of welfare programs and high taxes. The three societies split about evenly on this question, about half the vote going to the Social Democratic or Labor parties and the other half going to the conservative opposition. Shifts of a few percentage points in elections steer the system first to a little more welfare, then to a little less or to holding steady.

Are there not other issues in these societies? Yes, but they tend to take second place to this welfare question. Region, religion, nationalism, and urban-rural cleavages play only residual roles, siphoning off votes to parties representing these interests, but seldom do these parties have great electoral strength or a major voice in government.[1] They are not "antisystem" parties.

Consider, for example, how a once-important issue in West German politics has shrunk into a residual issue. During the 1950s the division of Germany and the loss of eastern territories to Poland and the Soviet Union was a hot topic in West German politics. Refugees and expellees even formed their own political party in the Federal Republic and won seats in the Bundestag from 1953 to 1957. Since then they have been swallowed up by the Christian Democrats. The children of the refugees care little about their ancestral homelands and have been integrated into the Federal Republic. Willy Brandt's treaties of the early 1970s with the Soviet Union, Poland, and East Germany, confirming the postwar boundaries and renouncing any future claims, put an end to this question in West German politics.

Regional questions have also largely subsided in Northern European politics, although we must qualify this statement in regard to Britain, where Scottish nationalism has reappeared just in the last decade. With the discovery of major oil reserves in the North Sea off the coast of Scotland, a small movement has grown into a serious one. In 1964 the Scottish National Party won 2 percent of the Scottish vote, but in October 1974 it took 30 percent of the Scottish vote and eleven seats in the House of Commons. A 1975 poll showed 22 percent of Scots favored independence for Scotland, and 29 percent endorsed a federal relationship with England.[2] British political scientist Richard Rose believes the new Scottish nationalism is more economic than sentimental: Scots simply want to keep the oil revenues at home and not share them with the English.

The resurgence of Scottish nationalism underscores the point that no political system, no matter how well-integrated it was thought to be, is immune

---

[1] See Richard Rose, "Class and Party Divisions: Britain as Test Case," in *European Politics: A Reader*, ed. Mattei Dogan and Richard Rose (Boston: Little, Brown, 1971), pp. 167–71. Rose demonstrates that the British working class is little distracted by questions of religion, nationality, urban-rural splits, region, or race. The author freely acknowledges his debt to Rose's germinal article.

[2] Richard Rose, "Oil Based Scottish Nationalism," *The New Republic*, September 20, 1975, pp. 18–19.

to corrosive forces. Even more serious in the case of Britain is the question of Northern Ireland, the last remnant of the great question of nineteenth-century British politics. Britain is clearly the weak sister in the Northern European pattern in regard to regional problems. Sweden and West Germany have few such problems.

Now, those familiar with European voting patterns may object that region still plays a considerable role in elections. Certain districts of Great Britain, for example, are either durably Labor or Conservative in their long-term voting habits. Much of the Communist vote in Sweden is in the far North where seasonal unemployment in timbering tends to radicalize workers. The Christian Social Union holds sway in Bavaria rather than the CDU; Bavaria is sometimes described as the Texas of West Germany and takes pride in regional differences.

But in comparative perspective, how serious are these regional differences? Where can one find the equivalent of Basque separatist terrorists in Northern Europe? Aside from Ulster, nowhere. Region may influence votes in Northern Europe, but it is seldom as important as in Southern Europe where, for example, Spain and Yugoslavia have serious separatist problems. Bavarians may vote CSU, but none contemplates seceding from West Germany.

Religion may be seen in the same light in our Northern European pattern. It does influence voting, especially in West Germany, but seldom does it represent a clericalist frame of mind as in Latin Europe. We might compare German and Italian Christian Democrats in this regard. The West German CDU is a catchall party of the Center and Right without close ties to any church. Indeed, since the CDU attempts to lure Protestants it cannot have close ties to the Catholic Church. One could almost strike off "Christian" from the name Christian Democratic Union for an accurate description of CDU ideology. Now consider Italian Christian Democracy: a child of Catholic Action, strongly connected to the Vatican, supportive of Catholic causes and, rhetorically at least, striving for Catholic ideals in politics. The Italian DC is also a catchall party, but one that emphasizes "Christian" more than "Democracy."

In terms of political culture, our Northern European examples are on the integrated side of a fragmentation-integration continuum. Legitimacy is particularly high in Sweden and Britain (again excepting Ulster) and has been growing in West Germany since its shaky beginnings after World War II. Swedes and Britons are proud of their political institutions and such pride is also growing in the Federal Republic. Feelings of trust toward others and toward institutions predominate in the Northern European pattern. Feelings of "political efficacy," the ability to influence politics, are also rather high; there is little alienation from the system. The political culture of Latin Europe tends toward low feelings of legitimacy and efficacy, high mistrust, and much alienation.

In sum, while region, religion, nationalism, and other factors help structure the vote in our Northern European pattern, seldom do these factors dominate politics. Instead, elections largely—but never exclusively—turn on pocketbook issues with a good portion of the working class voting Left and much of the middle and upper classes voting Right. This question of class voting brings us to perhaps the most important distinguishing characteristic of Northern European systems, their tendency to be Social Democratic.

The Primacy of Labor   In the middle 1970s all three of our Northern European systems had Social Democratic (or Labor) governments; of our three Latin European systems none had. While the British Laborites and Swedish and West German Social Democrats could easily be ousted in the next election, their strength stands in marked contrast to the situation in Latin European societies.

A basic requisite of the Northern European pattern is a large, unified labor movement that encompasses the lion's share of the blue-collar workers and supports the Social Democrats. The best example is Sweden where the LO speaks for over nine-tenths of wage earners and is closely connected to the Social Democratic party. In Britain, the large Trade Union Congress (TUC) is a constituent member of the Labor party. The West German *Deutscher Gewerkschaftsbund* (DGB), although not officially bound to the SPD, generally supports it at election time.

This union-party linkup structures the political debate for the society at large. The Social Democratic party proposes a series of welfare measures, which the labor movement generally endorses. The conservative parties oppose these measures as too expensive, inefficient, limiting of private initiative, giving slackers a free ride, increasing bureaucracy, and so on, and they are supported by most of the middle and upper classes. The Social Democrats do not always or immediately triumph; their path is a zig-zag one, sometimes in power and sometimes out, sometimes militant but more often moderate. Their successes come piecemeal but once accomplished are seldom erased by a subsequent conservative victory at the polls, for the conservatives, whether they know it or not, are caught up in a largely social democratic game. The Social Democrats propose; the conservatives oppose. Indeed, the conservative political programs are little more than reactions to challenges thrown down by the Social Democrats. The conservatives are seldom *for* anything in particular; they are simply *against* the welfare and reform measures introduced by the Social Democrats. But once in power the conservatives largely continue to run the welfare programs, sometimes boasting that Tories run them better than Labor. The conservatives simply refrain from introducing new welfare programs. Thus, whether the Social Democrats are in power or out, they are the ones who establish the basic parameters of political controversy.

Represented by France, Italy, and Spain, Latin Europe still has many of the problems our Northern systems have largely overcome. In Latin European systems legitimacy is still not fully established; large sectors of the population doubt that the regime has the right to rule. Political upheavals occur periodically, and regimes tend to be personal creations (e.g., those of Mussolini, Franco, and de Gaulle) that often end with the demise of their creator. Welfare is not yet the leading issue in Latin Europe; many other problems push it to the rear. If there is one question we could use to characterize the complexity of Latin European societies it might be, "Should this system exist?" The conservatives who dominate most Latin European systems say yes and the leftist opposition says no, the entire system should be radically restructured.

Taking a cue from Spain, we may discern not only Two Spains but Two Frances and Two Italies as well. Roughly half of each country is Catholic, conservative, and favors strong executive leadership; the other half is anticlerical, liberal or radical, and favors a strong parliament.

Spain is the most extreme example of this pattern. France is rapidly becoming so modern that it may eventually leave the ranks of the Latin European countries and join the Northern European pattern; but France too has a long way to go. Italy occupies a middle ground and is a better example than France of the Latin pattern in transition.

The most obvious cleavage—indeed, one that can serve as a shorthand expression of all the divisions—is between pro-Church and anticlerical elements. A good deal more than religion is involved. Tied up with anticlericalism is the issue of making the state a purely secular institution with few ties to and no guidance from the Roman Catholic Church. The pro-Church elements are mostly conservative in economic, social, and political orientations. From the ranks of the anticlerical elements the parties of the Left (Communist, Socialist, Social Democrat) draw their supporters.

In France, much of the worst of the clerical-anticlerical split has been overcome, but the issue still simmers below the surface in the continuing question of state aid to Catholic schools. In 1974, after a prolonged campaign that included confessions of illegal abortion by some of France's best-known women, abortion became legal in France. The conservative, pro-Church forces fought it and lost, a measure of the relative strength of the clerical element in today's France. Civil marriage and divorce have been long established in France. In effect, the French anticlericals have won.

In Italy, on the other hand, the clerical-anticlerical dispute is still extremely lively. The battle for divorce was fought and won only in 1974 with the divorce referendum. It is interesting that the same year France was legalizing abortion, Italy was just getting around to legalizing divorce, again a measure of the relative strength of clerical forces in the two countries. A campaign in favor of legal abortion was mounting in Italy at the same time, and one can foresee Italy soon going the way of France. Italy's largest party, the Christian Democrats, has strong ties with the Church, and this in itself has become a factor in Italian political disputes. The French Gaullists have no such close relationship with the Catholic Church. The Italian anticlericals have not yet quite established themselves as the dominant force in Italian politics, but they seem to be winning.

Spain can be seen as the most retrograde example of this pattern. As in France, the clerical-anticlerical split simmers below the surface, but in Spain the pro-Church forces won, at least under Franco. France legalizes abortion and Italy divorce while Spain stands pat. If Spain continues to modernize, however, we may expect that first the issue of divorce and then that of abortion will make their way into the Spanish political arena in future decades. In Northern Europe both issues have generally been settled on the secular side, except in West Germany where a 1974 abortion law was overturned by the Constitutional Court.

Other issues besides the political position of the Church wrack our Latin European polities. Regionalism is still alive, ranging in seriousness from romantic demands for the restoration of the Bretagne and Occitanian languages to cries for Basque independence. Several persons were killed on Corsica in 1975 during riots demanding autonomy from France. Spanish police relentlessly hunted down Basque separatists. Italy attempted to appease regional differences by setting up twenty regional governments.

By the same token, our Latin polities still show sharp North-South differences. Their Souths are less industrialized and more agricultural than their Norths. Accordingly, the Souths are poorer and more backward in social organization than the Norths. This North-South difference has greatly diminished in postwar France, but is still quite large in Italy and Spain. In sum, the countries of Latin Europe are poorly integrated, those of Northern Europe generally well integrated.

While Northern European politics are given great coherence by large, unified labor movements backing Social Democratic parties, nothing so clear-cut exists in Latin Europe. A French worker is as likely to vote Gaullist as Communist or Socialist.[3] The Italian working-class vote prefers the Left but is divided among Communists, Socialists, Social Democrats, Proletarian Socialists, and even Christian Democrats. The fragmented Italian labor movement is unable to speak with one voice or support one working-class party.

It is in this area that France, statistically so close to the Northern European pattern in incomes, standards of living, welfare benefits, and the like, is still trapped in the Latin pattern. The French Left has not really been in power since

---

[3] For a graphic portrayal of incoherence in French voting see the table, "Voting Profiles for the Presidential Election of June 1, 1969," in *Modern Political Systems: Europe*, ed. by Roy C. Macridis and Robert E. Ward (Englewood Cliffs, N.J.: Prentice-Hall, 1972), p. 253. Indeed, the only clear pattern is the larger the city the smaller the Gaullist vote.

the 1930s. French welfare programs are not a result of steady trade-union and social-democratic input into the regime; such programs flow, rather, from the *largesse* and technocratic planning of basically conservative governments. An important component of what we are calling the Northern European pattern is the role of a large and reasonably cohesive labor movement linked with a large, moderate Social Democratic party, which in turn structures the political debate—more welfare or less—for the society as a whole. The French Left has not achieved this status and, given the existence of a large Communist party that insists on maintaining its own militant identity, is not likely to. The French Communists are able to cooperate only intermittently with the French Socialists; it is unlikely that a single party will be able to unite the French Left and link it to a labor movement in the foreseeable future. This same type of fragmentation is even more pronounced in Italy.

In the absence of a large, unified labor movement and a moderate, flexible social democratic party that engages its moderate conservative antagonists in a never-ending debate, the political dialogue in Latin Europe tends toward the apocalyptic. Doom is forecast if the Left opposition comes to power. The Left sees decay and ultimate collapse if the Right stays in power. Civility and courtesy seldom appear in the political arena; readiness to compromise is taken as a sign of weakness.

Any such polarized polity slides easily into authoritarianism supported by panicked middle and upper classes who fear for their status and property in the face of radical leftist advances. A single charismatic figure, promising to restore "order," may easily command their allegiance. While such tensions are endemic in our Latin polities, the catalyst of an authoritarian takeover is often a foreign military misadventure. The endless, frustrating Algerian war brought de Gaulle to power in 1958. Franco's (and earlier Primo de Rivera's) rise to power in Spain grew out of a similar Spanish effort to pacify part of Morocco. Mussolini climbed to power in the wake of Italy's nearly disastrous participation in World War I. Italy today is at least safe from domestic repercussions of colonial wars: she has no more colonies.

Overseas military actions, by the same token, can bring down authoritarian Latin regimes. The Salazar regime in Portugal collapsed in 1974 when finally even the army had had enough of unwinnable African wars. The Greek colonels lost their nerve in facing Turkey after bungling an attempt to take over Cyprus in 1974. Franco's smartest move was to avoid foreign military entanglement. He provided Hitler with only one division and stayed neutral in World War II. His successor, King Juan Carlos, simply pulled out of the Spanish Sahara.

The Latin polities are also characterized by fierce, paramilitary police forces to bolster the regime and crush antigovernment street demonstrations. The French government calls out the *Compagnies Républicaines de Sécurité*, the Italian government the *Carabinieri* and *Celere*, and the Spanish government the *Guardia Civil* and *Policia Armada*. The presence of such armed police forces is not coincidental; our Latin regimes require them to limit antisystem demands in their fragmented polities. The Northern European systems do not have paramilitary police because they do not need them.

Exemplifed by the Soviet Union, East Germany, and Yugoslavia, Eastern Europe represents a militant repudiation of both the Northern and Latin European patterns. The key questions of the latter two patterns may lurk under the surface but are not allowed to rise. Yugoslavia without the Communists would probably fit into the Latin pattern: low legitimacy, regional separatism, and large North-South differences, as indeed was the case with interwar Yugoslavia. East Germany without the Communists would probably fit into the Northern European pattern: a large Social Democratic party, much welfare legislation, and a strong bureaucracy. Such was the pattern of the eastern portion of Germany in the interwar period.

The possibility of the reassertion of these patterns gives the ruling Communist elites permanent nightmares. Yugoslav leaders are perfectly aware that their country could break up, that Croats both inside and out of the Communist party are more Croatian than they are Yugoslav. Indeed, the periodic tightening up the Yugoslav Communists go through is largely aimed at weeding out nationalist elements before they become a threat to Yugoslav unity. The tumultuous welcome given West German Chancellor Willy Brandt in East Germany in 1970 served to remind the Communist leadership that underneath the Socialist Unity facade there still beats many a Social Democratic heart.

But instead of letting these West European types of conflicts play themselves out in the political arena, the East European pattern is to smother them under an authoritarian blanket that claims to have eliminated the cleavages of the previous non-Communist system. The solutions are probably not nearly as deep or permanent as the regime likes to think. In any case, the questions of Northern and Latin Europe—welfare and legitimacy—are blotted out. Politics in the East European pattern by no means disappears. Instead, the key question becomes, "How much centralization?"

The several reforms and attempted reforms that have stirred Eastern Europe and the Soviet Union since World War II all revolve around the issue of how closely the economy and the society can be run by centralized administration. The two poles of this debate are the Stalinist model on the one hand and the Titoist on the other. The pure Stalinist model is no longer to be found in Europe, with the possible exception of Albania. But even Yugoslavia, at the other pole, has pulled up short of complete decentralization. "Self-management," so much touted in Yugoslav theory, has never been fully implemented. Instead, an invisible web of Communist party members, particularly the old Partisan combatants, still exercise considerable behind-the-scenes control. Nonetheless, as an idea, Titoism has had considerable impact in Eastern Europe, for it confronts the Stalinist model with an alternative path to socialism.

The Titoist model introduces (or sneaks in the back door) under a socialist banner the notions of a market economy, worker-managed enterprises, easy permission to travel abroad, loosened media controls, and an end to officially sanctioned standards in art. The brief 1968 Czechoslovak reform was strongly influenced by the Titoist model. Much more subtly than the Czechs, the Hungarians have been quietly introducing certain elements of decentralization, taking special care to not alarm the Russians.

East Germany has resisted such a path. There we have a system that might be called neo-Stalinist. While criteria of profitability have been introduced into East German economic decision making, things are still largely centrally run. Foreign travel is sharply restricted, the media have no autonomy, and artistic development proceeds cautiously. In many respects the East German system is a perfection of the Soviet system. With Prussian thoroughness and a more technological population to work with, the East German system has surpassed the Soviet Union in most sectors.

The tension between the two paths is likely to be nearly permanent in Eastern Europe. The alternations between tightness and looseness that we have seen in Yugoslavia could probably stand as an exaggeration of what goes on quietly within all the Communist parties of Eastern Europe. In Yugoslavia, the swings between decentralization and recentralization come more frequently —every few years—and are more public and more pronounced than in the countries still under Soviet tutelage. In much of the rest of Eastern Europe, reorientations and new departures come slowly and hesitatingly, usually requiring the dying off or retirement of the original Stalinist hacks and their replacement by a new generation of more flexible younger people who bill themselves not as reformers but as "pragmatists." These people must implement any such changes with great caution, always glancing over their shoulders at the Soviet reaction. If they go too far too fast, they risk Soviet intervention. But even the Soviet Union is not immune; the aging Soviet party elite, which has "effectively blocked any significant representation of political cadres born after 1920," cannot live forever.[4]

WHERE DOES THE UNITED STATES FIT?

Since we are comparing polities, let us consider where—if at all—the American polity fits into this threefold scheme. Elements of both the Latin and Northern

---

[4] John D. Nagle, "A New Look at the Soviet Elite: A Generational Interpretation of the Soviet System," paper presented to the Northeastern Political Science Association, Buck Hill Falls, Pa., November 10, 1973, i.

European patterns are found in U.S. politics. Although the great sectional schism was militarily settled by the Civil War, the South proved to be a sore loser with a long memory. The status of black Americans, the power of the Federal government and, until recently, peculiar one-party politics have been points of Southern resistance to the national pattern. The Southern monopoly of the filibuster is symbolic of this resistance on Capitol Hill. Every country has its South, and the United States is no exception. In some respects, the American South has been as distinctive and resentful as France's *Midi*, another conquered region that has never quite forgiven the France north of the Loire. The North-South differences in the United States, of course, are not as serious as those of Spain, Italy, or Yugoslavia.

On the religion issue, the American Catholic Church makes its voice heard in such areas as film censorship and abortion. We may note here that the United States legalized abortion (by a 1973 Supreme Court decision) only one year earlier than did France. A certain amount of Catholic-Protestant tension remained at least through the 1960 presidential election when the victory of John F. Kennedy was celebrated as a breakthrough. Still, compared to the clerical-anticlerical conflicts of Latin Europe or the Catholic-Protestant differences of Germany, the United States does not have a major religious issue.

While the United States system bears a weak resemblance to some facets of Latin European systems, it also bears a weak resemblance to Northern European systems in that—intermittently, at least—the key question of American politics becomes, How much welfare? The welfare question has never totally dominated American politics, though, and for several reasons. In the first place, relative to European standards, America was born rich.[5] Lacking much of the grinding poverty that plagued Europe, Americans did not focus their political thought on the wretched life of the underclass. Instead, it was assumed that everyone could, by hard work, ascend the social ladder, go "from rags to riches."[6] This assumption, of course, was never completely true, especially for racial minorities, but it has become the American national myth and one that refuses to die. While European social democrats attempted, with varying degrees of success, to enroll their working classes into parties that would lessen class differences by welfare measures, American politicians sought merely to perfect equality of opportunity (e.g., improved educational opportunities for the poor) so that each person could reach the level he or she deserved. Indeed, one of the major political debates of postwar America has centered around equality of education for blacks (e.g., busing).

American labor unions have seldom advocated a comprehensive program of welfare measures; instead they have concentrated on "bread and butter"

---

[5] For an illuminating contrast between European and American social thought see Hannah Arendt, *On Revolution* (New York: Viking Press, 1963).

[6] See Seymour Martin Lipset, *The First New Nation: The United States in Historical and Comparative Perspective* (New York: Anchor Books, 1967), especially chap. 6.

issues of higher wages and better fringe benefits. The early U.S. labor leaders deliberately avoided turning their movement into a political party, or even establishing firm ties to one of the existing parties. It is for this reason that the American system, even though it may wrestle with welfare questions, will probably never closely match the Northern European systems. In contrast to the strength of Sweden's LO or Britain's TUC, American labor unions enlist fewer than half of U.S. wage workers and, furthermore, stand for no particular program, ideology, or political party. Thus, although some of the political debate in America revolves around welfare questions, these questions are seldom posed by organized labor as is the case in Northern Europe.

The above is not to imply that the American system is inferior to or less developed than the Northern European model, only that it is different, possibly unique and fitting into no other pattern than its own. Indeed, in some ways the U.S. system, precisely because it is such a peculiar hybrid, may be better able to cope with the fast-changing demands of the modern world. Without a major input from organized labor and lacking a programmatic social democratic party, the American polity is capable of processing demands (if they are made loud enough) from a wide variety of social sources. Its very lack of programmatic coherence offers the benefit of flexibility. The U.S. system is unable to fit into the relatively neat Northern European pattern of how much welfare. Instead, if there is a key question in American politics, it might be, What's the question this year?

THE MEDITERRANEAN PENINSULAS

As we considered earlier, Yugoslavia in some respects still resembles the Latin pattern of European politics. Take away the Communist leadership stratum and Yugoslavia would fit into this pattern rather well—if there was a country left. Let us compare the three Mediterranean countries we have covered in this book, Spain, Italy, and Yugoslavia, neglecting for the moment the fact that the first is right-wing authoritarian, the second democratic, and the third maverick Communist. The three systems have much in common but have handled their common problems differently.

All three countries are characterized by a poor South and a rich North. The standards of living, backwardness of agricultural technique, unemployment, and underdeveloped infrastructure are quite similar in Spain's Andalusia and Estremadura, Italy's Mezzogiorno, and Yugoslavia's Macedonia, Bosnia, and Montenegro (and even South Serbia).

In these three lands, industry is heavily concentrated in the North. Indeed, if the northern parts of these countries are viewed separately—Spain's Catalonia and Basque area, Italy's Piedmont and Lombardy, and Yugoslavia's Slovenia and Croatia—they resemble the standards and styles of Northern Europe. Almost any industrial product one can name from these countries comes from their Northern regions.

Table 7–1   Three Mediterranean Countries in Comparison

	Spain	Italy	Yugoslavia
Poor South	Andalusia, Estremadura	Mezzogiorno	Macedonia, Bosnia, Kosovo
Rich North	Catalonia, Basque Country	Industrial Triangle	Slovenia, Croatia
Periphery resents central capital in	Castile	Rome	Serbia
Minority languages	Catalan, Basque, Galician	German, French	Slovenian, Macedonian, Hungarian, Albanian
Political Catholicism	Opus Dei, Catholic Action	Christian Democrats	Strong Croatian church
Internal migration	South to North	South to North	South to North
Workers abroad	Approx. 1 million chiefly in France, West Germany	Approx. 1 million chiefly in Switzerland, West Germany, France	Approx. 1 million chiefly in West Germany, Austria
Aid for South	–	Cassa per il Mezzogiorno	Fund for the Underdeveloped Regions
One-man rule	Franco	–	Tito
Income from tourism (1971)	$2 billion	$1.9 billion	$360 million
Inflation rate (1974)	25%	25%	32%

This North-South difference (as well as many other differences) gives the national government a great deal of trouble that comes under the heading, "center-periphery tension." All three of our Mediterranean lands suffer from tension between their centers and their peripheries, dangerously strong in the cases of Spain and Yugoslavia, not so serious in Italy. The problem in Spain and Yugoslavia is that their industrial areas are precisely the same regions that harbor old feelings of resentment at being ruled by an ethnically different central government. The dominant Castilians of Spain made Madrid the country's capital and have enforced their will on the Basque- and Catalan-speaking Northern industrial areas. In Yugoslavia, the dominant Serbs made their capital of Belgrade the nation's capital and, muted by Yugoslavia's federal structure, continue to limit Croatian desires for more complete autonomy.

One might say that the Yugoslavs have been more clever than the Spaniards in handling their respective center-periphery problems. The Yugoslavs, aware of the centrifugal tendencies of their multiethnic state, gave in to a considerable extent to local nationalism, hoping that federalism and local language rights would satisfy Yugoslavia's many ethnic groups. To an extent, this has worked. Croats are free to speak and publish in their variation of Serbo-Croatian, Slovenes in Slovenian, etc. The Belgrade authorities even brought in an American scholar after World War II to write the first grammar of the Macedonian language (in order to emphasize its distinctiveness from Bulgarian, which the Bulgarians deny). But staffing by local talent and language rights were not sufficient to fully appease local—especially Croatian—demands for *economic* autonomy. Ironically, the Yugoslav Communist leadership, followers of a doctrine that stresses the economic basis of social attitudes, failed to recognize the economic basis of Croatian demands, namely to retain the investment capital and foreign exchange earned by Croatian industries. Thus cultural federalism and a certain amount of political autonomy have not sufficed to erase Yugoslavia's center-periphery problem.

In Spain, the Franco government tried precisely the opposite tactic: allow no autonomy whatsoever and crush any movement in favor of even language rights. Only grudgingly did the post-Franco regime permit the use of Basque and Catalan. The Madrid attitude on language rights was, Give them an inch and they'll take a mile. To the regime, Basque and Catalan demands for the unfettered use of their languages were just the opening wedge for political separatism. If they gave in on cultural autonomy, they felt, it would lead to a full-scale breakaway movement. There may have been some truth to this view. The point here is that neither giving free rein to the local language, as in Yugoslavia, nor stifling it, as in Spain, is a sure-fire solution to either country's center-periphery problem.

Italy had this minority-language problem in a relatively minor way with its quarter of a million German speakers in the area won from Austria after World War I—Alto Adige to Italians, South Tyrol to Austrians. Many South Tyroleans resented the settlement of Italians in their area (with encouragement from the government in Rome), fearing the demise of their German language and culture. A handful of South Tyroleans even formed a neo-Nazi terrorist group and blew up power pylons in the 1960s. Tough Italian police measures plus a guarantee of language rights to German-speaking inhabitants appeared to solve the problem, however.

The rich Norths and poor Souths of Spain, Italy, and Yugoslavia mean considerable internal migration, from South to North, which has greatly increased since World War II. Now each of these three Mediterranean countries has a large minority of southerners working, invariably in the lower positions, in northern industrial towns. In addition, each of these three lands has roughly a million of its nationals working in Northern Europe. In West Germany alone there were close to half a million Italian and half a million Yugoslav workers and a sixth of a million Spanish workers—and these were just the ones registered and working legally. An estimated 10 percent might be added to include illegal migrant workers. Other big employers of Southern European labor were France, Switzerland, and Austria.[7] The economies of Spain, Italy, and Yugoslavia benefited greatly from the remittances of their workers abroad and indeed from having an escape valve for domestic unemployment. The economic turndown of the mid-1970s sent shudders through all three countries, for it meant that some of their workers were sent back from Northern Europe to unemployment at home. In this regard, all three of the Mediterranean lands we are considering were economically the weak sisters of and partially dependent upon the thriving economies of Northern Europe.

In varying degrees, our three Mediterranean lands try to do something about their poor Souths. Italy's Cassa per il Mezzogiorno invests government funds and encourages private industry to build new plants in the impoverished third of the peninsula below Rome. While there has been economic growth in the Mezzogiorno, it has not nearly caught up with Italy's North, which has grown even more. Yugoslavia's Fund for the Underdeveloped Regions is a counterpart to the Italian Cassa. Aiming initially to set aside 1.85 percent of Yugoslavia's total social product for economic development, the bulk of it to go to the poor South, the Fund repeatedly fell short and, furthermore, created a good deal of resentment on the part of the richer northern republics, which had to foot the bill. As in Italy, Yugoslavia's South has not narrowed its gap with the North; indeed, the gap continued to widen as the North surged ahead economically.

The best that can be said about the Italian and Yugoslav efforts to uplift their poor Souths is that the gaps would doubtless be even larger in the absence of their respective development funds. They have helped their Souths grow in absolute terms, but not relative to their booming Norths. Spain has done little in this regard. Instead of having new investments go to the poor areas, mostly in the South, Spanish industry has tended to concentrate more and more in the areas that are already industrialized, Catalonia and the Basque country. Capital in the backward areas seeks investments in the rich areas—returns are safer and surer—and labor migrates from poor to rich provinces, leading to more concentration of both capital and population in the rich provinces. Spain has done little to reverse this flow, believing that any economic growth is good, no matter what regional imbalances may come with it.

FRAGILE EUROPE

The fragility of all three of our Mediterranean countries should by now be apparent. In two of them, Spain and Yugoslavia, political stability depended greatly on the unchallenged power and long lives of, respectively, Franco and

---

[7] Robert Ball, "How Europe Created Its 'Minority Problem,' " *Fortune*, December 1973, p. 133.

Tito, both of whom were born in 1892. The forces latent in Spain and Yugoslavia that bubbled to the surface in the 1970s potentially threatened the unity of each land. On the one hand, the problem of regional separatism was probably stronger in Yugoslavia than in Spain. On the other hand, Yugoslavia had a better mechanism—the Communist party—to check and control separatist tendencies. Spain did not have quite the problem as Yugoslavia—Spain's Basques and Catalans had been Spanish for centuries; Yugoslavia has existed uneasily only since 1918—but likewise Spain lacked a serious political movement to cut off separatism at the grass-roots level. We cannot be sure, of course, that the Yugoslav Communist party, itself riven by regionalism, will prove equal to the task of holding the country together after Tito.

Both Spain and Yugoslavia, in many ways so similar, face the distinct possibility of military takeover in the post-Franco and post-Tito era. The probability is higher in Spain than in Yugoslavia. In both cases the army is formally charged with the preservation of national unity, and if that were threatened there can be no doubt the army of either nation would not hesitate to carry out its mandate. In both countries, threats to national unity—in the form of breakaway tendencies in the industrial Norths of each land—are quite real.

Italy, while lacking a separatist problem, is also not immune from a possible military takeover, although the probablity of this is markedly lower than in its sister Mediterranean peninsulas. The discovery of plots in Italy's several intelligence services and paramilitary forces raised the specter of eventual direct military intervention into the affairs of state. The possibility grew more distinct as the Italian Communists' power grew. Although the Communists bent over backwards to show their moderation and flexibility—indeed, becoming little more than Social Democrats in their avowed program—conservative Italians mistrusted the Communists' ultimate intentions and would support extralegal action to block the PCI from entering the cabinet. Many Italians believed the United States would support such action in the style of the 1973 overthrow of Chile's Marxist President Salvador Allende.

The factor that could push any or all of our three Mediterranean countries into domestic chaos is economics. All three suffered during the economic slowdown of the mid-1970s, experiencing inflation rates in excess of 20 percent a year. Part of this inflation, but only a small part, was due to the quadrupling of Middle Eastern oil prices from 1973 to 1974. A greater part was due to inflationary wage settlements and a budding taste for the good life among the middle and working classes. Automobile ownership and beef consumption, particularly in Italy, soared. All three of the governments, for reasons of their own, found it extremely difficult to bring down these inflation rates. A jittery Madrid regime hesitated to crack down on Spanish workers for fear of provoking them into militancy. The weak Rome government was relatively powerless to put the brakes on the large wage increases that militant labor unions were able to force from management. The Belgrade government, lacking the centralized administration of Soviet-style Communist systems, was content to let inflation spur consumption and erode welfare outlays.

To a considerable extent, the citizens of Spain, Italy, and Yugoslavia became used to chronic and hefty inflation. But at what point would they break? The London *Economist* and other worried commentators suggested that a democracy cannot survive for long with inflation running at over 20 percent a year. Although we would not classify Spain and Yugoslavia as democracies, the specter of long-term, major inflation raised the question of whether they could survive as relatively uncoercive authoritarian systems. Demands are felt even in authoritarian polities. "Politics is a game for boys," said one angry Yugoslav housewife as she looked at prices. "But when people find they can no longer feed their families, then watch out."[8] No doubt the same statement was made many times in Spanish and Italian. To give in to such demands, however, say, by raising wages, simply fuels more inflation. To ignore such demands invites civil disobedience, possibly leading to insurrection. To force people to accept a lower standard of living requires authoritarian controls—either right-wing or left-wing.

Severe inflation often pushes the upper and middle classes to the Right; they demand a conservative crackdown on what they perceive as the runaway power of labor unions. If conventional politics cannot do this, they sometimes look to a general or to a fascist movement to put labor in its place. At the same time, inflation often moves the working classes to the Left; when the market basket cannot be filled they demand higher wages, subsidies and government price controls. The United States suffered from this sort of polarization in the mid-1970s, but the situation was not nearly so difficult as in Spain, Italy, or Yugoslavia, and the American government institutions were much stronger.

The problem was not confined to Mediterranean Europe but manifested itself in greater or lesser degree throughout the Continent. The pressures and polarizations were so great in Britain that some began to wonder if the British system was immune to upheaval. With inflation hitting 26 percent a year in 1975, British society began to polarize into a militant Left and a reactionary Right. Labor unions, some of them with Communist leaders, struck for and sometimes got 30 percent wage increases. The attempts of the Labor government to restrain unions by means of a "social contract" generally failed, and Conservative critics charged the cabinet with handing over power to the unions. Fearing nationwide shutdowns, retired British army officers began setting up private armies to keep essential services going in a general strike. Adding to the misery was the civil war in Northern Ireland, which claimed over 1,600 lives. It was the worst British crisis since World War II, and some feared for the survival of British democracy.

The demise of parliamentary rule in Britain is unlikely, but the polarization

---

[8] Quoted by Malcolm W. Browne, "In the Twilight, Tito Is Creating a Rigid Legacy," *New York Times*, Feb. 16, 1975, p. E3.

of British society in the mid-1970s serves to underscore the fragility of what was previously supposed to be a durable political pattern. Just as France was possibly capable of moving up from the Latin to the Northern European pattern, so was Britain capable of dropping down from the Northern to the Latin European pattern. A Britain torn in two on the basis of social class, fighting a sort of Algerian war in Ulster, wracked by the explosion of IRA bombs, its famed two-party stability eroded, such a system may turn increasingly to the basic question—legitimacy—that characterizes our Latin polities. If Germany can progress from the Latin to the Northern European pattern, there is no reason why Britain cannot regress the other way.

EUROPE AS A DEVELOPING AREA

It has become customary to treat European systems as relatively mature, stable, settled, or "finished" polities. In contrast, the systems of the Third World are often analyzed in terms of tribalism, economic difficulties, corruption, malintegration, military takeovers, outmoded traditions and psychologies, and political institutions too weak to handle the heavy demands of change. Perhaps we should view polities in Europe and in the Third World as having a good deal in common.

We may not wish to call the separatist attitudes of Basques and Croatians "tribalistic," but are they really so different from the separatist tribalism that has wracked Nigeria and the Sudan? Are the murderous struggles of Catholics and Protestants in Northern Ireland qualitatively or merely quantitatively distinct from Hindu-Moslem warfare on the Indian subcontinent?

In some respects, a study of Latin American politics would serve as a useful background to the study of Latin European politics. The rise and fall of the Allende government in Chile (1970–1973) bears a resemblance to the founding and overthrow of the Spanish Republic (1931–1936). In both cases moderate leftists took over the reins of government unleashing mass demands for fast and radical improvements in the conditions of life. In both Chile and Spain the leftist regimes could not control extremist groups on the far Left. The middle classes panicked and welcomed military takeover. Even the subsequent executions, imprisonment, and harsh suppression of political opposition are similar.

The malaise of Italy resembles, to an extent, that of Uruguay, where labor unrest, economic decline, and urban terrorism led, in 1973, to a military-dominated civilian government that suspended constitutional rule, replaced the parliament with a Council of State, and closed the opposition press.

The centrifugal tendencies of Yugoslavia, which have plagued the country from its 1918 founding, might be considered in the light of other multinational federations. In 1965 the Malaysia federation, rent by Chinese-Malay rioting, fell apart and gave birth to an independent Singapore, dominated by ethnic Chinese. In 1967, the massacre of Ibos in Nigeria led to civil war as Biafra struggled to secede from the Nigerian federation. Pakistan, although not a federation, lost its eastern wing to Bengali separatists in 1971. India, a true federation, has experienced separatist agitation.

At first the reader might be tempted to reply, "Such things do not happen in Europe." The Nazi conquest of the Continent revealed otherwise. The German takeover of Czechoslovakia, Yugoslavia, and parts of the Soviet Union "liberated" with some local enthusiasm the short-lived states of Slovakia and Croatia and a major Ukrainian independence movement. The Germans knew perfectly well that the national unity of some of their neighbors was weak, and they took advantage of it. There is no guarantee that separatist impulses can be fully controlled in present-day Spain and Yugoslavia. Some parts of Europe have no more national unity than do parts of the Third World.

Observers of the Third World often point out how the "dead hand of the past" still blocks modernization, how traditional attitudes and an elite generation trained in old ways cannot come to grips with present-day situations. Europe is not really so different. Of the five countries we have studied in this book, three of them were ruled into the 1970s by men born in the last century who came to power along with the upheavals associated with the Second World War. Their psyches, one must presume, were still scarred by the cataclysmic events of this period. They had long memories; many seemed to be still fighting the battles of yesteryear against enemies long since slain or silenced.

This meant problems for the societies they ruled. For men such as Franco (born in 1892), Tito (also born in 1892), and Ulbricht (born in 1893), the memories of the battles their generation fought were increasingly dysfunctional to their societies' present-day problems. All three of these men were born and raised under a monarch: Franco under Alfonso XIII, Tito under Franz-Josef of Austria-Hungary, and Ulbricht under Wilhelm II. Their initial political experiences came when their respective monarchies were tottering, their attitudes set during the chaos of the interwar period. Two of our figures served time in prison: Ulbricht for a few months in 1918 as an army deserter, and Tito from 1928 to 1934 as a Communist organizer and agitator. All three experienced first-hand enormous political violence, and indeed they came to power as a result of that violence. All three have been responsible for killing their countrymen, Ulbricht perhaps hundreds, Tito some tens of thousands, and Franco hundreds of thousands.

The point of this is to emphasize that "old" Europe has not quite yet died. Human longevity is such that persons socialized politically in one period (in this case, under turn-of-the-century monarchies) are at the peak of their power perhaps half a century later (in this case, after World War II). It is almost comic how long-defunct monarchies still played a role in the politics of the 1970s. Thus Europe is not a finished product; it is rather a still-evolving mixture of the modern and premodern.

Despite the many differences of the five systems we have considered in this book, on one interesting point they tend to converge: most of the important decisions are made out of public sight. We may discuss political cultures, voting patterns, ideologies, parties, etc., at great length, but when we come down to the bottom line we repeatedly find crucial decisions reached in private among a handful of persons who are representatives of one or more elite groups.

This is true even of our democracies. In Sweden we considered how "Harpsund democracy" means informal meetings of the top elites of business, labor, and bureaucracy to steer Swedish society with little reference to parliament. In Italy we used the term *sottogoverno* to describe the behind-the-scenes arrangements made by business and bureaucratic elites.

What meaning then has democracy? It seems to mean that decisions made privately are eventually placed in the public arena for approval. This public discussion happens more frequently in Sweden than in Italy, but in both cases it is an auxiliary phase of the elite discussion that has taken place earlier in private.

In our authoritarian systems, of course, such a pattern is even more pronounced. The Franco cabinets were the arenas of interaction among military, monarchist, Catholic, and National Movement elites. In a similar fashion, the course of Yugoslav society was set by Tito and a handful of men around him in the upper echelons of the party. East German elite interactions have been between the older dogmatists and the younger technocrats. In authoritarian systems, the follow-up phase of public discussion and approval is much less important than in democracies. Franco preferred no public interest in politics; Tito sought mass support for his policies; Ulbricht simply orchestrated acclaim. We may notice, however, that the differences between democratic and authoritarian systems are ones of degree and not of absolutes in this regard.

How much of American politics is also conducted out of sight? Are we that different from the Europeans? The Pentagon Papers showed, among other things, how the operative parts of the 1964 Tonkin Gulf Resolution were actually drafted by the White House several months before the incidents at sea even occurred. Watergate showed that the 1972 election was only partly a matter of public campaigning. Crucial aspects were behind the scenes, in payments from oil, dairy, aircraft, and other interests. A great deal of government, even in a democracy, takes place privately, in interactions between political, military, and business elites.

Should we despair at such goings on? No, not if we have studied European politics, for such a study may help us to outgrow some of our native idealism. From our study of Europe we learn that life goes on under a wide variety of political arrangements, that politics out of public sight is the norm rather than the exception, and that we are not terribly different from the Europeans. We start out considering Europe and end up considering ourselves; this is the great merit of comparative politics. Such phenomena as "Harpsund democracy" and *sottogoverno* are not peculiar, alien phenomena. They are as American as cherry pie.

BIBLIOGRAPHY

ADAMS, JOHN CLARKE, and PAOLO BARILE. 1972. *The Government of Republican Italy.* 3rd ed. Boston: Houghton Mifflin.

ALLUM, P. A. 1973. *Italy—Republic Without Government?* New York: W. W. Norton.

ALMOND, GABRIEL A., and SIDNEY VERBA. 1965. *The Civic Culture: Political Attitudes and Democracy in Five Nations.* Boston: Little, Brown.

ANDERSON, CHARLES W. 1970. *The Political Economy of Modern Spain: Policy-Making in an Authoritarian System.* Madison: University of Wisconsin Press.

ARENDT, HANNAH. 1965. *On Revolution.* New York: Viking Press.

AUTY, PHYLLIS. 1972. *Tito.* New York: Ballantine Books.

BANFIELD, EDWARD C. 1958. *The Moral Basis of a Backward Society.* New York: Free Press.

BARTON, ALAN, BOGDAN DENITCH, and CHARLES KADUSHIN, eds. 1973. *Opinion-Making Elites in Yugoslavia.* New York: Frederick A. Praeger.

BARZINI, LUIGI. 1965. *The Italians.* New York: Bantam Books.

BAYLIS, THOMAS A. 1972. "In Quest of Legitimacy," *Problems of Communism,* XXI, No. 2 (March-April), 46–55.

BERTSCH, GARY K. 1973. "The Revival of Nationalisms," *Problems of Communism,* XXII, No. 6 (November-December), 1–15.

BLACKMER, DONALD L. M. 1972. "Italian Communism: Strategy for the 1970's," *Problems of Communism,* XXI, No. 3 (May-June), 41–56.

BOARD, JOSEPH B., JR. 1970. *The Government and Politics of Sweden.* Boston: Houghton Mifflin.

BURKS, R. V. 1961. *The Dynamics of Communism in Eastern Europe.* Princeton: Princeton University Press.

———. 1971. *The National Problem and the Future of Yugoslavia.* Santa Monica, Calif.: The Rand Corporation.

CARR, RAYMOND. 1966. *Spain 1808–1939.* New York: Oxford University Press.

CHILDS, DAVID. 1969. *East Germany.* New York: Frederick A. Praeger.

CHILDS, MARQUIS W. 1936. *Sweden: The Middle Way.* New Haven, Conn.: Yale University Press.

CHRISTMAN, HENRY M., ed. 1970. *The Essential Tito.* New York: St. Martin's Press.

CROZIER, BRIAN. 1967. *Franco.* Boston: Little, Brown.

DAHRENDORF, RALF. 1969. *Society and Democracy in Germany.* Garden City, N.Y.: Doubleday.

DEDIJER, VLADIMIR. 1971. *The Battle Stalin Lost: Memoirs of Yugoslavia, 1948–1953.* New York: Viking Press.

DE ESTEBAN, JORGE, et al. 1973. *Desarrollo Político y Constitución Española.* Barcelona: Ediciones Ariel.

DE MIGUEL, AMANDO, et al. 1972. *Sintesis del Informe Sociologico sobre la Situacion Social en España 1970.* 4th ed. Madrid: Fundacion FOESSA.

DENITCH, BOGDAN. 1973. "Notes on the Relevance of Yugoslav Self-Management," *Politics and Society,* III, No. 4 (Summer), 473–89.

DEUTSCH, KARL W. 1966. *Nationalism and Social Communication: An Inquiry into the Foundations of Nationality.* 2nd ed. Cambridge, Mass.: MIT Press.

———. 1974. *Politics and Government: How People Decide Their Fate.* 2nd ed. Boston: Houghton Mifflin.

Deutsches Institut für Wirtschaftsforschung Berlin. 1971. *DDR-Wirtschaft.* Frankfurt: Fisher Bürcherei.

DJILAS, MILOVAN. 1957. *The New Class: An Analysis of the Communist System.* New York: Frederick A. Praeger.

DJORDJEVIĆ, JOVAN. 1958. "Interest Groups and the Political System of Yugoslavia," in H. Ehrmann, ed., *Interest Groups on Four Continents.* Pittsburgh, Pa.: Pittsburgh University Press.

ELDER, NEIL C. M. 1970. *Government in Sweden: The Executive at Work.* Elmsford, N.Y.: Pergamon Press.

ELVANDER, NILS. 1974. "Interest Groups in Sweden," *The Annals of the American Academy of Political and Social Science,* 413 (May).

Federal Republic of Germany. 1972. *Bericht der Bundesregierung und Materialien zur Lage der Nation 1972.* Bonn: Bundesministerium für innerdeutsche Beziehungen.

FISHER, W. B., and H. BOWEN-JONES. 1966. *Spain: An Introductory Geography.* New York: Frederick A. Praeger.

FRIEDRICH, CARL J., and ZBIGNIEW K. BRZEZINSKI. 1956. *Totalitarian Dictatorship and Autocracy.* New York: Frederick A. Praeger.

GALLI, GIORGIO, and ALFONSO PRANDI. 1970. *Patterns of Political Participation in Italy.* New Haven, Conn.: Yale University Press.

GERMINO, DANTE, and STEFANO PASSIGLI. 1968. *The Government and Politics of Contemporary Italy.* New York: Harper & Row.

HANCOCK, M. DONALD. 1972. *Sweden: The Politics of Postindustrial Change.* Hinsdale, Ill.: Dryden Press.

HANHARDT, ARTHUR M., JR. 1968. *The German Democratic Republic.* Baltimore: Johns Hopkins Press.

HECKSCHER, GUNNAR. 1958. "Interest Groups in Sweden: Their Political Role," in H. Ehrmann, ed., *Interest Groups on Four Continents.* Pittsburgh, Pa.: Pittsburgh University Press.

HERR, RICHARD. 1974. *An Historical Essay on Modern Spain.* Berkeley: University of California Press.

HILLS, GEORGE. 1970. *Spain.* New York: Frederick A. Praeger.

HOFFMAN, GEORGE W. 1973. "Migration and Social Change," *Problems of Communism,* XXII, No. 6 (November-December), 16–31.

———, and FRED WARNER NEAL, 1962. *Yugoslavia and the New Communism.* New York: Twentieth Century Fund.

HOLM, HANS AXEL. 1970. *The Other Germans: Report from an East German Town.* New York: Pantheon Books.

HORVAT, BRANKO. 1969. *An Essay on Yugoslav Society.* White Plains, N.Y.: International Arts and Sciences Press.

HOTTINGER, ARNOLD. 1974. *Spain in Transition: Franco's Regime.* The Washington Papers, II, No. 18. Beverly Hills, Calif.: Sage Publications.

_____. 1974. *Spain in Transition: Prospects and Policies.* The Washington Papers, II, No. 19. Beverly Hills, Calif.: Sage Publications.

HUGHES, H. STUART. 1965. *The United States and Italy.* Rev. ed. New York: W. W. Norton.

HUNTFORD, ROLAND. 1972. *The New Totalitarians.* New York: Stein and Day.

JACKSON, GABRIEL. 1965. *The Spanish Republic and the Civil War, 1931–1939.* Princeton: Princeton University Press.

JOHNSON, A. ROSS. 1974. *Yugoslavia: In the Twilight of Tito.* The Washington Papers, II, No. 16. Beverly Hills, Calif.: Sage Publications.

KEEFE, EUGENE K., et al. 1972. *Area Handbook for East Germany.* Washington, D.C.: Government Printing Office.

KOBLIK, STEVEN, ed. 1975. *Sweden's Development from Poverty to Affluence, 1750–1970.* Minneapolis: University of Minnesota Press.

KOGAN, NORMAN. 1962. *The Government of Italy.* New York: Crowell.

LAPALOMBARA, JOSEPH. 1964. *Interest Groups in Italian Politics.* Princeton, N.J.: Princeton University Press.

_____. 1965. "Italy: Fragmentation, Isolation, Alienation," in L. Pye and S. Verba, eds., *Political Culture and Political Development.* Princeton, N.J.: Princeton University Press.

_____. 1974. *Politics Within Nations.* Englewood Cliffs, N.J.: Prentice-Hall.

LINZ, JUAN J. 1967. "The Party System of Spain," in S. Lipset and S. Rokkan, eds., *Party Systems and Voter Alignments.* New York: Free Press.

_____. 1968. "An Authoritarian Regime: Spain," in E. Allardt and Y. Littunen, eds., *Cleavages, Ideologies and Party Systems.* Helsinki: Academic Bookstore.

_____. 1970. "From Falange to Movimiento-Organizacion: The Spanish Single Party and the Franco Regime, 1936–1968," in S. Huntington and C. Moore, eds., *Authoritarian Politics in Modern Society.* New York: Basic Books.

_____. 1973. "Opposition to and under an Authoritarian Regime: The Case of Spain," in R. Dahl, ed., *Regimes and Oppositions.* New Haven, Conn.: Yale University Press.

LINK, RUTH. 1973. *Taking Part: The Power and the People in Sweden.* Stockholm: Sweden NOW.

LIPSET, SEYMOUR MARTIN. 1963. *Political Man: The Social Bases of Politics.* Garden City, N.Y.: Anchor Books.

_____. 1967. *The First New Nation: The United States in Historical and Comparative Perspective.* Garden City, N.Y.: Anchor Books.

LUDZ, PETER CHRISTIAN. 1970. *The German Democratic Republic from the Sixties to the Seventies.* Cambridge, Mass.: Harvard University Center for International Affairs.

_____. 1972. *The Changing Party Elite in East Germany.* Cambridge, Mass.: MIT Press.

_____. 1972. "Continuity and Change Since Ulbricht," *Problems of Communism,* XXI, No. 2 (March-April), 56–67.

_____. 1974. *Deutschlands Doppelte Zukunft: Bundesrepublik und DDR in der Welt von Morgen.* Munich: Carl Hanser Verlag.

MACKENZIE, LESLIE. 1973. "The Political Ideas of the Opus Dei in Spain," *Government and Opposition,* VIII (Winter), 72–92.

MACRIDIS, ROY C., and ROBERT E. WARD. eds. 1972. *Modern Political Systems: Europe.* 3rd ed. Englewood Cliffs, N.J.: Prentice-Hall.

MERKL, PETER H. 1970. *Modern Comparative Politics.* New York: Holt, Rinehart and Winston.

MEDHURST, KENNETH. 1969. "The Political Presence of the Spanish Bureaucracy," *Government and Opposition,* IV (Spring).

MOUNTJOY, ALAN B. 1973. *The Mezzogiorno.* New York: Oxford University Press.

PAVLOWITCH, STEVAN K. 1971. *Yugoslavia.* New York: Frederick A. Praeger.

PAYNE, STANLEY G. 1961. *Falange: A History of Spanish Fascism.* Stanford, Calif.: Stanford University Press.

PITT-RIVERS, J. A. 1954. *The People of the Sierra.* New York: Criterion Books.

PRITCHETT, V. S. 1954. *The Spanish Temper.* London: Chatto & Windus.

RAUSCH, HEINZ, and THEO STAMMEN, eds. 1974. *DDR—Das politische, wirtschaftliche und soziale System.* Munich: Verlag C. H. Beck.

ROSE, RICHARD. 1971. "Class and Party Divisions: Britain as Test Case," in M. Dogan and R. Rose, eds., *European Politics: A Reader.* Boston: Little, Brown.

———. 1975. "Oil Based Scottish Nationalism," *The New Republic,* September 20, 1975.

RUSTOW, DANKWART A. 1955. *The Politics of Compromise: A Study of Parties and Cabinet Government in Sweden.* New York: Greenwood Press.

SANI, GIACOMO. 1975. "Secular Trends and Party Realignments in Italy: The 1975 Election," paper delivered at the 1975 meeting of the American Political Science Association, San Francisco.

SÄRLVIK, BO. 1970. "Voting Behavior in Shifting Election Winds," *Scandinavian Political Studies 1970,* Vol. 5. New York: Columbia University Press.

SCHNITZER, MARTIN. 1970. *The Economy of Sweden.* New York: Frederick A. Praeger.

———. 1972. *East and West Germany: A Comparative Economic Analysis.* New York: Frederick A. Praeger.

SHOUP, PAUL. 1968. *Communism and the Yugoslav National Question.* New York: Columbia University Press.

SMITH, JEAN EDWARD. 1969. *Germany Beyond the Wall: People, Politics . . . and Prosperity.* Boston: Little, Brown.

STOJANOVIĆ, SVETOZAR. 1973. *Between Ideals and Reality.* New York: Oxford University Press.

SZULC, TAD. 1972. *Portrait of Spain.* New York: American Heritage Press.

TAMAMES, RAMÓN. 1973. *La República, La Era de Franco.* Madrid: Ediciones Alfaguara

THOMAS, HUGH. 1961. *The Spanish Civil War.* New York: Harper & Row.

TIERNO GALVÁN, ENRIQUE. 1966. "Students' Opposition in Spain," *Government and Opposition,* I (August).

TINGSTEN, HERBERT. 1973. *The Swedish Social Democrats: Their Ideological Development.* Totowa, N.J.: Bedminster Press.

TOMASSON, RICHARD F. 1970. *Sweden: Prototype of Modern Society.* New York: Random House.

TRYTHALL, J. W. D. 1970. *El Caudillo: A Political Biography of Franco.* New York: McGraw-Hill.

ULAM, ADAM. 1952. *Titoism and the Cominform.* Cambridge, Mass.: Harvard University Press.

U.S. Arms Control and Disarmament Agency. 1975. *World Military Expenditures and Arms Trade, 1963–1973.* Washington, D.C.: Government Printing Office.

VERBA, SIDNEY. 1965. "Germany: The Remaking of Political Culture," in L. Pye and S. Verba, eds., *Political Culture and Political Development.* Princeton, N.J.: Princeton University Press.

——— and GOLDIE SHABAD. 1975. "Workers' Councils and Political Stratification: The Yugoslav Experience," paper delivered at 1975 meeting of the American Political Science Association, San Francisco.

WELLES, BENJAMIN. 1965. *Spain: The Gentle Anarchy.* New York: Frederick A. Praeger.

WOLFE, JAMES H. 1974. "Corporatism in German Political Life: Functional Representation in the GDR and Bavaria," in M. Heisler, ed., *Politics in Europe: Structures and Processes in Some Postindustrial Democracies.* New York: David McKay.

ZARISKI, RAPHAEL. 1972. *Italy: The Politics of Uneven Development.* Hinsdale, Ill.: Dryden Press.

INDEX